Date Due

FEB 2 9 2000			
FEB 2 2 '00			

PRINTED IN U.S.A.   CAT. NO. 24 161   BRO DART.

Jim Bunning

In the series *Baseball in America*, edited by Rich Westcott

Jim Bunning

*Baseball
and Beyond*

Frank Dolson

Temple University Press
PHILADELPHIA

Temple University Press, Philadelphia 19122
Copyright © 1998 by Frank Dolson
All rights reserved
Published 1998

Printed in the United States of America

⊗ The paper used in this publication meets the requirements of
American National Standard for Information Sciences—Permanence
of Paper for Printed Library Materials, ANSI Z39.48-1984

Library of Congress Cataloging-in-Publication Data

Dolson, Frank.
Jim Bunning : baseball and beyond / Frank Dolson.
p.   cm. — (Baseball in America)
Includes index.
ISBN 1-56639-636-0 (cloth : alk. paper)
1. Bunning, Jim, 1931- . 2. Pitchers (Baseball)—United States—
Biography. 3. Legislators—United States—Biography. I. Title.
II. Series.
GV865.B83D65   1998
796.357'092—dc21
[B]   98-14655

To Allen Lewis, a Hall of Fame baseball writer and a good friend whose encouragement helped make this book possible and whose tireless research and support as a member of the Hall of Fame Veterans Committee played a major role in Jim Bunning's long overdue election.

Contents

Introduction   1

1   The Best Day   9

2   Turning Pro   19

3   Mary   25

4   The Winter Game I (The Player)   31

5   The Tigers   36

6   Champs—for 150 Games   54

7   The Crash of '64   73

8   Trying to Win 20   85

9   A Star among Stars   93

10   A Union Man   100

11   The Competitive Edge   115

12   Farewell to Pitching   126

13   Back to the Minors   135

14   God's Country   147

15   Jim Bunning, Mud Hen   158

16   The 89ers   175

17   The Firing   179

18   The Winter Game II (The Manager)   196

19   The Political Game   202

20   Man of the House   230

21   Love of the Game   262

22   The Biggest Challenge   276

      Appendix: The No-Hitters   285

      Index   291

Photos follow pages 30, 96, and 204

Introduction

Jim Bunning wasn't born to be a great pitcher. He wasn't blessed with an overpowering fast ball that rocketed into the high nineties. As a young pro he was told that he couldn't be successful with the sidearm pitching motion that became his trademark. And yet, after spending seven years in the minor leagues, he won more than a hundred games in each major league and earned a place in baseball's Hall of Fame.

Jim Bunning wasn't born to be a politician. He simply was not a political animal. Not a man who was comfortable shaking hands and making small talk with strangers. Not a man who found it easy to be nice to some media type who asked a foolish question or wrote a story Jim considered unfair. Not a man who was only too ready to say what the polls said was popular to say, or what he knew the person he was talking to wanted to hear. Jim Bunning wasn't merely honest when he spoke; he was often *brutally* honest. A second successful career as a politician? You had to be kidding. At least, that's what many of us who knew him in his baseball days thought. Well, we thought wrong. This man who didn't set out to be a politician, and only became one after his bid to become a big league baseball manager hit a dead end, is now a six-term congressman running for the United States Senate.

There is no mystery about Jim Bunning. He is what you see—unfailingly direct, sometimes to the point of being abrasive. There is no better friend than Jim Bunning; the hard part is proving to him that you deserve his friendship. If he doesn't like you or respect you—whether you're the president of the United States, a baseball manager he once played for, or a sportswriter or political writer who doesn't do his or her homework—you'll find out in a hurry. He is a man who makes loyal friends and bitter enemies.

Bunning has accomplished many things in his life. As a ballplayer, he lasted seventeen years in the big leagues and turned down a chance to make it eighteen. If he had to wait an inordinately long time to make it to the Hall of Fame, that's probably because he never went out of his way to charm the writers who do the voting. As a leader in the early years of the Players Association, he helped put together a pension plan that, to this day, is second to none in professional sports. As a politician, the conservative Kentucky Republican became a United States congressman.

His accomplishments are impressive, the man behind them even more so. In an age when professional-sports stars and politicians too often make headlines for the wrong reasons, Jim Bunning is a breath of clean, fresh air—even if that clean, fresh air can seem awfully cold to someone he doesn't like.

I was a sports columnist for the *Philadelphia Inquirer* when I first met Bunning in the mid-1960s. Jim was pitching for the Phillies then, and I was writing about them. Believe me, there were few tougher interviews in baseball than Jim Bunning after a 1-0 or 2-1 defeat, and pitching for some of those Phillies clubs gave a man ample opportunity to lose by such scores.

"I was never an easy interview," he says now. "I was pretty intense after I lost. Even after I won, if somebody asked a dumb question I told him it was a dumb question. If somebody asked, 'Why did you throw that hanging curve ball on 3 and 2?' I'd say, 'Well, that's a dumb question. If I thought I was going to hang it, I wouldn't have thrown it.'"

Thanks in large part to Jim, I learned not to ask so many dumb questions during the rest of my sportswriting career. For that alone, I am deeply in his debt.

To someone who covered Bunning in his baseball years it's amusing to hear the comments of political reporters who cover him today. Kit Wager, of the *Lexington (Ky.) Herald-Leader*, came up with a gem: "Baseball is a metaphor for his life. And everyone else is wearing the uniform of the other team."

Yes, Jim holds strong views. But to suggest that you have to agree with everything he says or does to gain (or keep) his trust and friendship simply isn't true. If Jim Bunning were the type of person some say he is, he would have stopped talking to this registered Democrat years ago—at least from the day he learned that I voted for Bill Clinton. Bunning would rather throw a hanging slider to Henry Aaron than vote for Bill Clinton. I vividly remember a casual political discussion shortly after the 1992 presidential election when he suddenly asked me how I voted. I took a deep breath, quickly glanced around the room to check the location of the nearest exit, and replied—rather bravely, I thought—"I voted for Bill Clinton."

Jim did not raise his voice in anger. He did not order me to leave and never return. True, his face showed the disappointment he clearly felt that someone he knew so well could do such a thing, but the look soon passed and our relationship remained the same.

Four years later, while visiting the Bunnings in Kentucky, Jim's wife, Mary, asked me the same question, although she phrased it a little differently. "You didn't vote for Clinton, did you?"

"Yes," I told her, "I voted for him twice." Then, seeing the look on Mary's face, I hastily added, "but not in the same election."

The low esteem in which Jim Bunning holds the president of the United States is like his feelings about some reporters. Said Al Smith, a former newspaperman who hosts a weekly political television show in Kentucky, "I think Bunning feels like reporters don't like him, and reporters feel Bunning doesn't like them."

If Bunning's dealings with the media—in sports and in politics—have been a bit edgy at times, that's largely because he has an extremely low tolerance for stories he considers unfair or flat-out untrue and for those reporters who write things or say things without checking the facts. As someone who was in the business for forty-one years, I can appreciate his concerns.

"I don't understand why people deliberately try to stir up problems for people when they quote certain sources they know are prejudiced because I'm a conservative," he told me. "And they do the same thing the other way. I won't be drawn into it any more. I know when not to say anything. In forty-seven years of dealing with the media I have learned a few things."

I was lucky. I got to know Jim well. I discovered how special he was as a human being once you scrape through that often hard exterior.

This is a guy who married his childhood sweetheart, helped her raise nine kids, and somehow found time along the way to embark on careers as a baseball player, a stock broker, a players' agent, and a minor league baseball manager before turning to politics.

The minor league managing job tells you a lot about Bunning. He had established himself as a big league star, winning 224 games, becoming the second man (Cy Young was the first) to win 100 games in each league. He pitched no-hitters in each league (matching Cy Young there, too), and made his second no-hitter the first complete perfect game in the National League in 84 years. He struck out 1,000-plus batters in each league, and when he retired he was second only to Walter Johnson in career strikeouts, with 2,855. He was a workhorse, too; from 1957 through 1967, he made 299 starts without missing a turn.

He was a genuine star, a pitcher who soared to the heights in All-Star competition, holding opposing hitters—the very best the sport had to offer—to four hits and a walk and no earned runs in his last fourteen innings of All-Star game pitching. And yet, unlike most established big league stars who think about managing when their playing days are over, Bunning didn't expect the job to be handed to him; he was willing to learn, the hard way. He rode around the northeastern United States and Canada on buses as manager of the Class Double A Reading (Pa.) Phillies in the Eastern League. Bunning then managed Triple A teams for the Phillies in Eugene, Oregon; Toledo, Ohio; and Oklahoma City.

For a total of five mostly difficult years he did it, and when he finally became quite good at it, he was fired. If there was bitterness at the time, it has vanished. By cutting short his baseball days, the Phillies opened the door to a far more important and satisfying career.

Not everyone enjoyed playing for Jim Bunning in his five minor league managerial seasons. Some players savored the experience, some hated it. Looking back on it now, most seem to appreciate what Bunning was trying to do: make them successful big league ballplayers, drive them to the limit with that goal in mind.

Mike Rogodzinski, a lefthanded-hitting outfielder who went on to have a fine year as a big league pinch hitter for the Phillies, was one who enjoyed playing for Jim. "A great pitcher, a great man," he said about his former Triple A manager in Toledo. Although Bunning's stern, all-business approach never seemed to bother Rogodzinski, Mike recognized that it bothered some players. "Jim was from the old school," he observed. "You do what you're supposed to do. If you did a good job, Jim wouldn't say, 'Good job.' That wasn't Jim's way. Sometimes you like to have someone say, 'Great job!' It would've meant a lot to some of the guys."

And a kind word from Jim Bunning did mean a great deal to those who played for him in the minors. Eddie Molush, a relief pitcher for Jim's Toledo Mud Hens, still remembers how good he felt when Bunning actually praised him after an especially strong outing. Molush relieved with Toledo trailing the Richmond Braves, 5-0, in the first inning, the bases loaded, and nobody out. He retired the side without another run scoring and went on to pitch four and two-thirds innings of no-hit, no-run ball.

His relief stint over, Molush was in the dugout when he heard Richmond manager Clint Courtney yell across the field, "Who's that kid, Jim?"

"His name's Molush," Bunning called back.

"The kid did a great job for you," Courtney replied.

As Molush recalled two decades later, "Jim turned to me and said, 'You impressed him, man.' It was real short, but coming from him. . . ."

Mike Paul, now an advance scout for the Texas Rangers, was nearing the end of his pitching career when he encountered Bunning for the first time in Toledo in 1975. He remembers how tough Bunning was on a young outfielder named Jerry Martin, a future big leaguer who was Paul's roommate that season.

"Jim would bark at him when Jerry had trouble hitting a breaking ball," Paul recollects. "He'd say, 'Shorten up your swing, hit the breaking ball.' Jerry would say, 'I'm trying.' Jim was a hard man. When I got there I'd just been released by the Cubs. I didn't know what to expect. I found this rigid personality. But I have no hard feelings."

What Mike Paul and others gradually discovered was that Bunning had another side. "I remember we were busing to Charleston [West Virginia] and he had the bus come by his home [in Fort Thomas, Kentucky] to pick us up," said Paul. "He had the whole team over for dinner. He didn't have to do that."

One man who got to know Jim extremely well was Scott Reid. Once an outfielder in the Phillies organization, Reid had the rare distinction of being the only man who played with Bunning on the 1970 Phillies, played for Bunning on the 1973 Eugene Emeralds, and coached for Bunning on the 1975 Toledo Mud Hens.

The year with Bunning at Toledo wasn't easy. "We had a terrible club," he said. But as bad as the club was, Reid called working with Jim "a good experience."

As the coach, Reid became "the middle guy." When there was a complaint—and there were plenty—the players would come to him.

"I'd say, 'This is the best guy you could ask to be playing for,'" he recalled. "I'd tell them, 'Number one, if you can play he'll get you to the big leagues. Number two, if you can't play he'll send you home and he's doing you a favor. So just bust your ass. Go play for the man. Give him everything you've got and that's all he'll ask for.

"I said, 'He's not going to be your buddy. He's not going to fraternize with you. He's just going to treat you like a man, and that's all you can ask.' Well, you know how pro baseball players are. They don't want to accept that."

The older ones—those who had spent some time in the big leagues—were accustomed to being pampered. As Reid put it, "They had an attitude." It made for some difficult times.

"Jim was Jim," Reid said. "He was trying to treat minor league players like major league players. . . . The thing that was good about Jim, there was consistency. He was that way and he was going to be that way day in, day out."

In retrospect, I really got to know Jim Bunning during those minor league managing days. Each summer I spent two or three weeks of vacation time traveling with his ball clubs, watching him work, getting to know his players. I was with him in Denver the day the Phillies' assistant farm director met with him and assured him the club wanted him back as its Triple A manager the following year. And I was with him in Kentucky the day after that same assistant farm director had phoned and told him his services were no longer required, and went on to deny saying what he had, in fact, said at their earlier, face-to-face meeting.

I have no doubt as to why the Phillies fired Bunning. As their top minor league manager, he was the logical choice to become their next big league manager, and they were reluctant—"frightened" might be a better word"—to give him the job. He was too brutally honest for their taste, too quick to say what he thought, too likely not to follow the party line when he felt the party line wasn't worth following.

As Scott Reid put it, Jim was Jim. I recall flying to Eugene in 1973 to spend a couple of weeks with Bunning's first Triple A team, the

Eugene Emeralds. One of the pitchers was Mike Fremuth, a free-spirited Princeton grad who had passed over Harvard Law School to continue his baseball career. Fremuth was the last pitcher sent down by the Phillies that spring. We were friends, and Jim knew it.

The day I arrived at the Eugene ball park Jim was standing in front of the home dugout, arms folded across his chest, watching me walk across the field. His opening line, delivered with a stern face, went something like this: "I imagine you want to see Mike Fremuth. For your information, I just released Mr. Fremuth yesterday. I left his phone number on the desk in my office."

With that, he pointed me in the direction of the office. He had, indeed, left the phone number on his desk in anticipation of my arrival. That was Jim. He didn't tell you what you wanted to hear. He told you the way things were; if you couldn't handle it, that was your problem.

To Bunning's way of thinking he did Fremuth a favor by cutting short his pitching career in the Phillies organization, opening the door for him to pursue his legal studies. Jim felt this extremely bright young man was wasting precious time playing baseball when he could be going to a top law school instead. Fremuth did enroll in Stanford Law School after his release and is now a successful lawyer in Washington, D.C. He retains his love for baseball and holds no ill feelings toward the manager who steered him away from the game.

The weeks I spent flying around Kentucky with Bunning during the fall of 1983 when he ran for governor were especially memorable. He lost that race, but three years later he was elected to Congress and he's been winning ever since. I vividly remember those cold early mornings with Jim, Mary, and some of their kids, handing out campaign literature to Kentucky commuters arriving at the bus station in downtown Cincinnati. I marveled at how far this oh-so-private man had come in shaking hands and making small talk and doing the things that politicians have to do and that so many of us thought Jim Bunning could never do.

That's the thing about Jim; he does what has to be done. Nothing is left to chance. Whatever the job, he works at it. As a pitcher he had a good arm, not a great one. This was no Walter Johnson or Bob Feller or Bob Gibson throwing virtually unhittable fast balls. Bunning threw hard, but not *that* hard. Yet he struck out all those big league hitters, won all those big league games, and wound up enshrined in Cooperstown. Not bad for a guy who was repeatedly told, early in his pro career, that he wouldn't be successful throwing the way he did—sidearm with a stiff front leg. They worried about his ability to get out lefthanded hitters. They were concerned about the way he flew off the mound after delivering a pitch, which made it difficult for him to field his position.

"They tried for three years in the minor leagues to get me to 'break' my front leg when I hit [the ground] so I could come up and be fielding," he told me. "I tried my darndest to do that."

He was advised to throw more overhand to get overspin on his breaking ball so it would break down. He tried doing that, too. But it wasn't until he went back to throwing the way he always had that he achieved success. He learned to throw a curve ball that broke down, no easy task considering the angle from which he released the ball. He came up with a slider that was more deceptive than an ordinary slider because it looked *exactly* like his fast ball on the way to the plate. "I'm not saying I was right and they were wrong," he remarked. "I just couldn't do it [their way] successfully."

So he did it his way. In his first full big league season, Bunning won twenty games pitching for the Detroit Tigers in a ball park known as a hitters' paradise, especially for lefthanded power hitters, who could take aim at a short right field porch with an overhanging upper deck.

Rep. Robert Borski, a Democrat from Pennsylvania who served with Bunning on the House Ethics Committee, said of Jim in a newspaper interview: "He comes at you with the high hard ones. He's a good guy, very principled, but a tough hombre. He's not out there to make friends. It was said of him that if his mother dug in on him with two strikes, he'd knock her down. I believe it."

I don't believe it. Jim loved his mother very much. At most he might have brushed her back a little. But then, I've had the opportunity to see the other side of Jim Bunning, a man who demands no more from others than he demands from himself. This is a bright, multitalented, incredibly determined man with a most understanding wife (without whom he never could have made it through those early political campaigns), nine fine kids, and—at last count—thirty-one grandchildren.

It's a rare person who makes it to the big leagues in two vastly dissimilar professions. Jim Bunning is a rare person. Those who know him, above all those who played against him in the big leagues, or played for him in the minor leagues, or sit with him in the House of Representatives, would be hard-pressed to dispute that.

The Best Day

Perhaps "good things come to those who wait," but this was getting ridiculous. Jim Bunning was convinced he would never make it to baseball's Hall of Fame.

He was accustomed to elections. But not this kind of election. Run for political office and you need only a majority of the votes to win, maybe even less if more than two are in the race. In baseball's annual Hall of Fame balloting, the magic number is 75 percent. No exceptions. No rounding off percentages. Fail to get three-quarters of the votes and it's wait 'til next year. Jim Bunning got fed up with waiting.

In politics, you wage a campaign, you cast your vote on election day, and then you wait, eyes glued to a television set, an ear pressed against a telephone as the results roll in. Win, and you give a victory speech to your cheering, adoring supporters; lose, and you deliver a concession speech. Either way, it was your campaign. Your victory. Your defeat. You played the major role in the outcome.

Baseball's Hall of Fame election is different. Ten-year members of the Baseball Writers Association of America do the voting. A player doesn't become eligible until five years after his last hurrah. Most Hall of Famers are forced to wait much longer than that. Despite being honored as baseball's "outstanding living player," Joe DiMaggio didn't become a Hall of Famer until his third year on the ballot. Juan Marichal, one of the premier pitchers of his era, also had to wait until his third year. Eddie Collins made it in his fourth year, Eddie Mathews his fifth. Mickey Cochrane needed six years, Joe Medwick seven, Joe Cronin ten, and Ralph Kiner fifteen.

Jim Bunning almost made it in his twelfth year of eligibility, falling four votes short (for 74.2 percent of the votes cast). Nine writers turned in blank ballots, in effect voting against everybody. Had they simply failed to return signed ballots Bunning would have made it, which only heightened his disappointment and made him more certain than ever that he should have insisted his name be removed from consideration years before.

Bunning never could understand why the support a man got varied so greatly from one year to another. His record didn't change from his first year of eligibility to his fifth, or tenth, or fifteenth. Why should he get 20 percent of the votes one year, 50 percent another year, and 74.2 percent another year?

When he didn't come close in 1976, his first year on the ballot, Jim asked to have his name removed from future consideration.

"Do me a favor," he said over the phone. "Get me off the ballot. I don't want to go through this for fifteen years."

"But you might make it some day," I told him. "A lot of people don't vote for somebody the first year, or the second year. Later on, though, they do."

"Why should I get more votes ten or fifteen years from now?" Bunning replied. "I'm not going to win any more games."

It isn't easy to argue with Jim Bunning under any circumstances, and he clearly had common sense on his side this time. Fortunately, he finally gave in (very reluctantly) and allowed his name to remain on the ballot. Several times in the years that followed Jim regretted that decision and made it a point to say so. "I shouldn't have listened to you," he would say.

Bunning received 143 votes his first year, 187 his second year, and 147 (34 percent) his third year. If the increased support in his second year had been encouraging, what happened in the third year was a terrible letdown.

"I'm not going to worry about that damn thing," Jim said. "I've seen too many guys eat their hearts out worrying about getting in the Hall of Fame. I'm not angry. Aggravated is more the correct word. My family is hyper about it. I'm not. I'm not going to campaign . . . I feel I've accomplished certain things in my career. What I did in baseball they can't take away. The fun I had playing the game, the money I earned, the accomplishments—no matter if I'm never voted to anything, they still can't take that away."

That was the second time Bunning asked to have his name removed from the ballot, and the second time he was talked out of it.

By 1984, his eighth year of eligibility, Bunning's vote total was climbing again . . . even if it wasn't climbing enough. It jumped again in 1985, which led many to believe that 1986 would be the magic year. Jim, of course, had doubts, although the sudden interest of the television networks made him wonder if they knew something he didn't know.

Jim and Mary Bunning were driving to their Fort Thomas home from Florida when word got to them that NBC and CBS were trying to contact him. So Bunning called.

"We want you to come on the *Today* show Thursday morning," the person from NBC informed him.

"We want you on the *CBS Morning News*, the voice over the phone from CBS said.

"Why?" Bunning asked each time.

Twice the answer came back loud and clear.

"We've been informed there's a very good chance you'll make the Hall of Fame," they told him.

He was to fly to New York after the vote was announced Wednesday night. There would be a limo to pick him up at his midtown hotel at 6:30 A.M. It sounded, for all the world, as if the two networks had been tipped off. One problem. The votes wouldn't even be counted until Wednesday evening. The networks were lining him up—together, no doubt, with such other hot Hall of Fame prospects as Willie McCovey, Billy Williams, and Catfish Hunter—just in case.

It's a cruel way to do things.

Bunning found out while eating dinner shortly before 10 P.M. that he had failed to get the necessary 75 percent, missing by forty votes. At 11:30 the networks called back.

"They told me, 'Forget it,'" Bunning recalled. "You know how the girl [from one of the networks] put it? She said, 'Maybe the next time.' I said, 'Fine.' You know what I wanted to tell her?"

A year later came another big buildup to a letdown. As the day drew near his phone kept ringing. Sportswriters and sportscasters from around the country wanted to know where he would be on the night of decision. They all made it clear they thought he had an excellent chance to make up the forty votes he lacked in 1986. Bob Lemon, a twenty-game winner seven times, had made it in his twelfth year of eligibility; maybe Jim would make it a year sooner.

Excitement grew. Get enough phone calls, have enough people build up your hopes, and, despite all those years of disappointment, it's hard not to catch the fever.

And then, two nights before the results were to be announced, Jim's mother suffered three strokes and went into a coma. Suddenly, Cooperstown didn't seem all that important.

It seemed plenty important to the television crews and the reporters who showed up at the Bunnings' home on Hall of Fame election night, however. There Jim and Mary sat, together with the media types, making small talk, waiting for the happy news from New York. Only there was no happy news. This time Jim had missed by twenty-one votes. The camera crews and the newspaper reporters tiptoed out.

Not surprisingly, Jim and Mary Bunning got as far away as they could on the night the votes were counted in 1988. Waiting for a congratulatory phone call that never came, while a mob of reporters and would-be well-wishers sat in your living room, got to be downright embarrassing.

So the Bunnings solved the problem by going to Maui for a short vacation, telling only a few close friends where they could be contacted. It turned out to be a good move. This was the year of the blank ballots, the year Jim lost by four votes and eight-tenths of a percentage point. Needing 321 of the 427 votes cast, he got 317. Although Bunning had three more years on the writers' ballot, he never came close again.

The 1988 failure was the hardest to take. Athletes are geared to make things happen, not to wait for somebody else to make them happen. That's what makes baseball's Hall of Fame election so difficult for many of them to endure.

Jim Bunning couldn't pick up a baseball and try to get his 2,856th strikeout or his 225th victory. For a man of action, the waiting, accompanied by a feeling of helplessness, is a darn sight rougher than facing Ted Williams with two out in the ninth inning at Fenway Park and a no-hitter on the line. Or throwing a 2-2 curve ball to the Mets' John Stephenson with two out in the ninth inning at Shea Stadium and a perfect game hanging in the balance. On those occasions success or failure was in Bunning's hands, not in the hands of several hundred baseball writers with varied opinions and prejudices and levels of knowledge.

This election night was a far cry from the ones Congressman Bunning had grown accustomed to in his political life. No reports from outlying areas. No network projections. No sense of how things were going. Just waiting. And waiting. And then, nothing.

I had the unpleasant duty of calling Jim in Maui with the results.

"Sorry, you missed by four votes. Yeah, four votes."

"I think I was right the first time," he said. "If you don't make it right away you should take your name off the ballot so you won't have to go through this bull every year."

In the end, though, all that he and Mary went through on those Hall of Fame election nights made his eventual 1996 election by the Veterans Committee that much sweeter. In a way it meant more, too, Bunning would say later, because the men on that committee were his contemporaries. They had seen him pitch; in some cases they had hit against him. They knew firsthand what he could do, how fine a pitcher and how tough a competitor he was.

The Veterans Committee included former major league general managers Joe L. Brown, Buzzie Bavasi, and Hank Peters; former Negro League player/manager/scout Buck O'Neil; former players Ted Williams, Stan Musial, Monte Irvin, Yogi Berra, Pee Wee Reese, and Bill White, the latter recently retired as National League president; the writers Allen Lewis, Bob Broeg, Leonard Koppett, and Edgar Munzel; and the broadcaster Ken Coleman. Under the rules they could elect just one player, who had to get 75 percent of the votes. As it turned out, two players hit the 75 percent mark: Bunning received thirteen of the fifteen votes, Nellie Fox twelve. (Fox was elected a year later.)

So it was that the call came in to Congressman Bunning's Washington office. Jim wasn't even thinking about the Hall of Fame on this day. Not after enduring all those past disappointments.

"I had put it away, put it out of my mind," he said. "I thought I'm not going to make it. Even though I had advocates—people like Allen Lewis [the retired *Philadelphia Inquirer* baseball writer] on the committee, and some of the people I played against—I never thought I could get 75 percent of everybody. I had put it so I would never let it become so big in my life that it would make me upset or get me disturbed. I had done, I think, a pretty good job of putting it away."

And then all of a sudden it happened. Ed Stack, president of the

Hall of Fame, placed the call from the Airport Marriott in Tampa, Florida, where the Veterans Committee meets each March. At the moment the phone rang in Bunning's office, Jim was meeting with delegates from the union that represents the treasury employees at the Internal Revenue Service, not exactly his most rabid boosters. "They said I'd never meet with them, so I said I'm going to meet with them," Jim recalled.

There were fifteen of them in Bunning's private office. The meeting was going hot and heavy—too hot and too heavy to be interrupted by a phone call from Tampa.

"They told me it's the president of the Hall of Fame," Bunning said. "I said, 'Take a message. I'll call him back.' And I didn't pay any attention to it."

All those years Bunning had waited for a phone call that never came. Now it had come and he was too busy to take it. He left Stack hanging on the other end and went on with the meeting. Finally, one of Jim's associates came in and said, "He won't hang up. He's holding."

Stack had held for ten minutes. When Bunning finally took the call, Stack handed the phone to Allen Lewis of the Veterans Committee, the former baseball writer for the *Philadelphia Inquirer* whose thorough research and presentation of Bunning's Hall of Fame qualifications played a major role in Jim's election.

"I picked up the phone," Bunning recalled, "and he said, 'Congratulations, you have just been elected to the Hall of Fame by the Veterans Committee.' And I said, 'Tell me one thing now—this is for sure. They can't take it back.'"

Lewis, himself a Hall of Famer in the writers' wing, assured him the deed was done. Twenty-five years after his final season as an active player, Jim Bunning had become a Hall of Famer.

"After waiting so darn long I didn't know how it worked on the Veterans Committee," Bunning said. "I didn't know that if I got one more vote than Nellie Fox, and both of us had enough votes to get in, only one gets in."

Now he knew. In the next few minutes Bill White, an old friend and onetime Phillies teammate, got on the phone to congratulate him. So did a fellow Kentuckian, Pee Wee Reese, the former Dodger shortstop and Hall of Famer. His first at-bat against Bunning came in an exhibition game in Miami; Jim, just a kid at the time, drilled him in the elbow with a pitch. Reese later told Bunning it was the hardest he'd ever been hit, but—letting bygones be bygones—Pee Wee voted for Bunning and joined the parade of well-wishers on the phone. Yogi Berra was the next to welcome Bunning to baseball's most exclusive club. Yogi always had a soft spot in his heart for Jim. "I hit good against him," he said.

That afternoon the new Hall of Famer was a hot topic on the floor of the House of Representatives.

"Mr. Speaker, I have a very special announcement to make," began Congressman Henry Hyde of Illinois. "One of our colleagues, the gentleman from Kentucky, was just named to the Baseball Hall of Fame." Added Hyde, "His selection was not by baseball writers, but by the veterans themselves, which makes it, it seems to me, a little loftier in stature."

Congressman Curt Weldon of Pennsylvania called Bunning "my boyhood idol when I was a Phillies fan growing up in the suburbs" and said, "Jim Bunning represented the same ideals that Cal Ripken stands for today. Mr. Speaker," he went on, "while we acknowledge Jim Bunning's leadership as a professional baseball player, let us also acknowledge his stature as a human being and as a father and as a husband and a man. As the proud parent of nine children, and who knows how many grandchildren, Jim Bunning really epitomizes what is right with this country. I am proud to call him not just a colleague, but someone that all of us can look up to in this country as a true role model for America."

And so it went on what, for Jim Bunning, was an unforgettable day, one he thought would never come. When it was his turn to speak, his voice cracked from emotions he seldom displayed in public.

"Mr. Speaker," he said, "it is hard to speak after twenty-five years . . . None of the numbers that were on the back of my [baseball] card have changed in that time. They are all the same numbers that I retired with, so it has been a long waiting process. Thank God it happened while I was still on my feet. Sometimes it happens posthumously. I really appreciate the Veterans Committee. As the gentleman from Illinois, Henry Hyde, said, 'Those are some of your peers that voted you in.'

"Particularly, I talked with Yogi Berra, who was on the committee, and I talked with Pee Wee Reese, who was on the committee. I talked to Bill White, one of my teammates from Philadelphia, after the vote was taken today . . . I would be remiss if I did not mention Allen

Lewis, who happened to be a beat writer in Philadelphia when I was playing. It was through his efforts that this happened, nobody else's. Thank you very much."

The man who had wanted to be removed from consideration nearly two decades earlier was deeply touched by the honor. And deeply grateful that he had been talked out of doing what he wanted to do. Shortly after his election he phoned and said simply, "You were right."

"Jim wanted it so bad, but he never let on," Mary Bunning said.

But nobody wanted it more than Mary. On the day Jim was elected his wife was getting her hair done in Washington. "I knew he was going to find out at 2 or 2:30," she remembered. "So I called down there . . . and Jim said, 'We won.' I was so excited, I kissed the guy that did my hair."

From the beauty parlor, Mary drove to Jim's office. "I said, to Jim, 'What should I do?' And he said, 'Well, I guess go home.' So I was driving down route 66 in Washington and I thought, 'Go home my foot. I went through his whole career with him.'"

Mary Bunning wasn't about to miss anything that happened on this day. So she turned around and headed back for the office. Her husband, the Hall of Famer, was doing an interview when she got there. "So I went in," Mary remembered, "and I sat on his lap while he was talking to this newspaperman about the Hall of Fame."

After that, the staff brought in the champagne, and the celebration was on. It was a beautiful day in the lives of the Bunnings, but an even more beautiful one was to follow: induction day in Cooperstown.

It was a family affair. All nine Bunning kids were there: Barbara, Joan, Jim, Cathy, Bill, Bridget (who sang the National Anthem at the induction ceremonies), Mark, Amy, and Dave. Twenty-one of the grandchildren were there, too.

Each day, Mary took a walk through the streets of downtown Cooperstown. "It was neat," she said, "because I kept running into the kids."

The morning after the induction Mary Bunning was out walking at 7, still too revved up to sleep late. She went over to the Hall of Fame; it wasn't open yet, but already there were people outside, some of them sleeping. Mary caught the attention of someone at the gate, told him who she was, and said, "I'd like to go in before anybody else, if you'll let me."

One look at Mary Bunning, at the joy and excitement in her face, and nobody could turn down that request. So inside she went, dressed in her jogging suit. Jim's plaque was already in place.

"I stood there," she said, "and I looked at the plaque, and I cried."

On each of her walks, Mary searched for memorabilia. When she returned to the big hotel on the lake, where the Hall of Famers stayed, she was loaded down with things for her husband to sign.

"I'd stop and look at the store windows and see what they had of Jim's," Mary said. "And then they'd see my pin [identifying her as a member of a Hall of Famer's family] and they'd say, 'What part of the family are you?' I'd say, 'I'm Mary. I'm his wife.' 'Oh,' they'd say, 'then get this signed and that signed.' Jim's been very good about signing."

The Bunnings loved every minute of that weekend in Cooperstown. "To watch Jim," his wife said, "it was just a transformation of him. We had many, many wonderful highlights in our married life and during his baseball career and congressional career, but this was it. This was the pinnacle. This was just wonderful."

Best of all, they could share this moment with the rest of the family. In that sense, Mary decided, "I'm glad it happened later. If it hadn't been later our grandsons and granddaughters wouldn't have seen it. I only felt bad about his mom and dad not seeing it, but they were there in spirit."

Jim's parents may not have lived to see him inducted, but they had a feeling it was just a matter of time. On Christmas Day, 1971, they presented him with two huge scrapbooks, filled with stories of his baseball exploits. Pasted on the first page of the first scrapbook was a typewritten letter:

"We wish to dedicate these two scrapbooks to our middle son, James Paul David Bunning, who we held as a tiny infant, loved as an exploring child, disciplined as a young boy, and tried to guide as a young man. But before we realized it he was grown up, married, and with a family of his own.

"But even as a boy he had big dreams, and by his hard work and devotion and determination and the help of a loving and understanding wife, he made a success of what he wanted to be.

"May this be an inspiration to his children in the future, or any young person with big dreams.

"We are thankful for the great moments he gave us and the millions of people who followed his outstanding career.

"We hope as the years pass he will be enshrined in baseball's Hall of Fame."

It was signed, "Lovingly, your devoted mother and dad."

Little wonder that Jim Bunning had to fight back tears as he spoke of his parents in his induction speech.

"My mother and father are the first on my thank-you list," he said. "I thank them for their loving care and guidance, for always being there when I needed them, and for their keen and constant interest in my career.

"My biggest regret is that they can't be here to share this day with me. But I know they're watching from somewhere up above us. And I know they're cheering today . . . just like they did in Richmond, Indiana, in 1950. [when Jim broke in as a professional baseball player at age 18]."

Among those who did share this day with Jim Bunning was his old friend and teammate, fellow Hall of Famer Al Kaline.

"That was great," Kaline said of Jim's election to the Hall of Fame.

At the time, Kaline was telecasting Detroit Tigers games with George Kell, another Hall of Famer. Since both couldn't skip their telecasting duties and go to Cooperstown on the same day, they alternated each year.

"I wasn't scheduled to be there that year," Kaline said. "Because of Jim, George Kell and I switched. I wanted to be there. Jim and I were real close."

Bunning said thank you to a lot of people that day. He worked hard on his speech, and the hardest part, he said, was trimming it to its final twenty-nine minutes.

Al Kaline and several more of Jim's big league teammates were not the only ones to go to Cooperstown to see him inducted. Marvin Miller, retired head of the Players Association, as well as some of the young men who had played for Bunning in the minor leagues, were there too. All in all, the day couldn't have been much better.

"Ladies and gentlemen, thank you very much," an emotional Jim Bunning told the crowd. "You have made this the best day of my life."

Turning Pro

It didn't make a splash in the local paper, just a couple of paragraphs: "James Bunning, son of Mr. and Mrs. Louis A. Bunning, has signed a contract with the Detroit Tigers, it was announced this week. He has been serving as pitcher for the Bavarian Beers in the K.A.G. semi-pro baseball league."

Not much coverage for a kid who had been a three-sport star (basketball, football, and baseball) at Saint Xavier High School. Bunning was good enough in basketball to make the All-Greater Cincinnati team and attract the attention of college scouts. He could have gone to Louisville or Miami of Ohio or even Oregon State for basketball, but he wanted to stay as close to home—and to Mary—as possible. So he chose Xavier of Ohio, just across the river.

Bunning played freshman basketball at Xavier, having a so-so season, and his thoughts turned to baseball. His freshman basketball coach, Ned Walk, was also the freshman baseball coach. Jim pitched three games for him and Walk, who went on to gain considerable fame as basketball coach at Arizona State, advised Bunning to concentrate on baseball. "You're good enough to make it," he told him.

The Tigers were interested and Jim was ready to sign, but his parents wanted him to complete his college education. What if he bombed as a pro baseball pitcher? What then?

The Bunnings reached a compromise with the Tigers. Their son would turn pro on the condition that he could skip spring training until he had his degree. For three years he reported to his minor league team only after completing the spring semester at Xavier.

That explains, in part, why this future Hall of Famer spent five full seasons and large parts of two others in the minor leagues before becoming a full-fledged Detroit Tiger.

Baseball was different then. There were fewer teams; the need for qualified pitchers was less acute than it is today. Now big league teams, desperate for pitching help, rush kids up to the majors with minimal experience, often hurting them in the process. In Bunning's day it wasn't unusual for a promising young pitcher to spend four or five years in the bushes, honing his skills, waiting for his big chance.

Frank Lary, another Tiger standout of the period, spent five seasons in the minors. Art Mahaffey, who would room with Bunning years later as a Phillie, needed four full years and most of a fifth to reach what ballplayers call "the Show." But *seven* years? Even then, although hardly unprecedented, that was a lot.

The money wasn't a lot. Jim got $4,000 for signing and a salary of $150 a month, which helped buy an engagement ring for Mary and pay for the basketball scholarship he no longer had. A year later the Tigers boosted his salary to a whopping $225 a month. The only baseball millionaires in those days owned ball clubs; they didn't play for them.

The young Jim Bunning was no sure-fire, can't-miss pitching star of the future. "I didn't throw the ball 98 miles an hour," he said. "I was 90, 91, 92 tops."

Still pretty good; a number of successful big league pitchers don't throw that hard. But hardly a guarantee that Bunning would make it to the big leagues, no less the Hall of Fame.

His professional career began in Richmond, Indiana, in the Class D Ohio-Indiana League, with the lowest of the Tigers' nine minor league teams. Jim could have gone to either of Detroit's other two "D" clubs (in Thomasville, Georgia, or Jamestown, New York) but the decision was a no-brainer. Richmond was an hour from home. Jim and Mary saw a lot of each other that summer.

Bunning had no difficulty staying out of trouble in his first pro season; after joining the club at the end of the school year in June, he lived with the Richmond chief of police. Jim won his first five decisions, then discovered it wasn't that easy. He lost his next seven and wound up 7 and 8. It would be the first of four consecutive losing seasons.

Bunning showed flashes, though. The following year, pitching for the Quad City Tigers (Davenport, Iowa) in the Three-I League, the nineteen-year-old righthander blanked the Quincy (Illinois) Gems on two hits, 5-0, in his first start. His first day in Davenport after arriving from college, however, hadn't been quite as promising. Jim was sitting in the stands behind home plate between teammate Charley Moore and Mrs. Moore, eight months' pregnant. A foul ball came drifting back, back, heading right for them. Mrs. Moore ducked. Mr. Bunning gallantly hollered, "I'll get it," and got to his feet. He got it all right; the ball hit him between his mouth and nose. "I forgot to close my hands," said Bunning. He never won a Gold Glove in the big leagues, either.

Jim won eight games his second year (losing ten), but he had not yet become a household name, even in Three-I League circles. A case in point is this headline that appeared in the local *Daily Times*, heralding the news that Jim had held the Terre Haute Phillies hitless for eight and one-third innings: "Singles Spoil No-Hit Bid by Don Bunning."

Hey, he's been called worse. Besides, the rest of the facts were accurate. Bunning did, indeed, come within two outs of a no-hitter, Terre Haute finally getting to him for three straight hits in the bottom of the ninth. It would be stretching the point to call his performance a pitching gem, however. Jim issued fourteen walks that night.

Ten days later, the paper informed its readers about another Bunning triumph, this one in Waterloo, Iowa. This time, the account began: "Behind Dick Bunning's four-hitter and the slugging of Bob Erps, the Tigers blanked Waterloo, 10-0, here Thursday night."

Even then, apparently, sportswriters were having a hard time getting to know Jim Bunning. More important, Jim was starting to show signs of becoming a pitcher with a future. That second pro year he gave up just two home runs, a seemingly fantastic achievement for a guy who, like so many hard throwers, yielded more than a few gopher balls in his career. According to Bunning, though, it wasn't all that fantastic. "We pitched with a Wilson ball that was kind of dead," he recollected.

Still, just two home runs. . . . Seems impossible. Maybe the others Jim gave up that season were charged to Don and Dick.

Back to college went Bunning, taking twenty-two hours the next year in order to speed up his graduation. Then off to Williamsport, Pennsylvania, after marrying Mary in January.

Marriage was fine, the team was awful. "Probably the worst team I played on," he said.

It wasn't all bad, however. His teammates included righthander Paul Foytack and second baseman Frank Bolling, both of whom went on to enjoy productive big league careers. Wins were hard to come by, though; Bunning went 5 and 9. But he was making progress of a sort. The sportswriters in Williamsport and around the Eastern League referred to him as "Jim."

Best of all, he graduated from Xavier the following January, doing it in three and a half years. So for the first time in his pro career, Bunning went to spring training in 1953. In fact, he was the second player ever to report to Tigertown, which had just been completed in Lakeland, Florida. At long last, Jim would get to meet *all* the players in the Detroit organization. "I'd been to 'D' ball, 'B,' and 'A' and never met anybody in the Tiger organization except those I played with," he remembered.

Initially, he was assigned to the Triple A Buffalo team, managed by Jack Tighe. "It was the oldest Triple A team in the history of the world," Bunning said. He and Frank Lary were the "kids" on the team —"the only ones under thirty. That Triple A team won everything."

Most of the time Bunning did nothing but watch. He pitched a total of five innings the first month, then got optioned to Little Rock in the Southern Association. There he did a lot of pitching, and a lot of ducking. "I never got hit harder in my life," he recalled.

Paul Campbell, who had managed him in Williamsport and later became traveling secretary for the Cincinnati Reds, was the Little Rock skipper, and he kept throwing Bunning out there every fourth day. Bunning wondered where that dead Wilson ball was when he needed it.

"They used a ball called the '97,'" said Jim. "It was made by McGregor."

And it was last seen flying over Southern Association fences, which weren't that far away. Lots of "little bandbox ball parks," Bunning said, ticking them off. Let's see, there was Nashville and Memphis and New Orleans and Mobile and . . . Well, you get the idea. The heat didn't help, either. Jim won five games and lost twelve that season. The following year the Tigers gave him a major league contract. They must have been impressed by his rising strikeout figures (124 in 158 innings) and his dwindling number of walks (66).

Freddie Hutchinson was the manager of the Tigers when Bunning reported to his first big league camp in 1954. Jim had a good spring and impressed Hutchinson, who went out of his way to have a good long talk with Bunning when he was sent down.

"Hutch called me in and said, 'Here's what you have to do if you want to be a major league pitcher,'" Jim recalled. "He said, 'You've got to have a breaking ball to get over when you're behind hitters, and you've got to get better command of your breaking stuff.' He's the only manager I ever had who called me in and told me what I had to do to get to the big leagues. He was great."

Bunning returned to Little Rock in 1954. The ball was still lively, the fences were still short, the weather was still hot. But he had a manager, Bill Norman, he really liked. For the first time in his professional career, Jim Bunning became a winning pitcher (13 and 11).

"It was because of Norman's confidence and direction," he said. "Every time I would pitch poorly he would get me aside and say, 'You've got to think more on the mound. You've got to get control of yourself. When you do, you'll get control of the ball and everything will work.' He's the first manager I ever had a relationship with."

Bunning returned to the big league camp the next spring. The Tigers had a new manager, Bucky Harris. Bunning had no relationship with him. "He had yet to say hello, speak, or even acknowledge that I was with the club," said Jim.

Bunning pitched three innings with the big club that spring, then was sent to Buffalo. He returned to the minor leagues angry with the way he had been ignored in the big league camp and determined to show the Tigers they had made a mistake. He went 8 and 5, gave up just 106 hits in 129 innings, struck out 105, and earned a trip to Detroit. The Tigers were terrible. Harris was still managing. And Jim didn't exactly set the American League on fire, going 3 and 5 with a 6.35 earned run average and winding up in the bullpen. But it was a taste of the major leagues, and once a man finds out what it's like up there he can't wait to make it his permanent address.

A winter's worth of pitching in Mexico City prepared him to make the move. Or so he thought. Bunning went 9 and 4 for a championship team in the Mexican Winter League and fully expected to begin the 1956 season in Detroit. Unfortunately for him, he had one option left, so the Tigers shipped him out again—this time to Charleston, West Virginia, the home of their new Triple A team.

That would be Bunning's final minor league stop as a player. Recalled by the big club in July, he would remain a major leaguer for the next fifteen full seasons. Getting there had been a long, hard struggle. Overly long, in Bunning's view.

"I pitched 1,000 innings before I got to the big leagues," he said. "We used to joke that I was the all-time strikeout leader in baseball [at the time of his retirement] if you counted the 700 strikeouts in the minor leagues."

Actually, Bunning pitched 1,050 innings in the minors, striking out 788 batters. Added to his 2,855 big league strikeouts, that would give him a total of 3,643. Walter Johnson, who never pitched minor league baseball—he began his storied pro career as a major leaguer at the age of twenty—had 3,508. If it's true, as some have said, that a pitcher has only so many innings in his arm, Jim Bunning wasted a lot of precious innings in the minor leagues.

Bucky Harris stuck Bunning back in the bullpen when the pitcher returned to Detroit. Jim appeared in fifteen games, winning five of six decisions. From there he went to Cuba for another round of winter ball. He was 11 and 4 there, and did it while pitching against many major league-caliber hitters. He was ready to be a starter in Detroit—so ready that he won twenty games for the Tigers the following season.

James Bunning, son of Mr. and Mrs. Louis A. Bunning, former star pitcher for the semi-pro Bavarian Beers, was about to make some big headlines. Neither Don Bunning nor Dick Bunning was ever heard from again.

Mary

Jim Bunning should run for president for one reason above all others: his wife would make one of the best, most caring First Ladies this country has ever known.

Her name was Mary Theis. She was tall and slender and lovely, with a disposition that made anyone in her presence feel just a little bit better. She and Jim lived a mile apart in Southgate, Kentucky — "a minute away by bike," he recalled. "All I had to do was ride down a hill."

That hill was extremely well traveled. Mary was in the fourth grade at Saint Terese Parochial Grade School and Jim was in the fifth when they met, even though their families had known each other for years.

"We liked each other and fell in love in high school, I guess," Mary said. "But we liked each other all the way through grade school."

"She was very tall and very pretty," Jim said. And she had a strict father who wasn't thrilled about having young boys going steady with his young daughters.

"We started dating in the seventh and eighth [grades]," Bunning recalled, "but not with the cooperation of her father. He was very protective. He had four daughters and he didn't trust any of the guys that dated his daughters."

Mary's father wanted her home at midnight every time young Jim Bunning escorted her out of the house. The rule was in force at all times, New Year's Eve included. Mary's mom came to the rescue, though. Sometimes she would arrange for Mary to stay overnight at a friend's house, enabling Jim and her daughter to stretch the curfew on special occasions.

From the beginning they were about as perfect a pair as you're likely to find. It takes a special woman to be a baseball wife. All the moving. All the traveling. All the uncertainties. All the lonely days and nights when your husband, the pitcher, is on the road. Mary made it look almost easy, even if it wasn't.

Without a devoted, understanding wife Jim Bunning couldn't have survived those seven years bouncing around the minor leagues—from Richmond, Indiana, to Davenport, Iowa, to Williamsport, Pennsylvania, to Buffalo, New York, to Little Rock, Arkansas, back to Buffalo, and finally to Charleston, West Virginia—a tour of the country interrupted only by brief trips to Detroit.

Nor could he have made it through that culture shock known as winter ball. And how many wives, after living through all those minor league seasons, and seventeen years in the big leagues—while raising nine children—would say, "If that's what you want, hon," when her husband announces upon his retirement as an active player that he wants to return to the minors to learn how to be a manager?

She was home with the kids when he was on the mound, trying to establish himself as a pitcher good enough to face big league hitters. He was able to concentrate on what he had to do because he knew she was doing what she had to do.

Later, when baseball left their lives and politics entered, Mary Bunning was there again. Without her, there's no way Jim could have made it through those early campaigning efforts. Mary had this knack of walking up to strangers and making them feel like they were old friends in minutes. Her warmth, her enthusiasm were ideal for the taxing job of being a politician's wife. And God knows that Jim Bunning, no slap-on-the-back, glad-hander type by any stretch of the imagination, needed someone to lead the way on those door-to-door precinct walks to get him out of his shell.

They dated eight years before they were married, and they've been married forty-six years. That's a long time together, and a lot of mostly terrific memories.

Mary was not a baseball fan when she became Mrs. Jim Bunning. "I really hated baseball," she said. "I hated it because it took him away from me."

She watched Jim pitch semi-pro ball for twenty-five dollars a week and decided that wasn't so bad because it provided them with date money. But, really, she went to the games because she wanted to be with him. "And then," she said, "when he signed professionally the only thing baseball did was take him away. He missed so many things at home."

Especially in those difficult early years. As Mary put it, "The minor leagues were horrible."

Only rarely did Mary see Jim pitch in the minors. The kids were small. She didn't have anybody to help her with them. So while Jim was at the ball park, Mary would prepare dinner for them, get them all in bed, and wait for her husband to come home.

For a while, Mary didn't get to see Jim pitch in the big leagues, either. "He said I made him nervous," she recalled. "I thought, 'That's stupid. If I'm going to be in this, I'm going to go.' So I had one of the other wives leave me a ticket."

The wives' seats were behind the Tigers dugout. Mary brought a newspaper along, and when Jim came striding off the mound back to the dugout at the end of each inning she hid behind it. "If he wins," she thought, "I'll stay. If he loses, I'll go home and he'll never know I was there."

Jim won. Mary stayed. End of stupid superstition.

"It was over," Jim acknowledged. "From then on she came any time she wanted."

And she didn't have to buy a newspaper to do it.

"It's our life together," Mary told him. "I went through all the minor leagues, and at least you're in the big leagues now and I'm going to go to the ball games."

Mary liked to be around people. Above all, she liked to be around Jim. That's what made the minor league experience so dreadful. Their first child, Barbara, was born in 1952, eleven months after they were married. Jim was in college at the time, and when the school year ended he had to leave to join his minor league team.

"Then we had Laura the next year," Mary said. "She's the little girl that died, and Jim had to leave again, and that was a horrible time for me. I had a lot of sorrow over that."

Laura contracted spinal meningitis and died when she was three days old. While Jim was away, pitching for Buffalo and Little Rock, Mary's parents and her sister Joan helped her through that difficult period.

No wonder Mary Bunning hated minor league baseball and the

separations that were so much a part of it. In 1956, when Cathy was born, Jim had to leave to play baseball in Cuba while Mary was in the hospital. He had little choice. They had bought a house the year before in Fort Thomas, Kentucky, and the extra money from winter ball was needed to meet the payments. "I knew that," Mary said, "but it was awful."

It takes a lot of patience, a lot of love, a lot of trust to be a baseball wife.

"I remember a trip Jim took," Mary said. "He'd been out in San Francisco, and he got a letter from this girl. He got home and showed it to me. She said, 'Dear Jim, I certainly enjoyed our weekend together in San Francisco.' He knew he didn't do that, so he got the schedule out and he wasn't even in San Francisco on the weekend she said."

"Our relationship," Jim said recently, "is better than it ever was and it gets better all the time. She's an unusual gal."

That's putting it mildly. Listening to some of their early adventures now you wonder how they ever survived them. Imagine packing all those kids in a car—and later, when the numbers increased, in two cars—and taking off from Kentucky to Eugene, Oregon, while dad was off pitching for a living. Young Jimmy was driving one car, his mother the other. In all, eight kids were along for the ride; Barbara was an exchange student in Mexico that year.

"Bill was the navigator," Mary recalled. "We each had a copy of where we were going to stay and what we were going to do. We really made a trip out of it. We wanted to go to the Painted Desert and the Grand Canyon. We all decided it was going to be fun."

Not quite. The cars got separated. Mary decided to drive to the Painted Desert, assuming—hoping—that Jimmy would follow the itinerary and be there when she arrived. But he wasn't. Mary was a nervous wreck until Jimmy drove up hours later.

"Then we stayed at the Grand Canyon one night," Mary remembered. "I don't know why, but I thought the Grand Canyon had a fence around it. Well, we were there and Mark (he was about eight) had a camera and he dropped the little lens cover down the canyon and he said, 'Oh, Mom, I'll get it,' and he started down that canyon. I got so nervous I said, 'We're not staying here. Take a good look because we're leaving.' I thought, 'I can't watch all these kids up here.'"

Goodbye Grand Canyon, hello Disneyland. There, at least, Mary Bunning knew there'd be a fence around the place.

"Those trips were all classics," Jim said. There was, for instance, the time the two-car Bunning "caravan"—minus Jim, who was with his Eugene ball club—took a sightseeing trip to Fisherman's Wharf in San Francisco on the way to Oregon.

Lunchtime came. They parked both cars and went to a restaurant. Everything was just fine. Lunch over, they were walking around the area when panic struck. Mary took a head count and came up one short. Little David was missing.

"He was five or six years old," Jim said. "Mary thought somebody had grabbed him and run off with him."

Finally, they went back to the car and found David, standing there, waiting for them.

Another time Mary stopped for gas. The kids went to the bathroom. "She got back in the car," Jim recalled, "started it and went off down the road. That's when one of the kids said, 'Mom, Barb's not here.' She had left Barb at the gas station. Things like that happened all the time."

So many memories. So many adventures. Most of them seem funny now. They weren't all so funny then.

"One year we went to Buffalo," recalled Mary. "We got all unpacked, and then three days later he was sent to Charleston. We had three kids and I was pregnant with Cathy. I said, 'This is ridiculous. I'm going home.' So I drove home."

Life was considerably easier when Jim got to the big leagues, but Mary's adventures as a family tour guide continued. There was that memorable trip to Philadelphia after the Tigers traded Jim to the Phillies. By then, the full complement of young Bunnings, all nine of them, were on hand.

"Traveling with nine kids, it takes you longer," Mary said from experience. "You've got to make a lot of pit stops. But we had it all mapped out. Somehow I went the wrong way on the Pennsylvania Turnpike."

Easy enough to do; the turnpike has more than one branch. Unfortunately, Jim's mother and Mary's mother, who were to meet the rest of the clan at a predetermined motel, didn't take the same branch. They waited, and they waited. When Mary and the second car full of Bunnings didn't show up, they worried, and they worried. Finally, they called the police. Eventually Mary arrived. The manhunt was called off. Their lives as Phillies could begin.

"Thank God for family," Mary said. "My mother and Jim's mother both would come and stay with the kids for a weekend, and I would drive or fly and spend a weekend with Jim. I used to pray that he didn't have a roommate that weekend."

Somehow, it all turned out wonderfully well, although, come to think of it, Jim's five-year fling as a minor league manager left something to be desired. Imagine Mary's reaction when her ever-loving husband told her what he had in mind. It's one thing starting out in the minors as a teenager, but quite another to subject yourself to that life at forty.

What did Mary say when Jim popped the news?

"As angry as I was about that, my initial reaction was, 'It's best to get this out of his system because if he doesn't he'll always wish he had and I'm not going to be the one to keep him from doing that,'" she said. "And you know, he's really good that way with me, too, and I think that's what makes a marriage work. Like with my painting. He is so encouraging to me, so supportive. I'm not saying we don't have arguments. We do. We've had times where Jim has walked out and taken a walk."

Raising nine sons and daughters can be hard on the nerves. "All year [while Jim was doing his job] I was the disciplinarian," Mary remembered. "I was the boss. I got tired of it. So when he came home I said, 'It's your turn.' That was difficult for us, and difficult for the kids."

It's a testament to the love in the Bunning home that the parents, and the kids, did so well.

"I've told our children this," Mary Bunning said. "I told them, 'You can't take anything for granted in marriage. You have to remember the good things and the good qualities and pursue them. I think it's important when Jim comes home that I greet him at the door and give him a kiss, and he's the same way with me. You can't just let things go. You have to work at marriage. It is not something that is just going to happen."

The better you get to know Mary Bunning the more you realize that Jim Bunning is a very lucky guy.

It's the 1996 Hall of Fame induction weekend in Cooperstown, New York, an experience Bunning will never forget. Here, he shares a table during one of the many functions with St. Louis Cardinal great Stan Musial while fellow Hall of Famers (from left) Reggie Jackson, Yogi Berra, and Tom Seaver look on. Musial's wife is on the right. *(From the collection of the National Baseball Hall of Fame Library, Cooperstown, N.Y.)*

Four all-time Phillies (from left, the late Richie Ashburn, Steve Carlton, Jim Bunning, and Robin Roberts) clasp hands on the lawn behind the Otesaga Hotel in Cooperstown on the day of Bunning's induction. Bunning was shocked some fourteen months later when a phone call from a friend in Philadelphia informed him that Ashburn, a long-time favorite of Jim's, had suffered a fatal heart attack in a New York hotel room after broadcasting a Phillies-Mets game. *(From the collection of the National Baseball Hall of Fame Library, Cooperstown, N.Y.)*

A pair of beaming 1996 Hall of Fame inductees, Bunning and long-time Baltimore Oriole manager Earl Weaver, pose with their plaques. *(From the collection of the National Baseball Hall of Fame Library, Cooperstown, N.Y.)*

A rainy evening didn't stop Jim and Mary from enjoying Jim Bunning Night at Philadelphia's Veterans Stadium in the summer of 1996. The Phillies honored Jim following his entry into the Hall of Fame. Here, Jim and Mary (holding one of the many Phillie Phanatic dolls presented to her for her grandchildren) ride around the Vet at the close of the ceremony. *(Photos this page courtesy of Jim and Mary Bunning)*

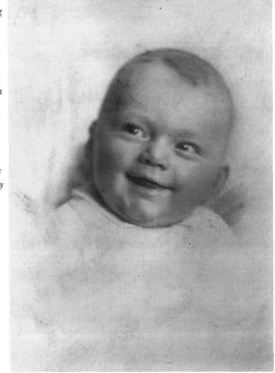

That smiling, chubby face belongs to a very youthful James Paul Bunning. Who'd have guessed it?

Mary Theis and Jim Bunning walk down the aisle at Saint Terese Church in Southgate, Kentucky, in 1952. *(Photo courtesy of Jim and Mary Bunning)*

4

The Winter Game I
(The Player)

One of the greatest challenges facing a minor league baseball player in Jim Bunning's day was trying to make ends meet. A man with a growing family could hardly exist on his minor league salary then. (Or, for that matter, now.) Come to think of it, existing on what Bunning made his first full season as a big leaguer took some doing. Jim made twelve thousand dollars in 1957, the year he won twenty games for the Tigers.

To augment his minor league income, Bunning, like many others, played "the Summer Game" in the winter—first in Mexico, then in Cuba.

In winter ball, a man earned whatever he made. For a young married couple with three children, the winter of 1954-55 in Mexico was a monumental undertaking. Jim had thought all the games would be played in Mexico City. He soon discovered that his team, the Mexico City Reds, would be making road trips to five other towns. He also discovered that some of those trips would necessitate four- and five-hour drives over roads that bore scant resemblance to American highways. According to Jim, "First time Mary found out, she panicked."

You couldn't blame her. The thought of being with those three little kids in a strange place, surrounded by people speaking a different language, while her husband was bouncing along some road in the Mexican hinterlands was terrifying.

"I can remember my mother when we left," Mary said. "She thought we were going to the end of the earth. She cried and cried." There were times, on some of those trips, when Jim thought Mary's mother was right. It *was* the end of the earth, or very close to it.

The Bunnings rented a first-floor apartment in Mexico City, thinking that would make it easier for Mary and the twins, Jimmy and Joanie, who were not yet a year old. Their oldest child, Barbara, was approaching her third birthday.

"We got the baby beds up," Mary recalled. "The first night I'm sitting in the living room. We've got venetian blinds, and they weren't quite together. I saw these eyes looking in and here I was sitting in my slip."

So much for the convenience of living on the ground floor. Next day, at Mary's insistence, the Bunnings moved to the third floor.

Life in Mexico for the uninitiated is no walk in the park on any floor. "You had to soak everything with these pills," Mary discovered. "If you wanted to buy strawberries, you took them home, washed them and then you had these pots, and you put in these little pills and soaked everything for three hours to purify it. We couldn't afford to buy the frozen stuff from the States."

Then came the crusher—realization that her husband would be gone for days at a time.

"After three days, Jim came home and he said, 'We're going on a road trip,'" Mary recalled. "I got livid. I thought, 'You brought me down here and now you're going to leave me.' I was ready to kill him. I said, 'You can't leave. I can't even speak this language.'"

There was no choice. Jim had to leave. Luckily for Mary, the team manager's wife lived above them. And then there was Natasha, the Indian maid Mary hired. "She couldn't speak English and I couldn't speak Spanish," Mary said, "but we got out these dictionaries and we would talk to each other through the dictionaries."

Despite the language barrier, Mary and Natasha became close. With Mary Bunning's loving disposition, it's hard for someone not to get close. The going wage for a maid was ridiculously small. "It wasn't a living wage," said Mary, who quickly decided to ignore the official pay scale, as specified by the agency that supplied Natasha. "I just paid her what I thought she should get, and they got very angry with me," Mary said. "And we weren't supposed to eat with them. I thought that was inhuman. She was darling. She would take the twins out for walks. I don't think I could have done it without her."

For a while there was no guarantee they'd be able to do it with her.

"We almost lost Jimmy, our oldest son, down there," Bunning said. "He had dysentery, and he was vomiting. We just got him to the hospital in time. He started to dehydrate; they put glucose in his arm and he turned out OK."

Bunning's teammate and friend, pitcher Paul Foytack, got sick, too. "He was living in a hotel," Mary said, "and he got deathly sick. I said to Jim, 'Have him live with us.' We had two bedrooms. Jimmy and Joanie slept in our bedroom, and Barb and Paul Foytack shared a bedroom."

Foytack still kids Barbara, now in her mid-thirties, about the time they were roommates in Mexico City.

Moving in with the Bunning family must have helped, because Foytack got better. At least until the team's first road trip, when all the Americans got sick. From then on, Mary fixed enough food for "about five of them" whenever Jim, Paul, and the rest of the Mexico City Reds took off on one of those four- or five-day road trips.

"First time we went on a trip, we went to the ball park and we look at the bus," Jim recalled.

What they saw did not fill them with confidence that they'd ever make it back in one piece.

"It was so rickety," Bunning said. "And we knew we were going over the mountains. The Americans said, 'We ain't getting on that bus.'"

They informed Bobby Avila, a former big league second baseman who owned the team, of their concern and decided to go by car. Eventually, Avila got rid of the bus and permitted the Mexican players to drive as well. Even then, Bunning was practicing for his future role in the Players Association.

"We [the Americans] took two cars," Bunning said. "I had a brand new nine-passenger station wagon. If I put that Mexican gas in it, it sounded like a machine gun. Even if I put super in it. But it still ran."

One road trip in particular remains a vivid memory.

"You can't imagine Jalapa," Bunning observed. "The hotel was depressing. My wife, if she hadn't cooked food for the three days we were there, none of us would have eaten. That's an experience I'll never forget."

Bunning's club battled the home team tooth and nail, and won. "A very tough game," Jim said.

It was so tough that the home fans were rather upset by the outcome, especially when a close decision or two went against their heroes.

"The umpires had a tough time," Bunning said. "Before we could get out of the ball park, the guy who owned the team locked us in . . . with padlocks. Jim Rivera took his bat and beat the locks off."

Why had they been locked in?

"I don't know," Bunning replied. "Maybe to save our lives. They almost had a riot that night. What they did, they shot a firecracker, one of those Roman candles—and it hit the catcher in the back."

The Mexico City catcher, understandably irate, thought he knew where the firecracker came from and went into the stands to confront the guy who threw it, a rather risky undertaking.

"He [the catcher] wants to fight," Jim remembered. "He's lucky he didn't get killed. They threw him out of the stands."

And what did his helpful Mexico City teammates do? Not much.

"We weren't going in those stands," Bunning said. "They could have had machetes. They could have had anything. So, anyway, Rivera beats us out of the ball park and we get back to the hotel and I told Foytack, 'I'm not going to the ball park tomorrow.'"

Jim finally relented, going to the park long after the rest of the team had arrived "when nobody knew I was coming. They had the military there. They had machine guns mounted in each dugout. We played. Nobody got killed."

At least the trip to Puebla was beautiful. Decent roads. Gorgeous scenery. The ball park made up for it. It was an old bullfight arena converted into a baseball field.

The Bunnings spent two winters in Mexico. Jim won a lot of games and was part of a pennant-winning club for the first time. Later, he played in Cuba, a hotbed for baseball, and pitched for a team that won the Caribbean Series. That, too, was quite an experience.

"They had bookies all over the stands in Cuba," Jim noted. "They bet on a pitch. They bet on anything. There were only four teams, and they all played in the same park with a doubleheader every Sunday. You'd go a little early to sit in the stands and here come the bookies up to you. They were always asking, 'How do you feel today?' and that kind of stuff. So finally you'd go in the clubhouse because you didn't want to sit around and be harassed.

"The fact is, it was a memorable experience pitching in Cuba, to know when you came back you were ready because you had faced major league hitters. Good major league hitters. There were four or five on each team."

The Caribbean Series, involving championship teams from Mexico, Puerto Rico, the Dominican Republic, Cuba, and Panama was a major event in Havana. "Oh gosh, it was a big deal," Bunning recalled. "We played in Gran Stadium. The crowds were right at thirty thousand. It was a round-robin. You played each team twice, and we lost one game. We were, I think, 7 and 1. I beat Panama two games."

Pitching in Mexico and Cuba helped Jim Bunning become a stand-out big leaguer. "It really helped," he said. "I got command of my slider in Cuba before I got back for the '57 season. That really was the difference between being successful and mediocre."

As one of the heroes of the Caribbean Series, Jim became something of a celebrity among baseball aficionados in Havana. The Bunnings celebrated their fifth wedding anniversary there, and it was an event to remember. They were guests at one of the top night clubs in the city—the master of ceremonies was a huge fan—and the star of the show, Nat (King) Cole, dedicated the evening to the happy couple.

The Tigers

Tiger Stadium in Detroit is a great place to play baseball—especially if you're swinging a bat and you're lefthanded. That short right field porch with the overhanging upper deck looks so inviting. You'd have thought a hard-throwing, sidearming, righthanded pitcher would hate the place. Not this hard-throwing, sidearming, righthander.

"I pitched in a park that was a lefthanded hitters' paradise," Bunning recalled years later, "and I won seven out of every ten games there. So I thought I had pretty good luck against lefthanded hitters, and I didn't think Detroit was a tough place to pitch, particularly if you pitched hard [and] away."

Center field was the pitcher's friend. At its deepest point, it was 440 feet from home plate. Keep the ball away, stop the batter from pulling, and Tiger Stadium (or Briggs Stadium as it was known then) swallowed up those long fly balls. But make a mistake and the customers in the upper deck in right field needed hard hats to be safe. And left field wasn't exactly out of reach, either.

Throw enough pitches and some are going to get hit hard. Bunning claims to be "the first guy to throw homers over both roofs" in Detroit, no small feat. Mickey Mantle, batting lefthanded of course, rocketed a Bunning pitch over the right field roof. Righthanded slugger Harmon Killebrew sent an American League baseball with Bunning's fingerprints on it soaring over the left field roof. Killebrew's homer was the first ever to make it in that direction. Even then, it should be noted, Jim Bunning was identifying himself with Hall of Famers.

For the record, Jim's first big league start (after getting called up from Buffalo in 1955) was in a home game against the Baltimore Orioles. Bunning led, 3-2, after seven innings and retired the first batter in the eighth. Then it all fell apart. Cal Abrams and Dave Philley singled. Two on, one out, and catcher Gus Triandos, a strong, righthanded hitter who would later catch Bunning in both Detroit and Philadelphia, was at the plate. Bucky Harris, the Tiger manager, decided to stick with his rookie pitcher, and Bunning threw a called third strike past Triandos. Then, he issued a four-pitch walk to load the bases.

Still, Harris stayed with Bunning. Dave Pope drove an outside, 2-2 pitch to left center for a two-run single. Hal Smith followed with a two-run double. The Orioles owned a 6-3 lead and the ball game by the time Bunning was yanked. The press, equipped as usual with 20/20 hindsight, criticized the Tiger manager for letting Bunning pitch too long. However, in all his time in Detroit, the Tigers never had a first-rate closer in the bullpen.

"I wanted to give Bunning every chance," Harris told the writers. "His pitching for seven innings showed he had stuff and determination. If he could have pulled out of that jam in the eighth it would have been a big help to his confidence. Too bad he didn't make it, but I still think he's going to make us a good starting pitcher."

Next time out, July 25, Jim Bunning became a winning pitcher in the big leagues for the first time, beating the Washington Senators 7-3 in the first game of a doubleheader. Al Kaline, who would help Jim win a lot of games down the road, hit one of the three Tiger home runs.

Bunning's other victory that season came in relief when his teammates rewarded him for a hitless top of the ninth against the Chicago White Sox in mid-August by scoring twice in the home ninth for a 9-8 win.

There was also a memorable duel with Boston slugger Jackie Jensen in a game the Tigers lost to the Red Sox, 18-3. Jensen knocked in nine runs that day and came up for the last time with two out and the bases loaded in the top of the eighth. The game may not have been in jeopardy, but Jim Bottomley's long-standing American League record of batting in twelve runs in a single game certainly was.

As the Associated Press report described the confrontation between

Jensen and the young Tiger reliever, "The 20-year-old muscleman swung so hard while missing Bunning's first offering that his cap flew off and he went to his knees. Once again he swung from the heels, but got only a small piece of the ball and topped it weakly to the mound for the third out."

Clearly, Bunning had his moments, but it would be two more years before he spent a full season in the major leagues.

And what a season that was! Twenty victories—the last in relief on the final day—against only eight defeats, a 2.70 earned run average, and three perfect innings as the American League's starting pitcher in the 1957 All-Star game. Bunning relished the challenge of facing the best hitters in the other league.

He also loved the challenge of pitching against the best hitter in his—or any other—league. The date was May 17, 1957. The Tigers were playing the Red Sox in Fenway Park, and the number-three batter in the Boston lineup was Ted Williams.

Bunning took a 2-1 victory, giving up only a tainted run in the bottom of the ninth when Al Kaline lost Williams's fly ball in the sun. But the big news that day was what happened the first three times Williams faced Bunning. Pitching mostly sliders, Jim struck him out all three times.

Things like that didn't happen to Ted Williams, least of all against a righthander in his first full big league season. "It was a front page banner: 'Ted Fans Three Times!' Not the score, not who won, not whether there was an earthquake someplace or a war, but 'Ted Fans!'" Williams said in his book *My Turn at Bat*.

Adding insult to injury, the third time Bunning fanned him the Red Sox had the tying run on third base with two out in the sixth. Williams did not take what happened lightly.

"Williams was so teed off he walked in the clubhouse and ripped his uniform off," recalled Gene Mauch, a utility infielder with the Red Sox that year who was an eyewitness. "I mean, he didn't bother with any buttons. Then he walked over to the schedule on the wall, ran his finger down it until he came to the next Detroit series. 'May 23,' he said. 'May 23. Bunning . . . I'm going to get you then.'"

Ted got him, too. "He hit two dingers," Bunning said. "I remember vividly. But did he say that I won that game despite the fact he hit two home runs? Damn right, 5-3. He hit a two-runner and a solo. That's all they got. But it's great to be remembered by a great hitter."

For his part, Williams always remembered that Bunning slider, which seemed to rise instead of drop as it approached the plate. At least that's the way it looked—a result of Jim's sidearm delivery that ended with him hurtling off the mound to the first base side, often with his gloved left hand actually touching the ground.

Bunning remembered the Williams swing, its smoothness and the awesome power it generated. He also would remember the intensity of the man, every bit as great as his own. "I determined early in my career if I pitched him down I kept the ball in the ball park," Jim said. "If I pitched him anywhere from the waist up he hit a home run unless I got it off the plate. . . . The only time he swung the bat against me one game he hit about a 450-foot home run. The *only* time. He hit it in the open part of the Tiger Stadium bleachers. We had a good battle for six years, a straight-up, honest battle. I struck him out more than any pitcher in six years and he hit more home runs off me."

Understandably, a lot of American League pitchers worked around Ted Williams. They'd take their chances with some of those right-handed bombers who hit behind Ted in the Red Sox lineup over the years—Jackie Jensen, Frank Malzone, Bobby Doerr, Rudy York, and Vern Stephens, for example. Never mind that chummy left field wall at Fenway. They'd rather take their chances with someone—anyone— other than Williams.

Bunning never approached it that way. It wasn't in his nature to duck a challenge, and there was no greater challenge in baseball than pitching to Ted Williams. "I never thought about walking him, ever," Jim said. "I didn't think about pitching around hitters."

Which explains why, with a no-hitter hanging in the balance, two out in the ninth inning, and the righthanded Malzone on deck, Bunning chose to pitch to Williams on July 20, 1958, at Fenway Park.

Somehow, walking Williams in that situation would have taken a little something away from one of the most memorable days in Jim Bunning's pitching career.

The Red Sox were hot. They'd banged out thirty hits in their two previous games. Bunning, on the other hand, had started slowly in 1958. Although he beat the White Sox 4-3 in the opener, Jim was 2 and 5 when Bill Norman was named manager of the slumping Tigers. By the time Bunning took the mound that July afternoon, he was 7 and 6.

It was "Vermont Day" at Fenway, with all sorts of gifts to be distributed to Red Sox players between the games of a doubleheader. Bunning forced a last-minute change in plans by the sheer brilliance of his performance. Before the game, however, he had no idea how special this day was going to be.

"I surprised myself," Jim said. "When I was warming up I had trouble with my fast ball and slider. Even in the first inning, I wasn't right. But after that, I had good stuff. And most of all, I had control."

The first inning nearly did him in as far as pitching a no-hitter was concerned. If not for a play in the top of the inning, the second batter to face Bunning in the bottom half almost surely would have had a hit.

Billy Martin, playing shortstop for the Tigers that day, helped make the no-hitter possible with a hard take-out slide that left Red Sox second baseman Pete Runnels with a pulled muscle. There was nothing dirty about it. "I've got to knock anybody down if they're in my way on a play," Billy told the press. "That's the way I've played this game all my life and when I don't it's time to quit baseball."

The damage was done, however. Runnels, who completed the double play despite Martin's efforts, was limping as the Red Sox came off the field for their first crack at Bunning.

Gene Stephens, Boston's lefthanded-hitting center fielder (who would draw the only two walks Bunning issued that day), led off the home first with a drive to deep right that Kaline caught near the fence. "In some parks it would have been a home run," Bunning said.

Next was Runnels, another lefthanded hitter and a particularly pesky one who hit a lot of balls to the opposite field. This time he topped a roller down the third base line. Ozzie Virgil charged it and fired to first, nipping Runnels for the second out. If not for the muscle pull, he would have beaten the throw for an infield hit. No big deal at the time, it became a very big deal as the game progressed.

Runnels, hitting .334, left the game after that at-bat, replaced by journeyman Ted Lepcio. Still, the Red Sox had plenty of tough outs left in their lineup, including such long-ball threats as Williams, Malzone, Jensen, and Dick Gernert. Throw in the left field wall, the "Green Monster," so close to home plate, and pitching against the Red Sox in Fenway was no picnic. But Bunning, after the shaky first inning, was in command. Jim didn't agree with all those pitchers who hated taking the mound in Fenway Park. He actually loved to pitch in the place, keeping the ball away from the righthanded sluggers in the Boston lineup and daring them to pull it deep to left.

He hit Jensen with one out in the second, walked Stephens with two out in the third and again with one out in the sixth. That was the extent of the Boston offense—three baserunners scattered among a dozen strikeouts.

The Tigers broke through for three runs in the fifth against Frank Sullivan, and now it was up to Bunning, who kept mowing them down. If anything, he seemed to be getting stronger, striking out two in the fifth, two more in the sixth, and another pair in the eighth. The Boston crowd was into it now. So was Bunning. "I knew I had a no-hitter going and I wanted it," he said.

Unless you're a Bob Feller or a Sandy Koufax or a Nolan Ryan, a great pitcher with *absolutely* unhittable stuff on a certain day, you've got to be more than a little lucky to pitch a no-hitter in the big leagues. Jim Bunning is the first to admit that. This time, the luck had come in the very first inning. After that it was simply a case of a power pitcher at the very top of his game.

There's an old superstition in baseball that makes it practically a federal crime to mention a no-hitter while one is in progress. The players don't talk about it on the bench, and, for many years, the vast majority of broadcasters didn't talk about it on the air. Van Patrick—"a great announcer," Bunning said—was the radio and television voice of the Tigers, and he wasn't about to be the guy who "cost" Jim Bunning a no-hitter. As the *Detroit Times* reported the next day, Patrick carefully skirted the issue. He'd say, "Well, let's see, there've been six hits so far in this game. They were all Detroit hits, by the way."

When the Tigers' Harvey Kuenn doubled in the eighth, Patrick threw out another hint. "Well," he said, "that's the eighth Tiger hit in this ball game, in which there have been eight hits."

And again in the top of the ninth after a Gus Zernial single: "Well, that's the ninth Detroit hit in this nine-hit ball game."

You didn't have to be a rocket scientist to figure out what was going on, but you did have to be paying attention.

Naturally, Jim's teammates were being just as careful not to breathe a word. Bunning had other ideas. Superstition be damned; Jim didn't believe in that nonsense.

"I talked about it; why not?" he said. "It wasn't a secret. I remember telling the fellows in about the seventh inning to get ready for some diving catches."

Six years later, at Shea Stadium in New York, Bunning would go

further in flaunting superstition. But what he said late in the game that
July afternoon in Boston must have shocked his teammates.

After throwing a third strike past pinch hitter Billy Klaus to end the
eighth, Bunning sidled up to Detroit first base coach Tommy Henrich
and told him, "Well, I've got to get three more." Henrich pretended
to misunderstand what Jim was talking about. "OK," he replied, "we'll
go out and get you three more runs this inning."

While Bunning was keeping his date with baseball destiny in Boston, his wife was back in Detroit, driving her sister, Lois, around town
on a little sight-seeing junket on the way to Willow Run Airport. They
had just switched on the car radio after leaving church to find out how
the game was going. It didn't take long to figure out it was going well,
but the voice on the radio wasn't about to divulge how well.

"The announcer gave the score, but he didn't say anything about
the number of hits the Red Sox had," Mary said.

But the clues kept piling up. Suddenly, it hit them: Jim was pitching
a no-hitter. "I almost bumped into somebody and finally stopped and
waited for the last out," Mary recalled.

That last out was baseball drama at its very best. The top of the
Boston order was coming up and that meant another showdown
with—who else?—Ted Williams.

"When I went out for the last inning, I told [my teammate] Paul
Foytack, and I was only half kidding, 'I suppose I'll get two out and
then the big guy will hit one out of the park and ruin everything,'"
Bunning said.

First, he had to contend with Gene Stephens, who had hit that deep
drive to right in the first and then drawn the only two walks. The
count went to 2 and 2. Stephens took a pitch he thought was outside.
Plate umpire Frank Umont thought otherwise. Stephens voiced his
complaint, banged his bat against the ground, and walked to the dugout. One out, two to go.

Lepcio was next, with the "big guy" looming in the on-deck circle.
The crowd was screaming now. "It was like Shea in '64," Bunning would
say years later. Lepcio took a strike, fouled the second pitch off catcher
Red Wilson's chest protector, took a ball, then went down swinging.

Two out, one to go. The big one. The biggest of the big, Ted
Williams, with a golden opportunity to gain more sweet revenge for
that three-strikeout humiliation the previous season.

As Bunning got ready to throw the first pitch, Williams stepped out and walked back to the on-deck circle to have a few words with Frank Malzone. He asked for the resin bag, patted his hands with it, threw the bag hard to the ground, and returned to home plate. The crowd, on its feet now, was eating it up.

Three times Bunning had faced Williams in this game. Twice Ted hit routine fly balls to Al Kaline in right, and once he bounced into a force play.

Williams was a dead-pull hitter, and a deadly one. Kaline braced himself. He and Bunning were good friends who often drove to the ball park together. Al had never been involved in a no-hitter before; like everybody else in Fenway Park, he was caught up in the excitement.

"The only thing I thought of was, 'I hope he hits it to me,'" Kaline said.

Bunning started Williams off with a high, inside fast ball. Ted stepped out, pounded his bat on the plate, and stepped back in.

Now Jim threw one of those nasty sliders that Ted had been getting under. He got under this one, too. In right field, Kaline signaled that he was going to make the catch.

"A routine fly ball," Kaline remembered.

The instant it dropped into the right fielder's glove, Bunning threw out his arms and screamed something unintelligible to Red Wilson, his catcher. Bill Norman and Tommy Henrich led the charge of Tigers out of the visiting dugout as the Boston fans—suddenly Bunning fans for a day—gave the no-hit pitcher a standing ovation.

As Roger Birtwell put it in the next day's *Boston Globe*: "Jim Bunning of the Detroit Tigers yesterday achieved a minor miracle of baseball. He pitched a no-hit game against the Boston Red Sox at Fenway Park."

Birtwell wasn't exaggerating. As baseball miracles go, this one wasn't at all minor, a fact that Bunning discovered many years later when he spent some time with Ted Williams on a trip to Florida.

"He told me, 'I've been keeping this for thirty-five years,'" Jim recalled. "He said, 'I have to tell you this because that no-hitter you pitched was the most amazing game I've ever been in.'"

The Red Sox, he explained, knew almost every pitch Bunning was going to throw, courtesy of that master sign-stealer, Del Baker, who was coaching at first base. Baker tipped off the batters verbally, hollering a key phrase toward home plate whenever a fast ball was coming. If Baker remained silent, it was a breaking ball.

"They knew everything that was coming," Bunning recollected

Williams telling him. "He said the only time he didn't know what was coming was the last at-bat. Everybody was screaming so loud that he couldn't hear Baker."

"What Ted says is a true story," Frank Malzone confirmed. "I remember it well."

Malzone, who played third base for the Red Sox, watched from the on-deck circle as Williams faced Bunning. A righthanded hitter, Malzone thought Bunning might pitch around Williams with two out in the bottom of the ninth and so much at stake.

"Normally, he would have walked Ted, but he knew I was tough," Malzone said kiddingly. "If Ted didn't make out I probably would have gotten a base hit and broken it up." He laughed, then grew serious. "No, Jim was tough that day. He was always tough, but that day he was something special. I don't think it ever entered his mind to walk Ted."

Nor did it enter Bunning's mind that he was tipping off his pitches on a day when the Red Sox weren't hitting them anyway.

"In those days a lot of pitchers held the ball in their hand [as they started their windup], and they'd show you more ball on the breaking ball than they would on the fast ball when they were coming up to their glove," according to Malzone. "I remember Dave DeBusschere—he pitched for the White Sox—he had good stuff, but you could read every pitch that he threw. Probably to this day he wonders why he wasn't more successful."

Sign stealing was an art. Another Boston coach, Billy Herman, was among the acknowledged masters.

"He was great," observed Malzone, now a Red Sox scout. "I was hitting one day against Don Mossi, when he was a starting pitcher with the Tigers. He gets me two quick strikes. I'm protecting the plate. All of a sudden I hear Billy Herman holler."

A fast ball was coming. "I hear him, I go, 'Whoops!'" said Malzone. "He threw a fast ball, I hit it in the net [atop the left field wall in Fenway Park]. To this day Mossi's probably wondering how the hell I hit that pitch. I went from a defensive hitter to an offensive hitter just like that."

That's how much it can mean to a batter if he knows what's coming. And yet, on a day when Williams, Malzone, and all the other tough Boston hitters knew, Jim Bunning pitched a no-hit, no-run game. Truly, it was an extraordinary achievement.

"Del Baker was good at stealing signs," Malzone remembered. "And he did have his [Bunning's] pitches that day. One of the signs, he would holler, 'Pop-it!' That meant fast ball. He didn't call the breaking ball, only the fast ball. If you fool around with two different signs [and get confused], you could get killed. Ted relied on Baker quite a bit in situations like that where he felt he wanted the edge. Which is normal. I felt the same way. . . . When you're talking about Ted Williams and Jim Bunning, you're talking about two special people in the game of baseball. You're talking about a great pitcher, Jim Bunning. As far as I was concerned, year after year he was the toughest righthander for me in the league. There's no question about it."

"I'm glad to see him finally get in the Hall of Fame. I thought he should have been there sooner. This guy did a lot."

What he did on that day was, in its way, every bit as remarkable as what he would do against the Mets at Shea Stadium in 1964. The Fenway Park no-hitter may not have been perfect, but it was surely miraculous. Bunning held one of baseball's top offensive teams hitless for nine innings in a notorious hitters' ball park on a day when the opposition knew what he was going to throw before he threw it.

Frank Sullivan, who absorbed the 3-0 defeat for the Red Sox, was so impressed he scribbled a note on a piece of cardboard after the game and had a clubhouse attendant deliver it to the winning pitcher.

"Jim, greatest I've ever seen," Sullivan wrote. "You were terrific all the way. I knew if I couldn't hit you, nobody could. [Signed] Sully."

The last line was meant as a joke. Sullivan was 5 for 38 at that point in the season. The game, of course, was played in the good old days before the designated hitter came to the American League. As Bunning laughingly put it, "He couldn't hit his way out of a wet paper bag."

Sullivan could, however, exhibit consummate class after losing a tough ball game. When the press found out about the note, the Boston righthander was the object of considerable attention. Cornered on a bench in the Red Sox training room, Sullivan told the writers, "It was the greatest game I ever saw."

Asked why he wrote that message to Bunning, Sullivan replied, "I can't be mad at a guy when he pitches like that. I think that game by Bunning was one of the greatest ever pitched in this park. This is no pitcher's paradise. It is anything but.

"There are so many things that can happen here, and we ain't exactly been playing dead these days. We had a dozen hits in one game and eighteen in another, a lot of them for extra bases, and we were shooting for our seventh straight win. Then Bunning comes along and knocks us off. That's a real feat to me."

This was no bosom buddy of Bunning's speaking; it was a fellow professional admiring a job supremely well done.

"I'm not too friendly with Jim," Sullivan told the press. "Oh, I know him and I've pitched against him. I remember the time I beat him when we got two hits off him and they got ten off me. Ted Williams' home run gave us a 1-0 victory, and that night I was sitting around by myself and I said, 'How would I feel if I was in his shoes?' Pretty low. So when he does something big I think everybody in baseball should recognize the fact. The only thing I could think of at the time was to write him a note and tell him so. There's not enough of that stuff in baseball. This is no war. We are not shooting at them or them at us. We are all in this together and I think it was my place to tell him that he did a good job. Our team had four men hitting over .300. One of them, Pete [Runnels], leads the league. Jackie Jensen leads in homers and runs batted in. Ted Williams won the game the day before and is tough for any pitcher in baseball. Then you've got Frankie Malzone. Half the order is about as tough as there is in the league right this minute and Bunning pitches his no-hitter against them and in this park. He couldn't find a much tougher test, as I see it. I don't think there is one."

The folks in charge of "Vermont Day" that afternoon at Fenway Park thought so, too. Stuck with a flock of prizes—for the first hit, the first run, the first RBI, and so on by a member of the Red Sox—they decided to unload all those goodies on the man who prevented their heroes from collecting. Among the prizes was a living, breathing, mooing, milk-giving cow. Jim thanked them for their thoughtfulness, but wisely decided he didn't need a cow on a road trip and left the poor beast in Boston. For Bunning, pitching the fourth no-hitter in Fenway Park history and becoming the third Tiger (after George Mullin and Virgil Trucks) to pitch a no-hit game was prize enough.

The exhilaration he felt the moment Williams's fly ball landed in Kaline's glove lasted until he fought his way through the crowd of jubilant teammates into the clubhouse. Once there, Jim felt emotionally drained. "You know, the euphoria and everybody running out on the field and stuff like that," he recalled, "and then I got in the clubhouse and it was unbelievable. I felt like I had a near miss with an accident."

Bunning has repeated that rather unusual analogy many times. When his friend Allen Lewis, the retired *Philadelphia Inquirer* writer, asked him to put in writing how it felt to pitch a no-hit game, Jim expressed it as, I'm sure, no man had ever expressed it before.

"As far as I am concerned, pitching a no-hitter is a lot like participating in an automobile accident that almost happened," he began. "If you have ever been in a car during a near miss, you know the feeling.

"You've spun the wheel; the brake pedal is to the floor. You smell the smoking rubber, hear the screeching brakes. Watching disaster approach at lightning speed, all you have left is that sinking, hopeless feeling that everything is beyond your control. And then—like a miracle—the roaring semi slides by with inches to spare, or you slide to a stop inches from the brick wall.

"Minutes later, you collapse in a puddle, shaken to the core but exhilarated beyond belief by the simple fact that you survived—you dodged disaster. That's the feeling of a no-hitter."

Although he would become the second pitcher in the history of the majors to pitch a no-hitter in each league, Bunning never thought of himself as a likely no-hit pitcher.

"For most pitchers like me, who aren't overpowering supermen with extraordinary stuff like Sandy Koufax or Nolan Ryan, a no-hitter is a freaky thing," he declared. "You can't plan it. It's not something you can try to do. It just happens. Everything has to come together—good control, outstanding plays from your teammates, a whole lot of good fortune on your side and a lot of bad luck for the other guys. A million things could go wrong—but on this one particular day of your life none of them do."

Adding to the emotional strain that day in Boston, Bunning pointed out, was the determination of the people around him—his manager, the coaches, his teammates, the trainer, every one of them—to say nothing about the drama that was unfolding.

"In fact, that's the main thing I remember about my first no-hitter," Bunning said. "There was tension, pressure, anxiety. It builds up to the point that you don't get any chance to enjoy your good fortune while it is happening. You're just waiting for the bottom to fall out. And to top things off, *no one will even talk to you.*"

Bunning was so drained after the Boston no-hitter that he "almost collapsed" in the clubhouse when it was over. The traditional silence he encountered as the game moved into its latter stages, he felt, was largely responsible.

"When it became clear that something special might be in the works, everybody started avoiding me," he recalled. "My teammates wouldn't look me in the eye. They wouldn't talk to me—all because of the fear that anything they would say or do might jinx me. On a normal day, in a normal game, pitching is a lonely job at best. But after inning five with a no-hitter going, you might as well be in outer space. Looking back, I always felt that the sad part of the whole thing was the fact that because of the tension I didn't get to enjoy it along the way."

The enjoyment would come later as the enormity of his achievement hit him. And what Ted Williams told him more than three decades later added to that enjoyment and satisfaction. In a sense, Bunning's no-hitter against the Red Sox served as a dress rehearsal for the historic perfect game against the Mets, six years later.

Occasionally a no-hit pitcher does extraordinarily well in his next start. Johnny Vander Meer produced the ultimate in 1938: another no-hitter. Ewell Blackwell came within an inning of doing the same. More often, though, pitchers who have just thrown a no-hitter struggle in their next one, two, or more starts. Maybe the strain Bunning was talking about takes its toll.

Whatever the reason, Bunning struggled, failing to complete his following nine starts. His next complete game did not come until the second week of September; it was a three-hit, 7-1 victory over the Washington Senators.

It was that kind of year for Bunning—up and down, reaching some lofty heights and plunging to some sickening depths. Overall, it was a disappointing year for a man who set such high standards the season before.

Among the other moments to savor in 1958 were a pair of impressive victories over a Yankee team that went on to win the World Series. On one particularly memorable Sunday afternoon, the Tigers embarrassed the home team in front of nearly fifty-five thousand fans in Yankee Stadium, blanking them in both ends of a doubleheader. Longtime Yankee nemesis Frank Lary pitched a four-hit, 2-0 victory in the opener; Bunning stopped them, 3-0, with a five-hit, eight-strikeout job in the nightcap, fanning Mickey Mantle three times. The following week Jim struck out fourteen Yankees in a 7-1 victory, losing his shutout on a Yogi Berra home run.

Held to fourteen victories in 1958, Bunning won seventeen for the Tigers in 1959. That was the first of two consecutive years in which Jim led the American League in strikeouts, recording 201 each season.

He also led the league in most home runs allowed in 1959, giving up thirty-seven. On the other hand, he did some pretty fair hitting himself, picking on his old Boston buddies in mid-May for four hits, including a home run and a triple, and knocking in five runs in a 14-2 Tiger victory. Ted Williams must have been impressed.

Statistics can be deceiving in baseball. Bunning's won-lost record in 1960 was 11 and 14; "that year," he said, "I pitched as good as I could in the American League." His earned run average was 2.79. In 252 innings, his strikeout-to-walk ratio was 201 to 64, and he gave up only 217 hits. But the Tigers were kittens when he was on the mound. Typical of his season, Jim pitched ten scoreless innings against the Senators in Detroit on May 18, striking out ten; he wound up with no decision in a game the Tigers lost, 3-0, in eleven.

Four weeks later, he faced the Red Sox at home and, as usual, rose to the occasion against Williams and Co., striking out thirteen in the first seven innings. One problem: Ted homered off him, the 498th of his spectacular career. The Tiger manager, Jimmy Dykes, pulled Bunning for a pinch hitter with two out and a runner on first in the bottom of the seventh.

"I had a chance to break the Tiger strikeout record and he took me out," Bunning said. "We had a few words."

The pinch hitter, Norm Cash, had the last word, though, hitting a home run. The Tigers, and Bunning, won. "I told Dykes, 'I won't fight you any more about staying in the game,'" Jim recalled. "I understand what you're trying to do, but I still don't agree with it."

An expansion year in the American League, 1961 was an exciting year for the Tigers, who battled the strongest Yankee team of the post–Joe DiMaggio era into September before fading out of contention. This was the year of the "M and M Boys," Mantle and Roger Maris. It was also the year that Norm Cash, a .286 hitter the season before, hit .361; Baltimore's Jim Gentile unloaded 46 home runs; and the Yankees, led by Maris's 61 and Mantle's 54, set a major league home run record by belting 240 of them—a mark that stood until the Orioles, playing in chummy Oriole Park at Camden Yards, erased it in 1996. In short, it wasn't exactly a great year to be an American League pitcher, but Bunning excelled. He won 17, lost 11, and, while big numbers flashed on scoreboards all around him, managed to post a 3.19 ERA.

Jim also got involved in a highly publicized fight with Cleveland's

Jimmy Piersall in late June. It happened in the fifth inning of the first game of a doubleheader, won by the first-place Tigers, 6-3. United Press International reported: "Piersall precipitated the brawl on the field when Bunning hit him on the shoulder with a pitch. . . . Piersall charged to the mound and began to throw punches as both benches emptied and players swarmed onto the field. Piersall, Johnny Temple and Bob Hale all were ejected."

Bunning, needing to complete the fifth inning to qualify for a victory, kept his head, ducked Piersall's punch, wrestled him to the ground and was allowed to stay in the game. "Bunning defended himself, that's all," explained umpire John Stevens.

For a change, Jim's club was in a pennant race, but his hopes of pitching in a World Series were dashed in a three-game weekend series with the Yankees in September before big crowds in the Bronx. Bunning pitched the Sunday getaway game after the Yanks had won the first two; he gave up first-inning homers to Mantle and Berra, then settled down.

When the Tigers rallied to take a one-run lead against Yankee relief ace Luis Arroyo in the top of the ninth it looked as if they might salvage a desperately needed victory, but the bullpen failed them. Mantle hit a solo homer to tie it, and Elston Howard socked a three-run homer to win it in the bottom of the inning. Only one other time in his big league career would Bunning pitch for a team that came within ten games of first place.

The next year was a big one for Jim. He won nineteen games, saved six, and once more pitched three shutout innings as a starter in the All-Star game. The six saves (in six tries) prompted Bob Scheffing, the Tiger manager, to toy with the idea of turning him into a full-time closer, an idea that hardly thrilled Bunning.

"He has the perfect equipment and an ideal temperament for relief work," Scheffing said. "He would be great at it—if there was some way to replace him in the starting rotation."

"Makes no sense," countered Bunning, secure in the knowledge that the Tigers had no way to replace him in the starting rotation. Even thirty-five years later, Jim gets annoyed when he reflects on it. "I made the All-Star game as a starting pitcher and Scheffing said I couldn't start any more," Bunning said. "Think about it."

Scheffing also annoyed Bunning with his second-guessing. In a game with the Red Sox at Tiger Stadium, "I got a three-run lead, top of the ninth," Bunning recalled. "Vic Wertz is sent up to pinch-hit with the bases loaded. Now it never entered my mind that I should pitch around Vic Wertz. It would never enter my mind to walk him [and force in a run]. I got in on him, shattered his bat, and he hit a grand slam, one of those home runs that *just* got in the [overhanging] top deck. When I came in Scheffing said something to the effect, 'Did you know if you walk him, they only get one run?' I said, 'Listen, if you wanted him walked why didn't you go like this—hold up four fingers, put him on?'

"He also did that one time in Chicago with me. Roy Sievers was the hitter. He hit a sacrifice fly off me, and we had an open base. When I came in he said, 'Did you ever think about walking Sievers?' I said, 'No, but you could've told me if you wanted him walked.'

"Another time in Chicago Sievers was the hitter, [Luis] Aparicio was on second, and [Nellie] Fox was on first." Aparicio was the league's premier base stealer, a threat to run at any time. "Everybody except our shortstop and second baseman knew if they ran we were going to second base with the ball," Bunning said. "We were going to throw Fox out, not Aparicio. So I struck Sievers out and we threw to third and nobody was covering [there either, two runs scored,] and he got on my butt about it. He just had some strange ways of saying, 'Why don't you take control of what's going on out there?' I said, "I have control of the mound. You have to have control of the game.'"

He may not have been wild about Scheffing's managing style, but Bunning liked him as a man. "He's the first [big league] manager I ever had who took a personal interest in people," Jim said. "Mary Scheffing and Bob Scheffing really, truly took an interest in you and your family. They made an extra effort to do that."

All things considered, Bunning would have been very happy if Scheffing had remained the Tiger manager through the 1963 season. The man who replaced him, Charley Dressen, was not one of Jim's favorites. And Dressen wasn't a charter member of the Jim Bunning Fan Club, either.

"The first thing he told us when he got there was, 'You hold them close for seven innings and I'll think of something,'" Bunning remembered. "To be undermined by Charley Dressen I thought was the highest of insults. Detroit always went out and got some of the oldest people in the world to manage the team—Dressen and Jimmy Dykes and Bucky Harris . . ."

It was loathing at first sight when Dressen arrived on the scene, loaded with bright ideas on how to turn the Tigers into winners again. "I didn't pay any attention," said Bunning. "I was not on the bench [when Dressen was there]. I went to the bullpen and just sat."

Bunning had one basic problem with Dressen: "He didn't think I could pitch any more."

The veteran manager made it painfully obvious that Jim Bunning, at thirty-one, no longer figured prominently in the Tigers plans.

"He didn't like the way I pitched," Bunning said. "He didn't think I could get hitters out. He didn't look at the numbers in Tiger Stadium. I had over a 70 winning percentage in Tiger Stadium. I didn't realize it was a bad place [for a righthander] to pitch."

Bunning was 12 and 13 when Dressen replaced Scheffing, and he didn't get another start the rest of the season. There was this kid named Denny McLain, and the Tigers wanted to see if he could pitch. By bouncing Bunning from the starting rotation they opened a spot for the pitcher who, five years later, turned the baseball world on its ear by winning thirty-one games. Remember, this was a different era in big league baseball. Teams used four-man, not five-man rotations. So Bunning went to the bullpen. He also went to the front office at the end of the season and asked general manager Jim Campbell if he could arrange a trade to get him out of town and far, far away from the latest in a long parade of Tiger managers.

"Your manager doesn't think I can pitch and I know I've got some good years left," Bunning told Campbell.

"I'll do everything in my power to make it happen," Campbell replied.

And he did.

The trade that gave Jim Bunning's pitching career new life was made during the winter meetings. Since Bunning was the Tigers' player rep, and the Players Association was holding its meetings at the same time and place, Jim and Mary were there.

"At about two o'clock in the morning Jimmy Campbell calls me," Bunning recalled. "He said, 'We just traded you to Philadelphia.' I said, 'For who?' He told me. I said, 'Thank you, Jimmy. I really appreciate it.' I was going right back to sleep and my wife said, 'What was that all about?' And I said, 'I just got traded to the Phillies.' And she started to bawl."

Jim was overjoyed at the news that he and Gus Triandos were heading for the National League in a deal that made Tigers out of pitcher

Jack Hamilton and outfielder Don Demeter. And there was Mary in tears. It wasn't going to Philadelphia that hurt, though; it was the prospect of leaving all the people she knew so well after spending fourteen years in the Tiger organization—especially Frank Bolling's wife, Sue, and Don Mossi's wife, Louise, both of whom had become good friends.

"I cried and cried," Mary recalled. "There we were, out in California, and I just thought, 'Philadelphia?' It's hard, the first trade. I guess it's because we came up in the minor leagues with the Tigers. But they weren't going to start him any more. It was the best thing that happened for him."

For a while, though, Jim and Mary Bunning had vastly different reactions to Jim Campbell's 2 A.M. phone call.

6

Champs—for 150 Games

Jim Bunning never made it to the World Series. Neither did Gene Mauch.

They should have made it together.

The year was 1964, Bunning's first in the National League. It was a memorable year for Bunning. And Mauch. And the Phillies. Three years before, in their first full season under Mauch, they were the laughingstock of baseball, losing 107 games in a 154-game season. That was the club that set a modern major league record by losing 23 in a row. Yet a year later, when the National League expanded, Mauch's Phillies went 81 and 80, and the year after that they finished fourth, 12 games over .500. So it was no sad-sack ball club that Jim Bunning was joining in the spring of '64, even if—on paper—it was hardly the team to beat.

Bunning pitched brilliantly that year, and Mauch managed the same way. For 150 games. If not for expansion—if the big league season was still 154 games long instead of 162—the Phillies would have won the pennant with something to spare. Bunning would have had his biggest moment on the national stage as the starting pitcher in the first game of the World Series against the Yankees. And Mauch wouldn't be remembered today as the man who managed the most games in the big leagues without winning a pennant.

Think of Gene Mauch and, almost immediately, three teams come to mind—the 1964 Phillies, who led by six and a half games with twelve to go, lost ten straight, and wound up tied for second, one game out; the 1982 California Angels, who took a 2-0 lead in their best-of-five playoff series with the Milwaukee Brewers and lost three straight; and the 1986 Angels, who had a 3-1 lead in their best-of-seven playoff series with the Boston Red Sox, had them beaten with two out and two strikes on the batter in the top of the ninth inning of game five, and lost that one plus the two that followed.

But no matter how devastating those two Angel collapses were, they paled beside what happened to the 1964 Phillies.

Time heals all wounds, at least up to a point, and as painful as those final days of the '64 season were, Jim Bunning has no trouble talking about them now. In fact, when he thinks back to that year when his last chance to be a member of a World Series team slipped away many of the memories are good ones. After what he had gone through with Dressen and the Tigers in 1963, Mauch and the Phillies represented a breath of fresh air.

"The reason I pitched so well for Mauch, he trusted me and he had confidence in me and I knew it," Bunning said. "The only thing Mauch wanted to know, was I getting tired, and we had a little sign between ourselves. If I was getting tired I'd signal to him—a glove on the nose or something like that. I think I told him I was getting tired five times in four years."

"What I remember most about Bunning, it's like the Mike Witt thing [with the Angels]," Mauch said years later. "I didn't have much success relieving Mike Witt. It was like that with Bunning, and after it became apparent that I had trouble relieving Bunning because nobody saved any games for him, then he and I talked about it and Jim said, 'Well, I'll relieve myself.'"

This meant taking a deep breath, getting a second wind, and some-how, some way making it through the last inning or two and saving the victory for himself. More times than not, that's precisely what Bunning did.

The change from a manager who didn't think he could pitch any-more to one who wanted him to be the leader of his staff was a tonic for Bunning. The Phillies had another top-flight starter on the '64 staff, lefty Chris Short. "But Shortie didn't want to be the number-one pitcher," Bunning observed. "He wanted to pitch, but he didn't want the responsibility [of being the top guy], and when he got someone to relieve him of that responsibility he became a heck of a pitcher."

Bunning was delighted to take over the leadership role. In Detroit, even through the good times, he always thought he was playing second fiddle to Frank Lary. It felt good to be appreciated.

"It was a tremendous year," Bunning said of 1964. "I never had four middle infielders that could do the things those infielders could do. [Bobby] Wine was a completely different shortstop than [Ruben] Amaro, but they both got the job done. And [Cookie] Rojas and [Tony] Taylor, you could interchange them at second base and they were marvelous."

No matter what infield combination played at a given time, they made the plays. Being a part of that Phillies team, through the first 150 games, was flat-out fun. "The thing I remember most about the season," Bunning said, "was the unselfishness of the players, their willingness to do anything they had to do to win. And the way Mauch used players, the way he used the irregulars to be ready to pinch-hit, to be sharp enough to be good."

Playing for Gene Mauch was a baseball education. The man they called the Little General was an extraordinary tactician, generally a couple of steps, often a couple of innings, ahead of the guy in the other dugout.

"I think over the period of the four years I played for him he managed better than any manager I ever played for," Bunning said. "He was way ahead of the other guy. I'm not talking about managing people as much as I am the game. He did that—manage the game—better than anybody I ever played for, including Walt Alston. He always had the right guy ready to hit."

And because he made sure they played enough to stay sharp, they produced.

For 150 games.

But that's getting ahead of the story.

Bunning was welcomed with open arms when the Phillies began spring training in Clearwater, Florida. The manager, the coaches, his new teammates made him feel like somebody special. Maybe Dressen didn't think he could pitch anymore, but they did.

Mauch wanted a leader and Bunning led. Not by a lot of talk; that wasn't Jim's style. "The only thing I made sure of in spring training," he said, "was that I led by example. I didn't say hardly anything to anyone. Just that I did my work."

Here was this hotshot, veteran pitcher, this five-time American

League All-Star working as hard as some kid trying to make the big leagues. Gene Mauch couldn't have asked for a better kind of leadership. Bunning became a role model for the entire team.

"My attitude was so positive," Jim recalled. "I never had good springs before. In 1964 I had a good spring."

Mauch, always thinking, decided not to pitch Bunning against National League clubs in Florida. He explained to his new ace that he had no intention of letting batters he would face in the regular season get a close-up look at him until the Phillies started north. The first time Bunning took the mound against National League opposition was in Asheville, North Carolina, against the Pittsburgh Pirates, shortly before the start of the season. The game meant absolutely nothing; Bunning was experimenting, working on various pitches. But the memory of that day lingers on.

"We were playing in a bandbox," Jim said. "I had a terrible outing. [Willie] Stargell hit one over the hill [beyond the right field fence]. [Roberto] Clemente hit one. I mean, they knocked the hell out of me."

For Bunning, it was supposed to be just a workout, a tuneup for his first official National League start against the Mets. For the Pirates, it turned into batting practice. And while they were at it, they worked on sliding hard into second base to break up double plays. Billy Martin would have approved. But when somebody went slamming into Tony Taylor with regular-season intensity, Bunning did what he had to do: he drilled the next Pirate batter.

"I took care of business," Jim recalled. "Whoever was at the plate, I took care of it. [Former American Leaguer] Mickey Vernon, who was a coach on their team, said, 'Aw, he does that all the time,' and all of a sudden Tony bunts to first base and runs right into the first baseman and we're out there fighting. It's a middle-of-the-summer brawl and it's spring training."

In retrospect, Bunning thought the timing was perfect because it brought his new ball club that much closer together. Bunning, his Phillies' teammates now knew, was a pitcher who would stand up for them. In Jim's view, "It got us going right into the season."

And what a season it was. The old ball park in North Philadelphia hadn't seen so much excitement since Robin Roberts, Richie Ashburn, and the rest of the Whiz Kids won the 1950 pennant. For five magical months, Mauch made all the right moves. He didn't miss a trick.

Not everybody was a fan of the Little General. Pitcher Art

Mahaffey, for one, never forgave Mauch for the way he handled him. But most of those '64 Phillies came to respect Mauch and his knowledge of baseball.

"To me, Gene Mauch was really instrumental in opening up my mind as far as the game was concerned," commented Ruben Amaro, the smooth-fielding shortstop who became one of Bunning's closest friends on the team. "I played with Ralph Houk and I played with Johnny Keane and I played with Fred Hutchinson and Bill Rigney, and that man was beyond those people [as a baseball strategist]."

"He was the best at keeping a club in the ball game," said Paul Owens, a Phillies' scout when Bunning joined the team. "He always found a way."

Having Jim around to start every fourth day didn't hurt. He had a great beginning with his new club in his new league. One can only wonder what Charley Dressen thought when he read through those National League box scores and saw what his "washed-up" former righthander was doing.

In Jim's first inning as a National Leaguer, he struck out the first three Mets he faced, getting Ed Kranepool looking and Tim Harkness and Ron Hunt swinging. Rumors that Jim Bunning had lost too much to be a successful starting pitcher in the big leagues were grossly exaggerated.

Bunning closed the game with a flourish, too. After Tony Gonzalez, a lefthanded batter with a knack for hitting opposite-field home runs, broke a 1-1 tie with a two-out, three-run blast to Connie Mack Stadium's lower left field stands in the eighth, Bunning fanned Larry Elliot, pinch-hitter Hawk Taylor, and pinch-hitter John Stephenson in order to close out the ninth. Two and a half months later Bunning would once again strike out John Stephenson to end a ball game . . . and make baseball history.

Jim's second start was a six-hit, nine-strikeout, 10-0 victory over the Chicago Cubs. Next time out, he blanked the Milwaukee Braves for eight innings before Short and Ed Roebuck put the finishing touches on a 5-3 victory.

Bunning was everything Mauch and Phillies general manager John Quinn hoped he would be. As good as he was in April, he was even better in May. Twice, eleven days apart, Jim flirted with no-hitters, not bad for somebody who insisted (and does to this day) that he didn't have truly overpowering stuff.

He pitched one of the best games of his career on May 18 at the old outdoor ball park in Houston, the one where attendants drove around in golf carts before the game spraying the stands with mosquito repellent. Bunning faced just twenty-nine batters that day and carried a no-hitter into the fifth. Jimmy Wynn, leading off the inning, smacked a single past third, the only hit Bunning was to allow. Nellie Fox, hit by a pitch in the first, was the other Houston baserunner. Bunning was so efficient that the game was played in an hour and forty-six minutes.

"That might have been the easiest game I ever pitched," he observed. "They didn't even come close to [another] hit."

The victory put the Phillies in first place, prompting Bunning to tell the press, "I've been in six All-Star games, had a 20-game season, pitched a no-hitter, but I've never been in a World Series. I promised myself I'd be in one before I'm through."

Facing Houston again on May 29, Jim pitched a game he will never forget—but not for all the right reasons. For six and two-thirds innings he was perfect, retiring twenty in a row. The Phillies were breezing along with a 5-0 lead. The only question seemed to be: Would Bunning get those final seven outs and complete not just his second no-hitter but a perfect no-hitter as well?

Baseball is an unpredictable sport. First, Bunning's perfect game blew up. Then he blew up.

Houston's third baseman Mike White lofted a fly ball to left field with two out in the seventh. Wes Covington got a late start, then came rushing in and made a diving try for a catch. The ball skipped past him for a double. When Walter Bond hit the next pitch to right for a clean single, the shutout was out the window, too.

The Phillies still led, 5-1, going into the eighth, but the strain of carrying a perfect game into the late innings must have taken its toll. By the time Mauch got Bunning out of there, Houston had scored five runs and led 6-5. The Phillies came back to score a pair of two-out runs in the bottom of the eighth—on Gus Triandos's game-tying pinch double and Cookie Rojas's triple—but Bunning had learned a painful lesson. He felt certain the pressure and tension that had built up as the perfect game moved along caused him to "blow sky-high" after Mike White's fly-ball double. "I didn't want that to happen again," he declared.

That experience was still fresh in Jim's mind a little more than three weeks later when he faced the Mets in the first game of a Sunday doubleheader at Shea Stadium. The date was June 21, Fathers Day.

Mary drove to Shea with Barbara, the Bunnings' oldest daughter, and Gail Cater, whose husband, Danny, was a Phillie outfielder and occasional first baseman. The plan was for Jim and Danny to drive back with them after the doubleheader. Dinner first, then a nice, leisurely trip on the New Jersey Turnpike. It would not be quite so simple, however.

The most spectacular pitching performance of Jim Bunning's big league career started innocently enough. He hung a couple of sliders to Jim Hickman, the Mets' leadoff man. Hickman lashed out at both of them, and fouled them back. Bunning's third pitch, another breaking ball, caught him looking. It was the start of something big.

The only thing close to a hit came with one out in the fifth. Jesse Gonder, a lefthanded-hitting catcher, smacked a ball toward the hole on the right side. Second baseman Tony Taylor broke to his left, made a diving stop, and threw out Gonder at first. There was also a hard-hit ball by Ron Hunt in the seventh, but it went right at rookie third baseman Richie Allen, who made the play.

Bunning wasn't going to let the mounting pressure ruin this day, not if he could help it. Determined not to keep his feelings pent up, by the fifth inning he was talking about the no-hit possibility, imploring his teammates to dive for the ball, if necessary. In Boston, and again in that perfect-game bid against Houston that blew up in his face, he had kept his hopes inside too long; only in the last couple of innings had he shocked his Tiger teammates by daring to talk about the no-hitter. This time he didn't wait—he talked a blue streak.

"The other guys thought I was crazy, but I didn't want anyone tightening up," Bunning remarked. "Most of all, I didn't want to tighten up myself."

That May 29 debacle against Houston was on his mind as he entered the last three innings against the Mets. One Houston hit—a cheap one, on a misjudged fly ball—and "I just came unraveled," Jim noted. "That was the tension that built up on the bench. Nobody talked about it. Nobody did anything [so long as the perfect game was going]. I said, 'The hell with that stuff.' I wasn't going to let that happen again. No way. I said, 'What is this? This can't be the way to do this. There's got to be a better way.'"

It didn't matter what his teammates thought. What he thought, and felt, was what mattered. He had to keep his emotions under control, do everything possible to maximize his chances for success. That was the Bunning way. Total focus. Be prepared. And if his idea of being prepared to face the closing innings of a perfect game was to yak up a storm on the bench in defiance of baseball superstition, nobody was about to stop him.

"He was really silly," his catcher, Gus Triandos, recalled. "He was jabbering like a magpie."

Nor was Mauch leaving anything to chance. By the fifth inning he, too, sensed that something very special was in the works. "I felt that Bunning himself sensed it by his attitude, the way he was moving his fielders around," Gene said. "I figured I'd try to make it easier for him, so I made a defensive change in the fifth inning."

Cookie Rojas, who could play anywhere and do a workmanlike job, moved from short to left, replacing Covington. Bobby Wine took over at short.

If all that talking on the bench was unusual, Bunning's constant chatter with his infielders when he was on the mound was not. "I always did that," he said. "I'd move Tony to the hole because I knew I was going to throw down and in to lefthanded hitters, and as soon as I turned around he'd move back the two steps. Ruben used to laugh at me. And I'd cheat my third baseman up all the time, figuring they would not hit the ball to third base, and so when I fell to the left [first base] side of the mound my third baseman could get anything into that area. Richie Allen didn't like to move up. I finally convinced him they weren't going to hit anything hard at him."

The thirty-two thousand Shea Stadium spectators, like the Fenway fans six years before, were cheering for Bunning as he took the mound in the seventh. The first Mets' batter, Jim Hickman, struck out for the third time. Ron Hunt was next.

Bunning knew all about Hunt's reputation for getting in the way of pitched balls. He had a knack for being nicked by them. What a way to ruin a perfect game.

"My biggest fear," Bunning said, "was that Hunt was going to stick an elbow out in front of a pitch. I think I kept all the balls away from him. He would've had to run across the plate to get hit."

That was risky because the book on Hunt was to pitch him inside, but if the second baseman was going to spoil Bunning's perfect game he would have to hit his way on. And he almost did. That was the shot Allen fielded at third. Aside from Gonder's fifth-inning grounder it was the only really hard-hit ball the Mets could manage in the game.

Next was Ed Kranepool, and Bunning struck him out swinging. Now he was six outs away.

Joe Christopher led off the eighth for the Mets and struck out. Gonder followed by swinging at the first pitch and bouncing routinely to Taylor at second.

Twenty-three down, four to go. The batter was Bob "Hawk" Taylor, the Mets' left fielder. The day before he had whacked four hits against the Phillies; now he battled Bunning through a long, tense at-bat.

Jim got ahead, 1 and 2, then missed outside for 2 and 2. Taylor fouled off the next pitch, then took one off the outside corner. The count was full. One more ball and the perfect game would be ruined.

Triandos signaled for a slider and Bunning aimed it toward the outside part of the plate to the righthanded batter. Taylor took the pitch, took a quick step toward first base, and stopped in his tracks when he heard plate umpire Ed Sudol bellow, "Strike three!"

Taylor opened his mouth to protest, then realized that Triandos had dropped the ball and began running to first. The Phillies catcher easily tossed him out. Twenty-four down, three to go. Later, Sudol would tell Mets broadcaster Ralph Kiner that he knew Bunning was working on a no-hitter, but didn't realize it was a perfect game. "Do you mean I umpired a perfect game?" he asked Kiner.

One more inning, three more Met outs, and that's just what it would be, as Bunning kept reminding anybody within earshot.

"It was the strangest thing," right fielder Johnny Callison remembered. "You don't talk when you have a no-hitter, right? But he was going up and down [the bench] and telling everybody what was going on. Everybody tried to get away from him, but he was so wired that he followed us around."

"Dive for the ball," he kept telling them. "Don't let anything fall in."

Bunning's primary concern as he walked to the mound for the final inning was George Altman, a tough lefthanded hitter who was certain to pinch-hit in the bottom of the ninth. "He was on the bench and I knew Casey [Stengel] was going to use him," Bunning said.

The question was when. Bunning hoped that Stengel wouldn't save Altman for last. Jim much preferred to have the Mets' other lefthanded pinch hitter, John Stephenson, represent the twenty-seventh out.

"I knew if I got Stephenson up there with two out, I had it," he said. "I knew I could get him out on curve balls, no matter what. I could throw him five, seven, eight curve balls and get him out. Altman, I wasn't so sure of. I didn't know if I could still jam him with the ball."

Bunning got his wish. Altman was in the on-deck circle as Jim faced Charley Smith in the bottom of the ninth. The New York shortstop popped the 1-1 pitch behind the plate. Triandos gave chase, but the ball landed just behind the screen. Bunning threw an outside curve ball for 2 and 2, then got Smith to pop the ball in foul territory beyond third base. Shortstop Bobby Wine ran it down. Twenty-five down, two to go.

That's when Bunning called his pal Triandos out to the mound for a high-level chat.

"He calls me out and says I should tell him a joke or something, just to give him a breather," the catcher remembered. "I couldn't think of any. I just laughed at him."

With that, Triandos went back behind the plate, promising himself, no doubt, to include a copy of *Joe Miller's Joke Book* among his catching tools next time Bunning pitched.

The second batter was the man Jim feared most. Altman was tough on righthanders. Bunning tried to pitch him inside, but didn't get the ball as far in as he wanted. Altman hit a long, high foul to right. Johnny Callison chased it, but ran out of room as the ball drifted into the stands. Strike one.

Altman fouled off another one. Strike two. And he missed the next one. The Shea fans were on their feet, screaming now. Bunning had his ninth strikeout. Twenty-six down, one to go. And the final Met batter, Jim Bunning felt certain, couldn't hit his curve ball with a paddle.

You never can tell in baseball, though. Even a guy with an average of .047 and an inability to hit a curve ball might get a hit off a good pitcher—even a pitcher good enough to be one out away from a perfect game. Accidents did happen. That was part of baseball's charm, the uncertainty of it all. Just when you thought you had the game figured out, something totally unexpected happened. But whatever John Stephenson did, he would have to do it against Bunning's curve ball. That much *was* certain.

Curve balls. Nothing but curve balls. Stephenson swung at the first one and missed. Strike one. He took the second one. Strike two.

A touch of the resin bag, and another curve ball. It broke outside. Ball one. And yet another outside curve. Ball two.

And yet another. Stephenson swung . . . and the ball landed in Gus

Triandos's mitt. "Can you beat that?" Stephenson told the press. "I'm looking for a fast ball and he throws me a change-up curve."

Twenty-seven down, none to go. It was over. A ten-strikeout perfect game. Not merely a no-hitter, mind you, but a perfect no-hitter, the first in the National League in eighty-four years, the first in modern National League history. Also the first regular-season no-hitter in the major leagues in forty-two years, Yankee righthander Don Larsen having pitched his against the Brooklyn Dodgers in the 1956 World Series.

Jim Bunning pounded his fist into his glove in a rare show of emotion. The way he felt at that moment was vastly different from that day at Fenway Park. "I knew what I had done," he said. "I was completely in control of myself."

Not so Mary Bunning, who came rushing out of the stands to join her husband, boosted over the railing by a helpful Shea Stadium guard after she identified herself.

The excitement ran throughout the baseball world. In Minnesota, where the Tigers were playing, the news was flashed on the scoreboard. The next day the *Chicago Tribune* ran a picture of Tiger manager Charley Dressen standing in the dugout, holding his cap in his right hand, rubbing the top of his head with his left hand as he looked out at the scoreboard message: "Bunning Hurled First Perfect Game Since 1922 Today."

Maybe the former Tiger pitcher did have something left, after all.

Jim Bunning's red-letter day was a long way from being over. Pitching a perfect game in New York meant having to deal with the city's news media, not one of Bunning's favorite pastimes. And then there was the call from Frank Scott—"He was kind of a general agent," Bunning said—in the clubhouse while a Phillie rookie named Rick Wise, who himself would pitch a big league no-hitter one day, was beating the Mets in the nightcap for his first big league victory.

Scott asked Bunning if he would appear on that night's *Ed Sullivan Show*, for which Jim would receive "either $1,500 or $1,000" for a few seconds' "work"; he couldn't remember which. So the Bunnings and the Caters changed their plans. First, they looked for a place to eat in midtown Manhattan. "We went to Toots Shor's," Jim recalled. It was closed. So they wound up going to the *Ed Sullivan Show* first and eating later.

It had been a big sports day, and Sullivan had booked another sports guest—pro golfer Ken Venturi, winner of the U.S. Open—for an appearance on the stage of his very big show.

"I went backstage when I got to the Sullivan show," Jim said, "and Ken Venturi came in. He had just won the U.S. Open and he had to play thirty-six holes [on the final day] in unbelievably stifling heat at the Congressional Country Club in Washington. They had flown him in after he won. So we met each other, shook hands and he said, "You son of a bitch, I win the U.S. Open and you knock me off the front page by pitching a darn perfect game."

Venturi was supposed to talk to Sullivan during his appearance. Thanks to Bunning—and Sullivan's love for baseball—he was relegated to second-banana, nontalking, just-take-a-bow status. Sullivan wanted to talk to Jim Bunning.

"The only thing I can remember is the producer saying, 'Stand still because Sullivan will bob and weave when he talks to you,'" Bunning said. "So instead of getting fifteen seconds [as originally planned], I got about a thirty-second appearance on the Sullivan Show."

Poor Venturi, his chances for an Emmy gone, merely walked out, waved, and retraced his steps off stage.

Venturi, of course, was only kidding when he got on Bunning for upstaging him. In the years that followed, the two men became good friends. Bunning even attended a roast for Venturi, at which the golfer told the Sullivan story. "Any time I see him that's the first thing he brings up, " Jim noted. "'You son of a gun . . .' he'll say."

The dialogue during Jim's big television appearance with Sullivan was quite tame. "He asked me how it felt to pitch a perfect game," recalled Bunning, who told him it felt pretty good. Time restrictions being tight, Jim couldn't explain to Ed and his vast audience why pitching a perfect game was tantamount to barely averting a serious automobile accident. Just as well. The nation probably wouldn't have understood.

The show over, the Bunnings—Jim, Mary, and (then twelve) Barbara—and the Caters, surely starved by now, went to dinner. At least they tried to go to dinner. "We drove home on the New Jersey Turnpike," Jim remembered, "and stopped at Howard Johnson's because we couldn't find anything open in New York."

That, too, may have established a modern record of sorts, marking the only time visitors to New York City couldn't find a place to eat.

No matter. Jim, Mary, and the rest of the Bunning clan were on cloud nine. The cap he wore that day and the "game ball" were shipped to the Hall of Fame, beating him there by thirty-two years. The *Detroit Free Press* ran this item three days later: "It was learned, through reliable sources, that the Phillies do not intend to return Jim Bunning to the Tigers."

And how did the New York press approach Bunning in the Phillies' clubhouse immediately after his perfect game? To hear one of them tell it, with fear and trepidation. Bunning's reputation as a tough interview had preceded him to Shea Stadium.

The veteran New York sportswriter Maury Allen was one of those who made a beeline for Bunning's locker to interrogate the perfect pitcher. Years later, when Jim was elected to the Hall of Fame, Allen reminisced about that experience in print.

"When it was over," Allen wrote, "he did not dance in the clubhouse, entertain sportswriters with giddy stories of his youth or share bubbly champagne with his teammates.

"Bunning remained in character, intense, a little angry, proud and contentious as he was being questioned.

"He bristled when it was suggested the Mets hardly resembled the 1927 Yankees. . . . He bristled when questioned about the failure of the Mets to bunt against him in an attempt to steal the perfect game from him.

"'How would you like to bunt against me?' he bellowed to this reporter.

"Only Bunning and Bob Gibson seemed to intimidate hitters as well as sportswriters with their violent pitching motion and abrasive interview style."

Clearly, not all sportswriters loved the guy. But then, he didn't love all sportswriters, either, so it was a draw. And even those who liked him the least had to admit one thing: Jim Bunning was consistent. He could be as tough an interview after a perfect game as he was after a 1-0 loss. Well, almost.

How did the Phillies reward Bunning for his perfect game? "There was a story in the paper that they were going to tear up my contract," he recalled. Whoever wrote it had a good imagination. "They didn't tear up the contract," Jim said. "But when they sent me a birthday greeting in October of '64 there was a check for two thousand bucks. That was for the perfect game."

The no-hit string ended quickly. His next time out, Curt Flood, leading off for the St. Louis Cardinals, doubled to center field. The Phillies pulled out a 6-5 win on Clay Dalrymple's two-run homer in the ninth, but Bunning didn't get credit for the victory. He did win the next two starts to boost his record to 9 and 2, and he came up with a big save for Mauch against the Braves to halt a four-game Phillies' losing streak. With his team clinging to a 3-2 lead, Bunning relieved Ray Culp in the ninth. There were runners on first and second and nobody out. After Woody Woodward sacrificed, Bunning retired pinch-hitter Gene Oliver on a pop fly, walked Eddie Mathews intentionally, and then got pinch-hitter Merritt Ranew to bounce to first, Jim hustling over to take the game-ending toss. The victory kept the Phillies within a game of the first-place San Francisco Giants.

Three days later, the Phillies were back on top, a 7-5 win in Pittsburgh moving them four percentage points ahead of the Giants. For the next seventy-two days, they remained in first place.

Those were heady times for Bunning and the Phillies. Jim's tenth victory, a 4-0 four-hitter over the Giants on July 28, saw yet another no-hit bid. This one lasted until the top of the sixth, when Hal Lanier cracked a one-out single.

Twelve days and two starts later, Bunning was at it again. Facing the Mets in Philly, he retired the first fourteen batters before Joe Christopher—no doubt following Maury Allen's instructions—beat out a bunt to third. The Mets didn't get another hit until Charley Smith singled in the seventh; they wound up with five in the game, which Bunning won 6-0. Five days later he faced them again at Shea and carried a no-hitter into the fourth. Ron Hunt ended that one with a clean, one-out single, but Bunning breezed to a five-hit 6-1 victory.

August was a terrific month for the Phillies. With Bunning and Short providing Mauch with a killer one-two punch in the starting rotation, the club went 19 and 10 and boosted its league lead from one and a half games to five and a half. A move by the front office helped greatly. On August 7 John Quinn, the general manager, acquired veteran first baseman Frank Thomas from the Mets, a move that paid immediate dividends. On the first pitch he saw as a Phillie, Thomas smacked a double down the left field line off the Mets' Al Jackson. The hits kept coming. "He carried us on his back for two weeks," Bunning recalled. In all, Thomas played first base for the Phillies in thirty-three games; he hit .302, with seven homers and twenty-six runs batted in. A freak injury ended his season in early September, however. In

Bunning's view, and in that of many other observers of the 1964 Phillies, Thomas's loss ultimately cost the team the pennant. Bunning remains convinced to this day that if Thomas had stayed healthy the Phillies would have won, and won big—by as many as ten games.

We will never know that, of course, but we *do* know this: if not for a questionable postponement in August, Frank Thomas wouldn't have been injured playing the Dodgers in September. It was a classic case of a ball club being a little too clever for its own good.

The date: August 3. The first-place Phillies were scheduled to close out a four-game series with the Dodgers with a Monday night game at Connie Mack Stadium. The weather outlook was fine. "Variable cloudiness and continued mild," said the official forecast. An ideal day for a ball game—except for one thing. Quinn and Mauch saw a most ominous-looking cloud on the horizon. His name was Sandy Koufax, and he was scheduled to pitch that night for the Dodgers.

Koufax was at the height of his considerable powers then, and Koufax at the height of his powers was a tough cookie to beat. So the Phillies braintrust put their heads together and came up with a solution. The game was postponed because of "threatening weather," which sounded better than admitting the game was postponed because of Sandy Koufax. They'd make it up the following month—hopefully on a day when Sandy Koufax was not scheduled to pitch.

The brilliant, if rather sneaky, move backfired. The makeup date was September 8, which happened to be a Jewish holiday. (Quinn and Mauch thought of everything in those days.) The deeply religious Koufax was definitely out of the picture, but the rest of the Dodgers showed up and beat the Phillies, 3-2. Far worse, the club lost Frank Thomas in a most ill-advised play on the bases.

"That was the thing that started us down," Bunning recalled as he bemoaned "the stupidity of that injury."

"He was going to fool [Dodger shortstop] Maury Wills by getting in front of him and distracting him so he couldn't catch [a ground ball]," Bunning remembered. "He got so far off second base that he had to dive back, and when he dove back, he broke his thumb."

Until that unfortunate incident, it was mostly full speed ahead for the Phillies. Bunning went from July 15 to September 16 without losing a game, winning eight consecutive decisions in that stretch. With a little luck, he could have won more. Jim's toughest no-decision came on August 28 in Pittsburgh. Going into the last of the ninth, he had a three-hit, ten-strikeout shutout and a two-run lead. Bill Virdon began the final inning with hit number four, a single. Roberto Clemente became Bunning's eleventh strikeout victim. Then Jim issued his first walk, to Jerry Lynch; Mauch glanced at the on-deck circle, saw Willie Stargell looming there, and decided to go with a fresh arm. It belonged to Ed Roebuck, who gave up a run-scoring single to Stargell and a game-winning, three-run homer to Smoky Burgess.

Next time out, Bunning had Houston shut out, 4-0, in the ninth at home. The Colt-45s put two men on base with two out, and this time Mauch stayed with Bunning. Joe Gaines promptly blasted a three-run homer off the upper-deck facade in center field, but Bunning hung in there, got the final out, and a 4-3 victory, his fifteenth. Number sixteen was a complete-game, 9-3 win over the Giants at home. The seventeenth was a ten-inning, route-going, 4-1 victory over the Giants at Candlestick Park that improved his record to 17 and 4.

Bunning's winning streak ended on September 16 in Houston, when Mauch got a little greedy and decided to pitch him with two days' rest, telling the Philadelphia press that Jim had asked to do it.

"No, that wasn't true," Bunning declared. "Absolutely not. Gene came and asked me if I thought I could pitch, and I said, 'Of course,' He thought we could steal that game."

Bunning didn't have his good stuff. A youngster named Rusty Staub tagged him for a two-run homer in the bottom of the first after the Phillies had scored twice in the top half. The Phillies took a 3-2 lead into the home fifth, but Bunning simply didn't have it. Houston routed him with a four-run rally, then held on for a 6-5 victory.

"Maybe he should have started somebody else," Bunning said. "I can remember that homer Staub hit like it was yesterday. In fact, we talked about it [during induction weekend] at the Hall of Fame. Rusty said, 'I remember that. I was just a kid.' I said, 'Well, I wasn't and I remember it, too.' He had just come back up from the minor leagues."

By pitching Bunning on that Wednesday night in Houston, Mauch figured he could start his ace with a full three days' rest against the much tougher Dodgers the following Sunday in Los Angeles, the final game of the road trip.

The night before Bunning faced the Dodgers, the Phillies lost one in a way that would rankle Mauch for years. Chris Short pitched a strong game and carried a lead into the late innings, but then gave up a booming, game-tying home run to his nemesis, huge Frank Howard.

The game remained tied until early Sunday morning, through fifteen and a half excruciating innings. In the bottom of the sixteenth the Dodgers had Willie Davis on third with two out and Ron Fairly at bat. Mauch went with the percentages, bringing in the lefthander Morrie Steevens, just up from the minor leagues, to face the lefthanded Fairly. Sure enough, Steevens got two quick strikes on the hitter. The strategy appeared to be working like a charm.

Whoops!

Willie Davis broke for the plate on the two-strike pitch. Ridiculous. You can't steal home with two out and two strikes on the batter. The guy at the plate swings, he's liable to kill the runner with a line drive. If he doesn't, and the ball is over the plate, the inning is over. It's an absurd play, a nonsensical play . . . and it won the ball game. Steevens panicked. The pitch went sailing to the backstop and the Dodgers earned the victory, 4-3.

It was a play Mauch will remember as long as he lives. "Two strikes on Fairly," he said many years later. "All he had to do was throw a strike. But Morrie Steevens, what the hell does he know? It's so absurd. Of course, Leo [Durocher] was coaching third that night, and apparently he thought Fairly wasn't going to get the run in, so let's take a chance. See, that's one of the things I always tried to do—eliminate the surprises for my players—but I can't prepare for two-strike steals of home. I can't handle that." And because Steevens couldn't, either, there was added pressure on Bunning to come up with a victory in the getaway game. Jim was reasonably well rested for the effort. While the Phillies and Dodgers were battling past midnight in their marathon, Bunning was back at the hotel.

"I was sleeping soundly in my room and some crazy fan from Philly called and woke me up at one, two in the morning [after Steevens's pitch had hit the backstop and the Phillies had lost]," Bunning recalled. "He said, 'What are you guys doing, giving it away?' I said, 'Who the heck is this?'"

It was a guy named Joe something-or-other. Bunning hung up the phone, then called the desk and requested that no more calls be put through to his room. He had an important game to win that afternoon.

Jim pitched well, carrying a 3-1 lead into the bottom of the ninth. Then, with two out and a runner on second, Frank Thomas's replacement at first, Vic Power, prepared to field a potentially game-ending ground ball. In his prime, Power was as slick a defensive first baseman as you were likely to see. But his best days were behind him.

Power was out of shape and his reflexes were a touch slow. The ball took a little skip on him, hit his bare hand, and rolled away. The runner scored from second as Bunning, who had run over to cover the bag, stood on first base waiting for the throw that never came.

Now the tying run was on, and the winning run was at the plate in the person of a tough lefthanded hitter, John Roseboro. Bunning was equal to the occasion. He struck out Roseboro on a 2-2 pitch, and the Phillies headed home feeling very good about themselves. They had survived the West Coast trip. Their magic number was down to seven. They were six and a half games ahead with twelve to go, and their next seven games were at Connie Mack Stadium. It was all over but the shouting. The pennant was theirs. They could feel it. They could taste it. Heck, the entire city of Philadelphia could taste it.

Paul Owens, scouting on the West Coast at the time, was so sure the Phillies would win that he went out and bought two suits he "couldn't afford." "I wanted to be dressed good for the World Series," he recalled. "They said the scouts would be coming back to see it."

Ruben Amaro placed a long-distance phone call to his father in Mexico. The elder Amaro had been a baseball star in Cuba, and he loved the game. Ruben wanted him to fly to Philadelphia, be part of the Phillies' victory drive.

"We come back from the road and I call him and I say, 'Father, it looks like we're in and I really want you to come here and enjoy the World Series and I want you to come early,'" Ruben declared. "I remember my father saying, 'I don't like to sound pessimistic or anything, but I wouldn't really be sure of playing [in the World Series] until I know you have clinched the pennant.'"

The older Amaro had been through some heart-wrenching defeats in pennant races in Cuba. He reminded his son of that, making it clear it wasn't a good idea to count your pennants until they're clinched.

But hey, Dad, this was different. I mean, six and a half games up with twelve to go and a big home stand coming up. Nothing could go wrong now. Or so it seemed. World Series tickets were being printed. Pennant fever was sweeping the town—just like it had fourteen years before when the Whiz Kids won the National League pennant.

Chances are, people had forgotten that the 1950 Phillies had a seven and a half game lead over the Dodgers with eleven games to go—and had to beat the Dodgers in extra innings at Ebbets Field on the final day of the season to win the pennant. Funny things happen in baseball.

But there wasn't anything funny about what happened in the next week and a half to Gene Mauch, Jim Bunning, Chris Short, Richie Allen, Johnny Callison, and the rest of the 1964 Philadelphia Phillies.

The Crash of '64

What happened still boggles the mind. Not one of the Phillies could have imagined on that flight home from Los Angeles what was in store. "We played 150 games as strong as you could play them, as well as you could play them," said Bunning.

The 151st, a Monday night meeting with the Cincinnati Reds, was another of those games you had to see to believe. Coming on the heels of that sixteenth-inning steal of home by Willie Davis, it set the pattern for disasters yet to come.

With Short and Bunning having pitched the previous two games, Mauch gave the start to Art Mahaffey, and the right-hander pitched a strong game. It was scoreless in the sixth as Mahaffey dueled with Reds' righthander John Tsitouris. Then came trouble. With one out, Chico Ruiz singled to right, and Vada Pinson singled off Tony Taylor's glove into right field. Johnny Callison charged the ball and, as Ruiz sprinted to third, the strong-armed outfielder gunned down Pinson at second. Two out, Ruiz on third base, and Frank Robinson, the Reds' most dangerous hitter—indeed, one of baseball's most dangerous hitters—at the plate.

What happened next was as unthinkable as what had befallen Morrie Steevens in Los Angeles. Ruiz broke for the plate. One of the game's great RBI men batting and the damn fool was trying to steal home, taking the bat out of Frank Robinson's hands. It was an absurd play—so ridiculous that Dick Sisler, the Reds' acting manager in the absence of the ailing Fred Hutchinson—was ready to strangle

Ruiz . . . until Mahaffey threw the ball away. For the second time in three days a bad play, a positively ridiculous play by the opposition, had turned into the winning run.

"I remember it distinctly," said Bunning. "I saw it but I didn't believe it. The coach at third base—I think it was Reggie Otero—saw him go and almost fainted. It was a complete freak."

What it was, was another of those plays that Gene Mauch hadn't prepared his troops to combat because it wasn't in any baseball book that Mauch, or anybody else, had ever read. So Ruiz scored the run and the Phillies lost, 1-0. The most agonizing losing streak in Phillies' history—yes, far more agonizing than the twenty-three-game streak of 1961—was under way. Night by night, day by day it grew until it enveloped the ball club, turning the sure-fire pennant winners of late September into shocked, shaken losers.

Short, a seventeen-game winner who pitched so well that year, went the next night; he gave up six earned runs in four and two-thirds innings. The Reds romped, 9-2. Then came Dennis Bennett, the sore-armed lefty. "He was hurting so bad, but he tried to pitch," Bunning recalled. No use. Bennett, who would take the ball no matter how much he hurt, gave it a game try. The Phillies carried a 3-2 lead into the seventh, but the Reds scored four and went on to win, 6-4, led by Vada Pinson's two homers. Still, Bunning refused to believe the Phillies were going to let this pennant slip away. "I was perfectly confident we weren't going to blow it," he said.

What followed was a four-game nightmare against the Milwaukee Braves. For the Phillies, it was a lost weekend to end all lost weekends, the series from hell. Bunning remembers it clearly. He started two of the four games.

Yankee manager Joe Torre remembers it, too. Torre was one of the Braves, who arrived in Philly nice and loose and proceeded to maul the home team in four straight.

Although they were out of the race, the Braves could hit. Hank Aaron and Eddie Mathews were murder in those days, and Torre was closing out a banner year, in which he hit .321. All he did that weekend was go 11 for 19 with seven runs batted in. Joe and his teammates were having a ball; beating Gene Mauch was a favorite pastime of National League clubs. Gene, it seemed, went out of his way to make the opposition hate him.

"You didn't feel sorry for Mauch in those days," Torre said. "Gene was an arrogant bastard. He'd scream at you from the dugout. I remember one time we're in Milwaukee. I'm in a slump and he's screaming, 'Knock this son of a bitch down.' I get a base hit. I'm at first base and I'm screaming at him. He comes out to change pitchers and I'm yelling at him, and [Phillies' first baseman John] Herrnstein, with his glove up [over his mouth] is going, 'Give it to him.'"

It didn't take much prodding. Mauch gave and Mauch received. But even if a few of his own players weren't too fond of him at times, Torre came to see in later years why Jim Bunning and so many others were big Mauch boosters.

"The next year he managed the All-Star game [for the National League because Johnny Keane, who managed the 1964 Cardinals, had gone to the Yankees]," said Torre, "and I loved playing for him. I went all nine innings in the '65 All-Star game. I like him a lot. I got pretty close to him when I broadcast out there [when Mauch managed the Angels]."

But on that September weekend in 1964 Torre and the rest of the Milwaukee Braves couldn't think of anything that was more pleasurable to do than knock Mauch's Phillies out of first place. For them, it was Gene Mauch payback time.

The Braves, with nothing to lose, could do nothing wrong. The Phillies, with everything to lose, could do nothing right. "They were so tight that weekend," Torre recalled.

Bunning opened the series and pitched decently, holding the visitors to six hits and three runs in six innings. But it wasn't good enough to halt the Phillies' plunge to oblivion. Behind 3-0, Bunning was lifted for a pinch hitter in the home sixth. Reliever Jack Baldschun gave up two runs in the eighth, enabling the Braves to survive a three-run Phillies' rally. The final was 5-3, the Phillies fourth loss in a row. All Joe Torre did in that one was go 2 for 4 (a pair of triples) and knock in three runs.

Criticism of the way Mauch was handling his pitchers began to be heard. Maybe he had worn out Bunning and Short by pitching them with less than their normal three days' rest. And why had he skipped over Bunning's road roommate, Art Mahaffey, so many times when Mahaffey was perfectly healthy, sticking all the while with Dennis Bennett, who wasn't healthy? They were legitimate questions. And they became louder when Short was unable to halt the team's skid the following night.

It was time for major concern. The city had been rocked by a violent riot in the north section, not far from the ball park, just a few weeks before. At a point when Philadelphians needed to focus on something pleasant, the baseball team, which had united the city and given its residents something to feel good about, was suddenly falling apart.

Out in Los Angeles, Phillies' scout Paul Owens kept checking the scores and getting more and more worried. Having already paid for two new suits he couldn't really afford, Owens (who would become the architect of the 1980 world champion Phillies and the field manager of the 1983 World Series team) was beginning to wonder if there'd be a '64 World Series involving the club at which to wear his new clothes.

For Owens, watching those Phillies-Braves scores come in from a few thousand miles away was almost as painful as witnessing the devastation at Connie Mack Stadium in person.

"Every night at Dodger Stadium [other] scouts would say, 'Don't worry. Don't worry,'" Owens remembered. "You know, we'd lost three, four in a row and they kept saying, 'Don't worry.' I said, 'Damn it, maybe you guys aren't worried. I'm worried.'"

By the time the Phillies lost the second game of the Braves' series and their fifth in a row—the club's longest losing streak of the season—Owens and just about everybody else following the year's most compelling baseball soap opera knew there was plenty to worry about.

The game that Short started was a gut-wrencher that ended in the wee hours, long after the lefthander had departed. The Phillies kept rallying and rallying, and still they lost. Callison, a tower of strength offensively and defensively all season, smashed a game-tying, two-run homer with two out in the eighth.

Torre, who had a home run, two singles, and three runs batted in, smacked his homer with a runner aboard in the tenth, seemingly dooming the Phillies. Not so. Richie Allen yanked them from the edge of defeat with two out in the bottom of the tenth, smoking a soaring drive to deepest center with one on. It rattled around off the scoreboard as Allen dashed around the bases for an inside-the-park homer that got his team even again. For sheer drama it was hard to beat. Unfortunately, for the Phillies that weekend the Milwaukee Braves were impossible to beat. Facing John Boozer in the twelfth, they scored twice on an infield hit, two walks, a run-scoring single by Eddie Mathews, and an error. The 7-5 defeat was excruciating; the game that followed wasn't much easier to take.

Desperately short of healthy, rested arms, Mauch gave Mahaffey another start and the pitcher turned in a solid performance. The Phillies opened up an early 4-0 lead, and still led, 4-2, going into the eighth. When the first two Braves reached base, Mauch pulled Mahaffey and the bullpen combination of righthander Jack Baldschun and lefthander Bobby Shantz held the Braves to a single run. For the moment at least, the Phillies had dodged the bullet, clinging to a 4-3 lead going into the ninth. But the Braves had more ammunition and they used it.

It was sheer torture. Aaron opened with a single and took second on Mathews's single. Bunning's old Tiger buddy, Frank Bolling, fouled off two bunts, then bounced the ball up the middle. Amaro made a diving stop behind second and flipped to Taylor, who dropped the ball. This loaded the bases for Rico Carty, who promptly unloaded them with a triple to center. That was the crusher. The Phillies' lead, three and a half games when the Braves arrived in town, was down to half a game. "After they lost that game," Joe Torre declared, "they were cooked." And Torre had helped cook them by going 3 for 4.

It was crazy. For five months the Phillies had done everything right; now they couldn't do anything right.

"We all must have been tired," Jim Bunning theorized. "I didn't feel tired because of the adrenaline, but I must have been. We all must have been because we all played bad. Our defense, which had been unbelievably good for 150 games, was terrible. A pop fly would go up, they'd drop the ball. A ground ball, a normal double play, we struggled to get one out. When we pitched good we didn't hit. When we hit good we didn't pitch. We had our losing streak the wrong time of the year."

The last home stand of the season had one game to go. Their once imposing lead was down to half a game over the surging Reds, a game and a half over the equally hot Cardinals. Both challengers were doing nothing but winning while the Phillies did nothing but lose.

If somebody tried to write that script, nobody would have believed it. But it was really happening—and the Phillies had nothing left with which to fight back. They had struggled mightily in the Friday night extra-inning thriller, and again on Saturday afternoon. By Sunday they were a beaten team.

With one last chance to win a game on their final home stand, Mauch asked Bunning to stop the bleeding and protect the slender league lead on two days' rest. It was too much to ask. Jim had nothing;

the Braves took what amounted to batting practice, banging out twenty-two hits in the game.

Bunning did manage to gut it out through three innings, taking a 3-2 lead into the fourth. Then those Braves bombers took over, knocking him out with a six-run outburst and continuing the assault in a four-run fifth against Dallas Green. In all, Bunning was charged with seven runs, all earned, and ten hits in three-plus innings. Green was charged with five runs, all earned, and seven hits in an inning and two-thirds. Once again, Joe Torre had a field day, hitting a home run and two singles in five at-bats. The homer came off Baldschun. Torre remembers it well.

"I got up against Jack Baldschun one time and I looked for a slider," Joe said. "I had no right looking for a slider against Jack Baldschun; he was a screwball pitcher."

But Baldschun threw a slider, and Torre smacked it into the upper deck in left field. It was that kind of a weekend for Joe Torre and the Braves, that kind of a weekend for the Phillies.

What made the 14-8 loss harder to take was that Callison hit three home runs out of Connie Mack Stadium, solo shots in the sixth and eighth and a two-run blast in the ninth. By the time Callison started playing long ball, however, the Phillies were out of the game, and out of first place. The team that had come home leading the league by six and a half games with twelve to go staggered out of town in second place. All that remained were five road games—three in St. Louis, two in Cincinnati—against the hottest teams in the National League.

Mauch held a lot of meetings during the season, so it was no surprise when he called one before the opening game of the Cardinal series. "He just tried to enrage us," Bunning recalled. "He said, 'You're letting it slip away, letting somebody take it away from you.' I remember him saying, 'Go start a fight. Do *something*.'"

Mauch was at his wit's end, desperately searching for a way—any way imaginable—to snap his team out of it while there was still time to salvage the pennant.

"He made so many talks during the year trying to charge us up that this one kind of fell flat," Bunning said. "I can remember Gus [Triandos] and I walking out of the clubhouse saying, 'I think he meant for us to start a fight with somebody on the Cardinals.' That's the only thing I got out of it. He could've started the fight. He was better at that than anyone. All you got to do is go out and chop a catcher [the way Mauch did one night when the Mets' Jerry Grote dared to go into the Phillies dugout in pursuit of a foul ball]."

To Bunning's way of thinking, this was no time for a pep talk, anyway. "We were busting our fannies trying to win," he said, "and we were playing just about as bad as we could play."

Was Mauch panicking? Bunning didn't see it. "But I didn't look for it," he added. "All I know is, the reason he started us [Short and Bunning] with two days' rest was because, first of all, he wouldn't give Mahaffey the ball [except when there was no other way to go]. There was no reason for him not to. Art should have been starting right along with Shortie and myself because he was sound and willing. Some of the others weren't. They were kind of glad Short and Bunning were pitching every third day."

Not Mahaffey. He wanted the ball. "He won twelve games," Bunning pointed out. "If Gene had a little more confidence in him he'd have won seventeen or eighteen. He should have been pitching in the last ten days of the season. He should have started the Dennis Bennett game [second game of the Cardinal series] or the Houston game [that Bunning pitched on short rest], or one of the games. He lost the 1-0 game to Cincy. He carried us into the eighth inning against the Braves, pitched very well, and then he didn't start the last ten days of the season. He should have because Dennis Bennett was seriously hurt and couldn't pitch."

Mauch, as stubborn as he is brilliant, never bought that argument. At least he never admitted it publicly. Before the St. Louis series began, the Phillies' beleaguered manager walked up to the *Philadelphia Inquirer*'s Allen Lewis and asked, 'What's wrong with my ball club?' And then he stood there, the way Mauch did so many times, with his arms folded, staring straight ahead, and listened as Lewis told him what he thought.

"I don't think anybody could have managed better for 150 games." Lewis began. "But every pennant that's blown is blown because the manager screwed up the pitching rotation."

Mauch just stood there as Lewis ticked off some examples. Then he said, "Aw, that's a bunch of bullshit," and walked away.

The game that night did nothing to restore his sunny disposition. Short started against Bob Gibson, gave up three runs in five and one-third innings, and was charged with the 5-1 defeat, the Phillies' eighth in a row. The next night, Bennett—sore arm and all—gave it a try. He lasted an inning and a third, giving up five hits and three runs, enough for lefthander Ray Sadecki to gain his twentieth win. Mauch used six pitchers in the 4-2 defeat. "Dennis couldn't even get the ball to home plate," Bunning said.

Desperate men take desperate measures, and Mauch asked Bunning to go again on two days' rest in the last game of the series against one-time Whiz Kid Curt Simmons. Again Jim didn't have it, yielding an early home run to Tim McCarver and lasting only three and one-third innings. By then the Cardinals had six runs and Simmons was mowing them down and making it look easy, baffling the Phillies with an assortment of off-speed deliveries.

"Curt Simmons pitched a no-hitter against us for six innings," Bunning remembered, "and he did it with the biggest array of zip [nothing] I have ever seen, and he's laughing at Mauch. He's having a ball."

The Phillies rallied late but came up short, 8-5. It was number ten in a losing streak that would go down in major league history as one of the all-time collapses in a pennant race.

Three years later, at a Gene Mauch roast in Philadelphia, Jimmy Dykes told him: "Nobody will ever forget what you did in 1964. No other manager in Philadelphia history has molded a championship team into a contender in ten days."

Even Mauch laughed—or pretended to.

The Phillies' 1964 season did not end in St. Louis, although the team looked to be hopelessly out of it as it headed for Cincinnati. But the Phillies, having blown that seemingly insurmountable lead, went out to prove that nothing was impossible, and Bunning maintained the hope, however faint, that the team somehow could tie for the lead and force a playoff. Mostly, though, Bunning and his teammates were "just kind of numb and disbelieving," Jim recalled. "We were actually behind."

Catching the Reds was still reasonable; the Phillies, trailing them by two games, could erase the deficit by sweeping the season-ending series in Cincinnati. But they trailed the Cardinals by two and a half games, three on the losing side. The only way the Phillies could catch them would be for the lowly Mets to sweep three games in St. Louis. Talk about wishful thinking . . .

And yet it almost happened.

The last weekend at old Crosley Field is fixed in Jim Bunning's mind. Just when the final nail was being driven into the Phillies' coffin, an amazing thing happened. The corpse came to life.

The Reds were rolling along, leading Short and the Phillies 3-0, after seven innings, and it could have been much worse. Alex Johnson, playing left field, ran up the terrace that fronted the outfield fences at Crosley, speared a long drive with two Reds baserunners (Vada Pinson and Frank Robinson) on the move and turned a likely two-run double into a triple play.

The turning point, in all likelihood, came in the bottom of the seventh. Chico Cardenas, batting with a runner on second and one out, was hit by a pitch and, apparently thinking Short had done it on purpose, started a fight that brought players rushing out of both dugouts and bullpens.

Bunning believes to this day that "if Chico Cardenas hadn't wanted to go out and hit Short and woke us up on that Friday night in Cincinnati we may not have won another game all year."

After the brawl was over, the Phillies erased the three-run deficit with a four-run eighth that the pouting Cardenas touched off by failing to make a play on a catchable pop fly to short center. Taylor's single with two on and one out knocked in the first run. Then, with two out, Allen tripled down the right field line to tie it and Johnson grounded a single up the middle to untie it. Baldschun held the Reds over the last two innings, and the Phillies had actually won a ball game. What's more, they were still mathematically alive; the Mets had knocked off the Cardinals in St. Louis.

The schedule was strange. The Phillies and Reds weren't scheduled to play Saturday, the Phillies' first off day since August 31. They had played thirty-one games in thirty days, a grueling test that Bunning felt contributed to their late-season collapse. Now, finally with a chance to rest, they had nothing to do but wait for the seemingly inevitable bad news from St. Louis, where the Cardinals certainly weren't going to permit the Mets to beat them two in a row. But that's exactly what happened, and it wasn't even close. So with one game to go, the Phillies were still breathing, a game behind the Cardinals and the Reds. Hope was springing eternal.

Reds' ace Jim Maloney wasn't going to face the Phillies on that final Sunday; he was waiting to pitch a possible playoff game against the Cardinals the following day. It would be Bunning against John Tsitouris in the last contest of the regular season.

Since Bunning lived just across the Ohio River in Fort Thomas, Kentucky, he spent that final weekend of the season at home. Jim went to church on Sunday morning and arrived at the ball park early. What happened when he got there remains a most vivid memory.

"I was in the clubhouse and [Phillies' trainer] Joe Liscio was giving me a rubdown," he said. "And here comes Hutch looking for Mauch."

Fred Hutchinson, the former Detroit manager who had treated the young Jim Bunning so well a decade earlier, was dying of cancer. He was once a fine big league pitcher, and always a highly respected man, and it was shocking to see him now.

"If you didn't like Hutch, you weren't human," Bunning said. "He was a man's man."

And if you didn't feel for Hutchinson when you saw him in his final days, you also weren't human. He walked bent slightly from the waist; his face looked drawn and tired. Two days earlier, when the Phillies arrived in Cincinnati with their ten-game losing streak, Hutchinson had phoned Mauch in the Phillies' clubhouse.

"The phone rang," Mauch recalled, "and I picked it up, and it was Hutch. He said, 'I wish there was something I could say to help.' Imagine him saying that to me."

That was the Fred Hutchinson who Bunning got to know and respect in the minor leagues during their brief time together. "He was the straightest guy who ever was," Jim said. In a game loaded with double-talkers and truth-benders, Hutchinson, like Bunning, was a straight shooter. Seeing him that Sunday morning, looking the way he looked, was a jolt.

"Cancer had really gotten to him," Bunning remembered. "I knew Hutch as one of the strongest guys I had ever known." The man he saw now was "just about done. You could tell," said Jim. "He couldn't control one of his eyelids. He . . ."

It was too painful to describe.

"He said, 'Where's the Little General?'" Or maybe he said, "Where's the little bastard?" Jim wasn't quite sure. Whatever Hutchinson's words, Bunning knew who he was looking for.

"You just missed him," Jim replied. "He's out on the bench."

Hutchinson nodded. "I want to say goodbye to him." And he went out and found Mauch.

Seeing Hutch that day put baseball in perspective. "Whatever we were going through was very slight [compared] to what Hutch was going through," Jim Bunning realized.

The game itself was a terrible anticlimax for both teams. The Phillies routed Tsitouris. Richie Allen hit two home runs and a double, driving in four runs. Bunning breezed to a 10-0 victory, his nineteenth of the year. Even now there are folks where he lives who remember how he shut out the Reds that day and ended their pennant hopes.

"I have people here who have never forgiven me for that game," Bunning said.

Ah, they were probably Democrats anyway.

The Phillies' victory came too late. The Mets led the Cardinals early, but soon fell behind. It grew very silent in the clubhouse as the news spread. The Cardinals were pulling away; there would be no World Series in Philadelphia.

"I remember the atmosphere in the clubhouse in Cincinnati when we finally heard the results of the [Cardinal] game," Ruben Amaro commented. "It was like everybody sat stunned. I mean, for an endless time. I can't tell you for twenty minutes, a half an hour, an hour; I don't know how long we sat there. But I know what I was praying for on the bench during the game. 'Please God, give us a shot. Give us one more game.'"

"I didn't say anything to anybody," Bunning recalled. "Nobody said anything to anybody. It was a total blah. We were out of it. We had it. It was ours. And we let go."

Nobody took it harder than the manager. He had done a spectacular job to put the Phillies in position to win, and then this happened. If only Frank Thomas hadn't gotten hurt. If only the Phillies had won two of the seven games on their last home stand. If only, if only . . .

Mauch would always be saddled with memories of the pennant that blew away.

"I will never forget his face," said Amaro, remembering the instant the Cardinal game ended and Mauch knew—they all knew—it was over.

Bunning didn't stick around until the race was officially over. He showered quickly, dressed and, ninety minutes later, was on a plane heading for New York and a Players Association meeting. His wife, upon hearing the Cardinal score, went into the ladies' room at Crosley Field, where she ran into Carolyn Rose, Pete's first wife. Their husbands had each missed tying for the pennant by one game. The two women put their arms around each other and cried.

The disappointment was such that, when Jim Bunning turned on the television to watch the first game of the Cardinals-Yankees World Series of '64, he quickly turned it off. "I didn't watch the Series," he remarked, "because Gibson was getting my starts. They had a great Series, the Cardinals [winning it in seven games], and I thought we could have had that Series, too."

Twenty-five years later the Phillies decided to hold a reunion of the 1964 team. To the surprise of many, Mauch showed up.

"I didn't really think he was going to come," Amaro said at the time, "because I know that hurt him so much."

Bunning, who was unable to attend the reunion, commented, "Mauch came? I can not believe it."

As for Mauch, he had this to say after reflecting for a quarter of a century: "Not winning [in 1964] is probably the only reason I'm still alive because I know I would have given fifteen years off the end of my life to win it."

Trying to Win 20

Despite what happened in 1964, Jim Bunning looks back on his four years under Gene Mauch as the happiest baseball years of his life, the years that convinced him to enter the Hall of Fame as a Phillie. Mauch respected Bunning, so much so that he let him call his own game. Until Jim arrived in Philadelphia, Mauch controlled what his pitchers threw, as Bunning discovered in a hurry.

"Clay [catcher Clay Dalrymple] had been trained to look for Mauch's every sign," Jim remarked. "As soon as Clay put down the sign, I changed it—by rubbing, adding or subtracting—and Dalrymple finally said, 'I'm not going to even look anymore.'"

Which was fine with Bunning and, as Dalrymple soon discovered, fine with Mauch as well. "Clay found out Mauch was not going to object if I changed the signs," Bunning recalled. "We played much faster games that way. It was so much easier."

If there was one thing Bunning wished could have been different in Philadelphia, it would have been the presence of a standout bullpen closer, a "hammer," as Jim refers to late-inning pitchers like Rollie Fingers and Bruce Sutter. The Phillies had some pretty good ones, at times. Jack Baldschun and Ed Roebuck had their moments. But Mauch, and Bunning, never had the luxury of putting the game in the hands of, say, a Goose Gossage in the last inning or two, which was tantamount to a guaranteed victory.

"I always thought if we'd had a Luis Arroyo or somebody like that it would have been different," Bunning said. "But we didn't. None of my teams had a 'hammer.' I always tried to pitch as long as I could. I think I may have won thirty or forty more games if I'd have had a 'hammer,' somebody who picked me up in the eighth or ninth inning."

He also would have had a lot more victories with better offensive support. Bunning won nineteen games in each of his first three Phillie seasons and seventeen in his fourth. The fact that he never reached that magical twenty-victory mark in the National League was undoubtedly a major element in his not being elected to the Hall of Fame by the baseball writers. Yet there's no question that Bunning should have won twenty in some, if not all, of those years.

Among the games he didn't win in 1964, for example, was a June 3 duel with the Dodgers' Don Drysdale at Connie Mack Stadium. Bunning pitched ten scoreless innings, striking out eleven, but was gone by the time the Phillies won, 1-0, on an unearned run in the eleventh. His next time out, four days later, Bunning had the Giants shut out, 3-0, after eight innings, then got tagged for a two-run homer by Duke Snider in the ninth. With no sure-fire "hammer" to close it out, Mauch stayed with Bunning, who gave up a game-tying homer to Jim Ray Hart. Only then did Mauch relieve the obviously tiring Bunning with Ed Roebuck, who lost the game in the tenth.

There was more of the same in 1965, including a July 28 start in Pittsburgh, where Bunning shut out the Pirates on two hits through eight innings. With the game scoreless, he was pulled for a pinch hitter in the ninth, and the eventual 1-0, fourteen-inning Phillie victory went to Jack Baldschun.

So Bunning, 19 and 8 in his first Phillie season, finished with a 19 and 9 record in his second. Maybe he didn't win twenty, but he was awfully good. On one memorable night at his favorite stomping grounds, Shea Stadium, Jim figured out a way to win those 1-0 games. He hit a sixth-inning home run over the right center field fence off future Hall of Famer Warren Spahn, then put an exclamation mark on the victory by striking out three Mets in the ninth.

There were other games to remember in '65, among them a no-hit bid against the Giants that ended when Tom Haller homered with one out in the seventh. Bunning, who won that one 10-2, didn't give up another hit until one out in the ninth. Two weeks later, on July 24, he allowed only two hits and three baserunners in a 5-1 win at Shea. Two starts later, against the Pirates, he pitched out of a bases-loaded, no-body-out jam in the first inning, striking out Willie Stargell and Donn Clendenon and getting Bill Mazeroski on a soft fly ball; Jim went on to fan twelve in a 4-0 victory, his 150th in the big leagues. Four days after that, Bunning was at it again, striking out nine and shutting out Houston 2-0. To win that one, Jim had to stop the heart of the Houston batting order with runners on second and third and nobody out in the sixth. His sixth shutout of the season, 2-0 over the Braves on September 14, was a two-hit gem, in which he permitted just two baserunners and allowed only three balls to reach the outfield. Two of the latter were soft doubles, an end-of-the-bat flare over third by Jesse Gonder in the second and an opposite-field looper down the left field line by Eddie Mathews in the seventh.

Gunning for his nineteenth win, Bunning struck out eleven Cubs on September 27 . . . and lost, 1-0, on Billy Williams's RBI hit in the eighth. He finally got number nineteen in his next (and final) start, beating the Mets 6-0 on a two-hitter and facing just twenty-eight batters to do it, striking out ten of them. His seven shutouts in a single season were the most by a Phillie pitcher since Grover Cleveland Alexander's eight in 1917.

From a team standpoint, the '65 season was a disappointment. No more pennant fever in Philadelphia. Johnny Callison had a second straight big year—with 32 homers and 101 runs batted in—and Richie Allen dodged the sophomore jinx with 20 homers, 85 runs batted in, and a .302 average, but the spark that flickered out in the final two weeks of the '64 season never returned. "We had a bunch of old people who couldn't play," Bunning remarked. Actually, they played well enough to win 85 games, but finished sixth in a ten-team league, eleven and a half games behind first-place Los Angeles.

There would be no more pennant drives for Bunning to live through; 1964, it turned out, would be his last chance to pitch in a World Series. Even though Allen had his finest year in 1966 (40 home runs, 112 runs scored, 110 RBI) and Bunning won nineteen more, against fourteen losses, the Phillies managed to finish no better than fourth, eight games out.

For Bunning, it was another year in which twenty victories barely eluded him, this despite finishing second to Sandy Koufax in strikeouts with 252 and in innings pitched with 314. Naturally, there was another of those extra-inning scoreless battles that he kept finding himself in during his first tour of duty with the Phillies. This one, at San Francisco, went fourteen innings before the Giants pushed across a run. Bunning went the first ten, holding the Giants to five hits. That effort was part of a streak of twenty-four scoreless innings for the Phillies' ace, who also won eight games in a row early in the season. After that his luck turned. On July 27, he went eleven innings in Los Angeles, striking out twelve Dodgers and holding the opposition to one run and six hits, only to wind up with another no-decision in a game the Phillies lost in twelve, 2-1.

But what really cost Bunning a twenty-win season, it might be argued, was the fact the Dodgers lost the first game of a season-ending doubleheader at Connie Mack Stadium, thus failing to clinch the National League pennant. Because the second-place Giants won their regular-season finale in Pittsburgh that day to stay alive, the Dodgers sent Sandy Koufax (plus a full lineup of regulars) against Bunning in the nightcap. Had the Dodgers beaten the Phillies' Chris Short in the opener, or the Pirates knocked off the Giants, Bunning would have faced a second-string Dodger lineup and a second-line Dodger pitcher in his bid for number twenty. But Short won, 4-3—and became a twenty-game winner himself. Some things are just not meant to happen.

It was quite a day at Connie Mack Stadium as the Dodgers fought to wrap up another pennant. The prospect of that happening was so enticing to a long-time Dodger fan named Danny Kaye that the entertainer had rushed to the Los Angeles Airport late the previous night to catch a red-eye for Philadelphia. Kaye wanted to be on hand when the Dodgers clinched, even if it cost him a night's sleep.

A tan raincoat pulled tightly around him, an old, scrunched-up rain hat covering his red hair, Kaye watched the first game from a seat adjacent to the Dodgers' radio booth under the third base roof. Chain-smoking cigarettes, occasionally removing the rain hat to smooth his tousled hair, Kaye looked like a television star whose option had just been dropped. The man obviously took his Dodger baseball seriously, and his heroes were losing to the Phillies.

By the ninth inning, with the Dodgers a run behind, Kaye squeezed into the visiting radio booth and stood guard next to a Teletype machine that was relaying the pitch-by-pitch description of the Giants-Pirates game from Pittsburgh. The Pirates had the bases loaded in the home ninth with the score 3-3; below, the Dodgers were down to their final out against the Phillies. It was nail-biting time.

By now, Vince Scully's radio booth was jammed with visitors. More than half a dozen Dodger fanatics were elbowing for position at the Teletype machine, seemingly oblivious of the broadcast going on a few feet away. They looked out as Tony Gonzalez raced to the right field line to haul in Maury Wills's game-ending fly ball, then turned back to the machine as one. They looked like spectators at a tennis match.

Their despair was evident seconds later when the teletypewriter made clicking noises and the word "out" appeared. "Clemente bounced out on a very close play," the message advised.

The Pirates had left the bases loaded. The Giants were still in business. Kaye put both hands on his head and tugged down viciously on the hat. "I had to stay up all night for this," he muttered. "Can you imagine?"

For the next twenty minutes, Danny Kaye, Buzzie Bavasi (the Dodgers' general manager), and assorted types from radio, television, and the newspapers wig-wagged signals from the booth to the Dodger dugout, where catcher Jeff Torborg, coach Preston Gomez, and others tried to interpret them. They needed to know, and know fast. A Pirate victory and the Dodgers could uncork the champagne and save Koufax for the World Series. A Giant victory and Koufax would have to pitch against the Phillies and Jim Bunning. For now, Koufax would have to begin warming up.

The Dodgers' problems were nothing compared to Danny Kaye's. He had suffered through a Dodger defeat in the first game, and now he wouldn't be able to stick around to watch them try to clinch the pennant. Kaye had to be in New York that Sunday night. Poor Danny was committed to be the "mystery guest" on *What's My Line?* If the television audience only knew what those mystery guests went through.

In Pittsburgh, the Giants won. Down below, it was Koufax versus Bunning in game two, the Dodgers' great lefthander pitching with two days' rest. He was up to the challenge. The Dodgers won the game and the pennant, depriving Bunning of his twentieth. While the jubilant Dodgers celebrated in the undersized visiting clubhouse, Danny Kaye—missing all the fun—was en route to Manhattan, where Dorothy Kilgallen and her fellow panelists were waiting, blissfully unaware of the sacrifice their mystery guest had made.

Although 1967 saw Jim Bunning compile the worst record of his first four years with the Phillies, numbers can lie. Granted, he won seventeen and lost fifteen. But he never pitched better. And Phillie hitters—the term is used loosely—never supported him worse.

The Phillies were noncontenders that season, fading to fifth place, two games over .500 and nineteen and a half games behind the pennant-winning Cardinals. Bunning's earned run average—under 3.00 in each of those first four Phillie seasons—dipped to 2.29, second only in the National League to Phil Niekro's 1.87. In addition, Jim led the league in strikeouts with 253 in a league-high 302 innings. He couldn't have been much better, pitching a succession of outstanding games. In one mid-May outing against the Cincinnati Reds, he retired the last nineteen batters in a row (and twenty-four of the last twenty-five) in a three-hit, 7-1 victory, spiced with eleven strikeouts. In a game in New York in late June, he retired the last seventeen Mets in a 1-0, three-hit victory.

If ever Jim Bunning should have won twenty or more games as a Phillie, this was the year. So why was he only 17 and 15? Five 1-0 defeats, three of them in one month, four of them in the span of nine starts, that's why.

His first 1-0 loss came on May 14 at Cincinnati. Bunning gave up four hits and struck out six before Mauch had to yank him for a pinch hitter in the eighth.

But the Phillie hitters saved the worst for last.

Their incredible, late-season run of nonsupport for their number one pitcher began on August 29 at Cincinnati. Bunning was brilliant, pitching a complete-game two-hitter and striking out eight. The Reds had one hit through the first six innings, a wind-blown, fly-ball triple to left by Pete Rose in the first. The run came in the seventh, when Vada Pinson opened with a ground ball over first base that rolled into the right field corner for a double. He moved to third on Rose's infield out and scored on Lee May's sacrifice fly.

One can only wonder how Jim Bunning managed to survive the ordeal that was September 1967. He pitched about as well as a man can pitch, but won just two games—both shutouts. As for the losses . . .

The Dodgers beat him, 1-0, on September 15 at Connie Mack Stadium. Bunning held them to four hits and struck out nine, but one of the hits was a two-out home run by John Roseboro in the fourth.

Four days later Jim lost to the Cardinals, 1-0, at Connie Mack

Stadium, giving up a first-inning run on three of the six hits he allowed in the eight innings he pitched before leaving for a pinch hitter.

Then, after shutting out the Dodgers in Los Angeles, 4-0, in his next start, Bunning lost his third 1-0 decision in four starts on September 27 at Houston. Jim kept the Astros scoreless on four hits through ten innings, then was beaten on a two-out run in the eleventh. This was his fifth 1-0 loss of the season, and it tied a major league record. Add to this that Bunning led the league with six shutout victories, and it's apparent his record should have been considerably better than 17 and 15.

Jim Bunning was never much fun to interview after a tough defeat; you can imagine what he was like after that game in Houston.

Yet, as many hard-to-take defeats as he had with the Phillies, Bunning remembers those years as his greatest. Mary came to love Philadelphia, and so did the kids.

"Philly was a wonderful place to play," Mary observed. "And I loved Connie Mack Stadium. I remember we had to go to the ball park early and we had to have a policeman take us across the street because of the bad neighborhood. But I loved that 'bad' ball park."

"I always liked waiting at the locker room for Dad to come out because all these kids were there waiting, too," said daughter Cathy. "I thought that was neat when he'd come out and you'd get to walk with him. They'd want his autograph and he wouldn't stop and I felt sorry for these kids. But he wanted to get home. He was tired, and I could understand. But I always thought he should give more autographs; I guess that just goes along with his whole personality."

Basically, as Mary pointed out, her husband was "shy."

One thing about Jim, no matter how tough the defeat, no matter how many times he lost 1-0 games, he never swore in front of the kids. For the longest time, Mary assumed he never swore in front of anybody. She was, of course, being naive. Jim Bunning was, after all, a ball player.

"I did not know that he ever said a four-letter word," Mary said, "because at home he never, ever did."

Then one time Jim slipped. "He used the Lord's name," Mary remembered. "I said, 'I don't appreciate you using my Friend's name that way.'"

Jim didn't do that again. But one day Mary was shocked to hear him utter a four-letter word.

"Jim," she said, "I never heard you say that."

"Well," he told her, "I've got two sets [of vocabularies] — my base-ball and my home."

"Well, I appreciate home," Mary replied, and that was the end of it. Jim hasn't slipped for years and years. Of course, he hasn't lost any 1-0 games for years and years, either.

A Star among Stars

His ambition to pitch in a World Series never realized, it was the major league All-Star game that provided Jim Bunning with the chance to perform on the national stage. He made the most of it. In eighteen innings of All-Star pitching—fourteen for the American League, four for the National—Bunning allowed seven hits and three runs (two earned) while striking out thirteen and walking one. It doesn't get much better than that.

"I didn't think about the national exposure at the time," Jim remembered. "The special thing about pitching in the All-Star game to me was that it meant I was one of the ten best pitchers in the American League or the National League at the time. It was just so exciting and awesome to be chosen . . . and then to have the honor to start three of those games for the American League, and then following [Don] Drysdale one game at Shea Stadium and following [Sandy] Koufax another time."

Jim had watched the 1956 All-Star game on a television set in Charleston, West Virginia. One year later, he was the starting, and winning, pitcher for the American League at old Busch Stadium (formerly Sportsman's Park) in St. Louis. For Bunning, it began a love affair with the All-Star game, an opportunity to play with, and against, the greatest players in baseball.

The 1957 game was special for Bunning. The American League manager, Casey Stengel of the New York Yankees, picked the Detroit youngster to start, a decision that raised a few eyebrows. Granted, the only reason Stengel didn't choose Early Wynn was because the Cleveland righthander had pitched two days before, but Bunning was thrilled to get the call. Also nervous. Very nervous. "I couldn't eat before the game," he said afterward. "I got the shakes."

That didn't prevent him from pitching three perfect innings against the National League's best. In the first, Jim got Johnny Temple, Hank Aaron, and Stan Musial on fly balls. In the second inning, he got Willie Mays looking at a third strike and retired Ed Bailey and Frank Robinson on infield grounders. In his final inning, he got Don Hoak on a grounder and Roy McMillan and opposing pitcher Lew Burdette on fly balls to Mickey Mantle in center. Bunning left with a 2-0 lead and was the winning pitcher in a 6-5 American League victory. His father, mother, wife, and two brothers were at the game, helping to make it an unforgettable event for Jim, who remained in the dugout when his three innings were finished. The shower could wait; he wanted to see the rest of the game. Stengel sent an attendant into the clubhouse to get a dry shirt for Bunning, who changed on the bench.

Two years later, the major leagues began playing two All-Star games, a practice that continued through the 1962 season. Bunning appeared in the first 1959 contest, taking over in the seventh inning with the score tied 1-1. Ernie Banks greeted him with a long double, stayed at second as Orlando Cepeda popped out and Wally Moon struck out, and scored on Del Crandall's single up the middle. Crandall took second on the throw and scored on Bill Mazeroski's single to left. Those were the only earned runs Bunning would give up in eight All-Star appearances.

There seemed to be no way Bunning could top his 1957 All-Star performance, perfection being hard to beat. But the man who retired the only nine National Leaguers he faced in '57 set down fifteen in a row in 1961, six in the first game, nine in the second.

The first game, played in San Francisco's Candlestick Park, is best remembered for the gale-force winds that swept across the field, at one point disrupting the delivery of Stu Miller, the eventual winning pitcher in the National's 5-4, ten-inning victory. Bunning came on in the sixth, retiring Roberto Clemente on a deep fly to Mantle and striking out Bill White. Then he saw his old pal and Tiger roomie, Frank Bolling, advancing to the plate.

"I saw Frank and I started to laugh," Jim recalled. "I had to turn away from the television [camera] to get my composure. I'm thinking, 'What am I doing here in an All-Star game facing my roommate?'"

The old friends had gone out the previous night, joining another friend—Ed Mosler, owner of the Mosler Safe Company and a big baseball fan—for dinner at Ernie's. Now Bunning pulled himself together, threw Bolling "a nice, high slider," and got him to pop it up to Norm Cash in foul territory outside first. Jim set down Smoky Burgess, Ken Boyer, and Maury Wills without a ball leaving the infield in the seventh.

Bunning started the second of the 1961 All-Star games, which ended in a 1-1 tie when rain swept across Boston's Fenway Park at the end of the ninth. Jim loved pitching in Fenway, with its inviting left field wall that lured righthanded batters into trying to pull outside pitches, and his love affair continued that day. It was nine up, nine down with only one ball—Clemente's second-inning fly to center—leaving the infield.

The first 1962 game, in Washington, another Bunning start, was almost as good. Clemente, the second batter he faced, drove an outside pitch down the right field line for two bases. The great Pittsburgh right fielder never left second base, staying there as Bunning retired Willie Mays and Orlando Cepeda on foul pops. In all, he set down the last eight batters he faced, leaving with the game scoreless after three. The National League went on to win, 3-1.

Being selected for that game gave Bunning a chance to meet John F. Kennedy, who visited the dugout and the clubhouse, shaking hands with the players. For Bunning, it was one of many pleasant All-Star memories.

"I didn't have any bad memories," he said.

Bunning's final appearance as an American League All-Star came in the 1963 game, which the National League won 5-3 in a nearly half-empty Cleveland Municipal Stadium. Taking over in the fourth with the game tied 3-3, Bunning retired the side in order, stretching his streak of consecutive scoreless innings in All-Star play to nine. He wound up the hard-luck loser, though, after issuing his only All-Star walk to Tommy Davis to start the fifth. Hank Aaron flied to center for the first out; when Bill White grounded to Frank Malzone at third, it appeared Jim would run his scoreless streak to ten innings. "A perfect double-play ball," he said. But Bobby Richardson dropped Malzone's throw, the ball rolled into short right field, and Davis wound up at third, from where he scored on Willie Mays's grounder to Joe Pepitone at first.

Bunning actually got booed in that game. Not for giving up an unearned run, but for getting Stan Musial to line out to right field for the final out in the fifth.

"Stan was making his final appearance," Bunning recalled. "He came up to pinch hit and he hit the hardest line drive you've ever seen, a frozen rope right at the right fielder, and they booed me for getting him out."

A year later, Bunning was pitching for the National League at New York's Shea Stadium, following Don Drysdale to the mound in the fourth. The first American League batter to face Bunning was Mickey Mantle. Trying to bunt for a hit, he popped to second. The next batter, Harmon Killebrew, ducked a high, tight pitch and the ball struck his bat, rolling toward third for an infield single. Brooks Robinson also singled, a two-out hit to right, but Bunning stranded the runners, striking out two; he recorded two more strikeouts in a one-two-three fifth. Jim left with a 3-1 lead and a chance to be the winning pitcher, but the American League rallied to carry a 4-3 lead into the bottom of the ninth. That's when Bunning's new Phillies teammate, Johnny Callison, capped a four-run rally that won the game with a three-run homer with two out that gave the Nationals a 7-4 win.

Johnny Keane, who led the St. Louis Cardinals to the 1964 pennant and world championship, was managing the Yankees in '65, so the honor of being the skipper of the National League All-Stars that year went to the Phillies' Gene Mauch. As a result, Bunning wasn't picked for the squad.

"Mauch said, 'I want you to rest,'" Jim explained. "He said, 'If I take you, I'll use you.'"

So Bunning stayed home. His next—and last—All-Star appearance was in St. Louis, at the new Busch Memorial Stadium in 1966. That's one neither Bunning, nor anyone else who was there on that brutally hot day, will soon forget.

"It was 115 degrees," Bunning recalled. "People were being burned by the little metal things on their seats. The television cameras were packed with ice so they'd function."

On the field itself, covered with artificial turf, the temperature must have hit 140 or more. But as hot as it was, Sandy Koufax, the scheduled National League starter, was having a terrible time getting his elbow

A young Jim Bunning in the early 1960s with the Detroit Tigers, who did the Phillies a huge favor by trading him away following the 1963 season. *(Photos this page courtesy of Jim and Mary Bunning)*

Jim Jr. with his dad in the Detroit clubhouse during the 1961 season. Looking on are outfielder Charley Maxwell and his son. The Tigers battled the Mantle-Maris Yankees deep into September before a three-game sweep in New York killed Detroit's pennant bid.

This is what a batter saw when Jim Bunning sent a baseball speeding toward home plate during his days with the Tigers. *(Photo courtesy of Jim and Mary Bunning)*

No, Jim Bunning wasn't always in great position to field the ball after delivering a pitch, as this photo of him falling off the mound to the first base side illustrates. But when you strike out 2,855 big league batters you don't have to field too many ground balls. *(Photo courtesy of the Philadelphia Phillies)*

A perfect Fathers Day is about to end. Jim Bunning delivers a 2-2 curve ball to the Mets'
John Stephenson, who swings and misses for the final out in the first perfect game pitched in
the National League in eighty-four years. *(Photos this page courtesy of Jim and Mary Bunning)*

Bunning's Phillie teammates mob the perfect-game hero moments after the final pitch.
That's manager Gene Mauch (second from left) and, next to him, a capless Dallas Green,
who would manage the Phillies to their first (and only) world championship sixteen years later.

The perfect daddy gets a congratulatory kiss from his daughter Barbara as Mary Bunning looks on shortly after Jim retired twenty-seven straight Mets in the first game of a Shea Stadium doubleheader in 1964. *(Photo used by permission of the* New York Times)

Mets' broadcaster Ralph Kiner, like Bunning a future Hall of Famer, interviews Jim on the field at Shea Stadium minutes after the perfect game. *(Photo courtesy of Jim and Mary Bunning)*

A study in concentration, Bunning looks for the sign before delivering a pitch for the Phillies. *(Photos this page courtesy of Rich Westcott)*

A smiling John Quinn, general manager of the Phillies' team that came agonizingly close to winning the 1964 National League pennant, presents Bunning with a plaque commemorating his winning a hundred games in each league. Only Cy Young had done that before him.

loose. "Walter Alston was our manager," Bunning remembered, "and he said, 'Jim, go down to the pen. I don't know when I'm going to use you, but you're going to be one of my pitchers.' So I went down."

Koufax, bad elbow and all, took the mound and pitched three strong innings, allowing one hit and one run, which scored on a wild pitch. Bunning got the call next and pitched brilliantly, retiring the first five batters he faced on three pop-ups, a ground ball, and a strikeout. The Tigers' Bill Freehan singled with two out in the fifth, but Bunning wrapped up his two-inning stint with another strikeout, getting Bobby Knoop swinging. Anxious to escape the blazing heat, Jim headed for the clubhouse, where he found Koufax sitting next to the television set with his elbow in ice.

"He said, 'Did you ever see such terrible stuff [as] I had?'" Bunning recalled. "Here he's complaining about the stuff he's throwing and he's throwing bullets. Whoosh! And a good curve ball, too. And his elbow's bothering him, really bothering him."

That's how Jim Bunning's last All-Star game ended: sitting next to Sandy Koufax in the National League clubhouse, watching the game on television. For Koufax, too, it would be the final All-Star game in a Hall of Fame career.

Pitching in both major leagues—and pitching in All-Star games for both leagues—provided Jim Bunning with plenty of opportunities to face the greatest hitters of his era.

The toughest out? No hesitation there. Ted Williams topped the list. "The hardest one for me to get out," Bunning declared, although he won his share of battles with the Boston slugger.

Another Williams was tough, too. Billy Williams of the Chicago Cubs, also a Hall of Famer, got some big hits off Bunning. "I seemed to make mistakes [pitching to him]," Jim said. "I didn't get the ball in on him as far as I should."

The late Nellie Fox, recently elected to the Hall of Fame by the Veterans Committee, was especially hard for Bunning to get out. So was the powerful Jimmy Ray Hart, one of the very few righthanded batters who enjoyed considerable success against Bunning.

"[Hank] Aaron, Willie [Mays] didn't hit me worth squat," Bunning pointed out. "I didn't throw Aaron anything hard that he could reach. I never let him hit something hard. If I threw something to Aaron that was a hard pitch it was out of the strike zone. I always flopped him a slow curve ball or took something off the fast ball. He hit one home run off me in my career. It was an inside-the-park homer at Connie Mack Stadium. Donnie Lock was our center fielder. Aaron hit a line drive that Lock thought he could catch. He came in and dove at the ball and it rolled to the wall.

"Mays was a different hitter if you put a guy on second base. He was a much tougher out then. He'd stay with you. If you got Mays up with no one on he was not a hard out for me. But if you put a winning run or a tying run on second base he would hit the ball the other way off you. He wouldn't try to do that much when he was hitting by himself. I didn't have that many problems with Mays."

Nor did he have problems with most of the top righthanded hitters of the time. "Kenny Boyer didn't even want to hit when I pitched," Jim recalled. "I got [Jackie] Jensen out fairly easily. When I had a good slider I could always get [Orlando] Cepeda."

With the help of that "good slider" Bunning did well against Willie McCovey, too. But if he made a mistake, the lefthanded-hitting McCovey pounced on it.

"I can remember McCovey hitting a ball *through* the Ballantine sign [atop the scoreboard at Connie Mack Stadium]," Bunning reflected. "It went right through it—through the wood, through everything. It was an unbelievable shot. And I remember McCovey hitting a shot over the roof in right field in Pittsburgh. Occasionally he'd hit a long ball, but he didn't really hurt me.

"[Willie] Stargell hit the longest ball off me in Veterans Stadium ever. It was a slider that didn't get in."

That came in 1971, Bunning's final season. "A lot of people don't remember that it had to be thrown fairly hard for him to hit it that far," the victim added.

With the exception of Ted Williams, though, there was no tougher out for Bunning than Yogi Berra. "Yogi hurt me," he said. "He drove in runs that hurt. He was like Williams, a guy you couldn't pitch to. You didn't know what to do. I'd get two strikes on Yogi and keep throwing them in there and he'd keep fouling them off and as soon as I'd go away [outside] he'd hit it hard somewhere, or if I'd go up here [high inside] he'd hit it hard."

If it came down to a clutch situation, Bunning had a better chance with Mantle.

"Mantle didn't like to hit off me," Jim said. "He didn't trust me to throw strikes. He knew if I got teed off on the mound I was going to go in on him. I pitched him in all the time, though. That's where you got him out lefthanded. Hard in, hard in, hard in, never on the outside. The only time I thought I was going to trick him, I threw a curve ball over the outside corner and he hit it over everything—over the roof in Tiger Stadium. So I never threw him a slow curve ball after that—ever."

A Union Man

Think of a conservative Republican and you're not likely to think of a union leader. Well, think again. One of the many proud accomplishments in Jim Bunning's baseball life was his role in the Players Association.

Even four decades ago, when management held the upper hand in baseball—God, it seems eons ago—Bunning fought for his rights and for the rights of his fellow players. When Jim discovered upon joining the Phillies in 1964 that the club made the players pay for parking spaces at the ball park, he promptly put his foot down; thereafter, he and his teammates parked free of charge.

Bunning was the player representative of the Tigers and the pension representative for the American League and then the National League for the last twelve years of his pitching career. Management detested union leaders in that era; Bunning's activities on behalf of the Players Association were seen by some as one of the reasons the Tigers traded him to the Phillies.

"Was Player Rep Bunning Too Busy?" thundered the headline on the first sports page in the *Detroit Free Press* when the trade was announced. "The trading of Jim Bunning," Joe Falls wrote, "should serve as a lesson to the rest of the players on the Tigers; it should, but it won't."

The "lesson": don't get too involved with union business.

"Bunning has a keen, analytical mind," Falls observed. "He can figure pension benefits and insurance premiums almost as quick as he can earned run averages. . . . There was a feeling in the front office that Bunning was devoting too much of his time to his job of player representative.

"Nobody ever said he gave less than his best on the field," continued Falls. "Nobody ever could. Bunning was one player who was always in shape and always gave 100 percent on the mound. The feeling, though, was that Bunning might have done better last season if he had concentrated on only one job instead of two."

As Falls pointed out, that criticism was leveled at Bunning by the Tiger front office after he went 12 and 13 in 1963, but "nobody raised any question about Bunning's dual role when he was a winning pitcher [19 and 10 in 1962]."

One Detroit newspaperman, Watson Spoelstra, called Bunning a "briefcase ballplayer," claiming that Jim's sub-.500 season was a result of his attention to union work. Bunning was furious when the story came out.

"I didn't have one problem with the press at all," he recalled, "until I got to Detroit and a writer wrote a story about me being more interested in what I was doing with the Players Association than I was in pitching, and I challenged his integrity a few times."

From the way he talks about it now, Bunning had all he could do to refrain from getting physical with Spoelstra, a veteran sportswriter.

"I reacted to the Spoelstra article so violently because it was a lie," Jim declared, "a total fabrication. I know somebody in the front office planted that story. It was not a friendly confrontation [with Spoelstra]. If he had been a little younger it would have been very unfriendly."

As usual, Bunning pulled no verbal punches. He said what was on his mind, and he could get very, very angry. He believed in standing up for his rights and, when necessary, for the rights of his teammates.

Bunning tried, in 1966, to help himself and his Phillies pitching partner, Chris Short, gain better contracts. The timing seemed ideal. Bunning won nineteen games the year before, Short won twenty. Also, Dodger aces Sandy Koufax and Don Drysdale had staged a joint holdout in 1965; why not Bunning and Short in '66? Or so Jim reasoned.

"'Shorty' was the worst negotiator," Bunning said. "I tried to get him to hold out because Drysdale and Koufax did it the year before. I said, 'Shorty, what are you making?' He told me. It was terrible. He always signed the first contract John [Quinn] sent him. I said, 'Shorty, you won twenty games last year.'"

Chris Short wasn't the holdout type. Bunning loved the guy, but they couldn't have been less alike. Jim battled as hard in contract negotiations as he did on the mound. And he was always ready to right a perceived wrong. With the Phillies, Bunning soon learned if he had a complaint the person to see was the owner, not the old-school general manger.

"In dealing with John Quinn I had no luck," he said, "but if I went to Bob Carpenter and said, 'Here's what we'd like, Bob,' whatever, he never would fight. Never would argue. He'd say, 'You think you'd like it that way? OK.'"

Unfortunately, the Bob Carpenters were a dying breed in baseball.

Bunning wasted little time making his presence felt in Pittsburgh when he became a Pirate in 1968. With the team ready to fly north at the end of spring training, Bunning found out that the front office personnel and their wives would be on the chartered plane. Jim went up to one of his teammates and asked, "Where's your wife?"

"Oh," the player replied, "they can't fly with the team."

That was enough to send Bunning flying into action. He met with the general manager, Joe L. Brown, and demanded equal rights.

"I said, 'Joe, if you're going to allow the front office wives to travel with the club, the players have to have the same opportunity.' He said, 'We'll think about it.' I said, 'You better think about it quick because my wife is going to San Francisco on the first trip Pittsburgh makes out there.' So it came to pass that the Pirates, for the first time, allowed players' wives to fly with the team."

Bunning was tough, and he was smart. So it stood to reason that when Harvey Kuenn stepped down as the Tigers' player rep in 1960, Bunning was elected by his teammates. At his very first Players Association meeting in that capacity he was elected American League pension representative, succeeding Eddie Yost. The National League pension rep was Richie Ashburn, whom Bunning had never met. Little did either man realize that years later they both would enter the Hall of Fame as Phillies.

Those were busy days in the Players Association, which was just getting its feet on the ground, preparing for what would be a knockdown, drag-out battle with baseball management. But, as Bunning recalls, the early meetings over pension matters were friendly.

"Working with Richie and [Pirates owner] John Galbraith and, believe it or not, [Washington Senators owner] Calvin Griffith was easy,"

Bunning remembered. "Mr. Galbraith was about as kind and gentle as he could be, kind of a benevolent owner."

The players were trying to diversify their pension, make it part fixed income and part variable that fluctuated with the market. Ashburn and Bunning asked Galbraith and Griffith if they would consider adding the variable component. "They said, 'Hey, it's your pension program; do what you want,'" Bunning recalled. "That's how cooperative it was."

It took a while to set up, but the change was made. "And it's been just a godsend," Bunning said. "When I retired I was earning a pension of about $24,000 a year after sixteen-plus years in the big leagues. Today I'm earning about $44,000 because of the variable. And it's going to continue to grow."

Meanwhile, the baseball world was undergoing dramatic change. The old, family-type owners were on their way out; corporations were on their way in. Bunning and the other Players Association leaders recognized the need for a permanent union office. Bob Cannon, a circuit court judge in Milwaukee who was later elected presiding judge of the Wisconsin appellate court, was appointed "volunteer legal advisor," for which he got expenses. Judge Cannon had a number of friends on both sides of baseball's labor fence; Bunning and Robin Roberts, among others, would come to feel he had too many friends on the management side.

"Judge Cannon determined that we needed an executive director," Bunning said. "He wrote the job description for himself."

And he was far and away the frontrunner. "We set up a five-person committee to look for candidates and interview candidates," Bunning said. "Marvin Miller was interviewed by Robin Roberts, Harvey Kuenn, and myself in Retirement Plans, Inc., an office in Cleveland, Ohio. I can remember it like it was yesterday." Also involved in the search were Bob Friend and Bob Allison.

Miller was the number-two man in the steelworkers union. He'd been recommended by a friend of Roberts at the Wharton School of Finance and Commerce of the University of Pennsylvania. The owners shuddered at the thought of a tough labor man taking over leadership of the players union; in fact, some of the players didn't like the idea, either.

Among other men interviewed for the top job was a rather well known public figure, Richard Milhous Nixon. "Bob Feller—kind of as an advisor—Harvey Kuenn, I think Bob Friend and myself, five or six of us in all, went to John Mitchell's law firm, where Nixon was special counsel," Bunning recalled. "This was between when he was vice president, had run for president and been defeated, and prior to him getting back and running again. We had a great meeting. I remember, John Mitchell was there, too. The fact is, Nixon had more ideas about baseball than anybody we talked to."

In his book, *A Whole Different Ball Game,* Marvin Miller wrote that Nixon was interviewed, not for the executive director's job, but for the position of legal counsel. Not so, said Bunning. "Marvin got a little confused. We interviewed Nixon to be executive director."

He loved baseball, but he had other, bigger plans. Nixon asked his visitors to join him for lunch. Thomas E. Dewey, the defeated Republican presidential candidate in 1944 and 1948, who was also a member of the law firm, went along, too.

"We knew when we left there that there was no chance [of Nixon's taking the job]," said Bunning. "We didn't put him on the ballot. All he told us was, he had other plans. He'd been going around the country making speeches, putting in chits that he was going to call back in 1967 and 1968."

Which was how Jim Bunning got involved in Athletes for Nixon.

"He was a very impressive guy, if you didn't know his private side," Bunning said. "If we had hired him, it would have been a coup."

Jim believes that Nixon would have been voted in "automatically" by the players, if he had chosen to run for the union office. "Even ahead of Bob Cannon." We'll never know.

"We could have changed history," Bunning reflected. "I think of that constantly. If he would have taken that job, American history is changed. I must have been a bad salesman."

Judge Cannon was kept fully apprised of the search for an executive director, and he had little doubt who the "winner" would be.

"I was so sure I was going to be elected I even picked out offices on Michigan Avenue in Chicago," he reminisced in his Clearwater, Florida, condo. "We lived in Milwaukee. No way am I going to take six children to New York. Our kids were young then."

Confident he was the obvious choice, the judge waited for word. "They went around the country," he said. "They interviewed Nixon, Jerry Ford, you name it. Every big name. Anyway, I'm elected."

Why not Miller? "That's kind of a drastic step for a players association," Bunning pointed out. "A lot of players didn't think we were ready to go right to a union type representative. So Cannon, being known by most of the people, won big time."

Bunning voted for him, too, and came to regret it.

"We called Bob Cannon up, told him of the results, told him to come in, that we wanted to make the announcement," Jim recalled. "We started talking to him—Bob Friend, Bob Allison, myself, Robin, Harvey, and some others, and we can see him backing up faster than he walked forward."

According to Judge Cannon, they offered him a five-year contract at $50,000 a year, but the office, they told him, would be in New York.

"I said, 'You've got to be out of your mind,'" he said. "'There's no way I'm taking this job in New York.' I was not going to New York under any circumstances."

He did agree to fly to New York to meet with them the next day. He didn't mind visiting the place; he just didn't want to live there.

"Next morning I had breakfast with Bunning at the Biltmore," Judge Cannon recalled. "I said, 'Jim, there's no way I'm moving to New York. I've got six children and that's it. I've got a lifetime job in Milwaukee. I run every six years, but I have no opposition. . . .' He finally said OK on Chicago [instead of New York]. Now I've accepted, but if they force me to stay in New York, I'm going to kiss them goodbye."

There was another problem. As Bunning recalled it, "He kept asking, 'What about my pension? Am I going to be included in your pension?'"

Indeed, Judge Cannon thought he should enjoy the benefit of the players' pension. He felt he was giving up too much security in leaving his post in Milwaukee to risk taking this job without a pension.

Bunning's feeling, to this day, is that the judge was playing hard to get because the job he really wanted was commissioner of baseball, not executive director of the Players Association. "See, we didn't realize, or I wasn't aware, Cannon was using this wedge to become commissioner," Bunning said. "That's what we found out. He had been playing very nice with us, but he had been a lot more friendly with Walter O'Malley and all the owners."

Judge Cannon admits to having had an excellent relationship with several owners that was so close, he declared, that he could call them, or meet with them, and get them to vote a certain way on issues involving the players. The morning after his meeting with Bunning, for example, he phoned Dodger owner Walter O'Malley in the hotel at 6 A.M. and arranged a 6:30 meeting in O'Malley's room regarding the division of the television money from the World Series and the All-Star game, which feeds the players' pension fund.

"I said, 'I want to know what you're going to do on this thing, Mr. O'Malley,'" Judge Cannon related. "He said, 'We've got to make you look good first day on the job. I'll give you a hell of an argument, but I'll vote for you on the thing eventually.' So I had it all wired."

The judge was proud of the way he handled it, and he informed the players of his arrangement. "We're in a cab," he said, "and I told them, 'I'll let you in on a little secret. I was in O'Malley's room this morning at 6:30. We talked this thing over and he said, 'OK, I'll vote for you.' I told them, 'That's the way we get things through.' So Bunning looks at me and he says, 'That's *our* money.' I said, 'Let me tell you something, my friend. As long as there's baseball the owners are going to say it's their money, and it *is* their money.'"

Obviously, the judge and the players' expert on pensions were not on the same wavelength. Bunning thought the new executive director was just a little too chummy with Walter O'Malley and the like. Judge Cannon thought a good relationship with the owners was a plus. Had he decided to keep the job with the Players Association, the game's labor relations—so stormy under Miller and Don Fehr—would have been far less confrontational. "No way was I ever going to permit them to go on strike, because I felt that I was smart enough to be able to negotiate in a sensible way that baseball would benefit, the players would benefit, the owners would benefit," he said. It was not a speech the hard-liners in the players' union enjoyed hearing. "For some reason or other, they just felt I was too close to ownership," Judge Cannon observed.

One thing we know: he was not close to Bunning. Talking to him today, it is apparent some animosity remains.

"Bunning is a great family man," the judge declared. "He's a wonderful person. Baseball has been good to him. But Bunning would no more be a congressman than the man in the moon if it weren't for baseball.

"When Bunning pitched his no-hit [perfect] game in New York, I was up in the pressbox in Milwaukee. When it comes over the wires I get down on my hands and knees and picked up the tape and put it together and put it on my letterhead and had my recorder type it out, saying this is the original tape announcing to the world the no-hit game between the Phillies and whoever it was on such and such a date, and put it in a frame and sent it to Bunning. I'm still waiting for a telephone call or a letter thanking me. But I mean, that's Bunning. We were never too close. He was influenced by Robin Roberts."

If the judge knew Bunning a little better, he'd realize Jim wasn't easily influenced by anybody.

Judge Cannon was also upset by the speech Bunning made the day he was inducted into the Hall of Fame. "I was disappointed in Jim and his acceptance speech," he commented. "He attacked baseball to a certain extent. He said it was rudderless."

Bunning actually said: "For over four years now, baseball has been rudderless. For God's sake and for the game's sake, find a rudder. Pick a course and stick with it, and get your internal problems resolved before the Congress of the United States gives up on you and intervenes. The only thing that could be worse is if the fans give up on you."

Judge Cannon was not the only person offended by Jim's remarks. Obviously, the truth hurts.

Bob Cannon may not have been seeking the commissioner's job, but it's easy to see how Jim Bunning and others came to that conclusion in the mid-1960s. In the interview in Florida, Cannon was asked, "Were you interested in being commissioner?"

"No, no, no," he replied. Then he added, "I had the endorsements of sportswriters on papers all over the country."

"And yet you weren't interested?"

"Sure, I was interested, and I was interviewed one time. I said, 'This is the biggest job in the United States, as far as I'm concerned.' I said, 'If I was offered it, I'd be interested.' One day O'Malley sent me a clipping from the *New York Daily News*. The headline was, 'I Want Job, Says Cannon,' and you read down the article, there was nothing whatsoever [to back up the headline]. O'Malley sends me this thing and in big, red pen he writes, 'Be careful.'"

The owners, Judge Cannon recalled, nearly voted him in as commissioner. "I missed by one vote in the National League," he said. "I got the necessary votes in the American League."

Whether the commissioner's job was what he really wanted or not, he was certainly the man the owners would have preferred as the union's executive director. Jim Bunning can hardly be faulted for thinking that. The man who wound up in the position was about as far removed from Judge Bob Cannon as baseball owners could imagine in their worst nightmares.

Marvin Miller had made a good impression on Jim Bunning and Robin Roberts when they interviewed him. He was a slightly built man who spoke in a soft voice, not at all the stereotype of a hard-boiled, rough, tough labor leader. But when it came to negotiating, there was nobody tougher.

For the players, it was time to take a long, hard look at this union man. Judge Cannon was unhappy with his arrangement. He had six children and, as he saw it, not much money. As a judge in Milwaukee he had a pension, security. The $50,000 annual salary the players offered wasn't enough to justify the move. "I'm giving up a pension," he remarked, "and they [the players] won't give me a pension. I said to Bob Friend, 'Bob, how can I fight for you, for your pension, better hospital benefits and all that when I've got nothing?'"

According to the judge, acting as "volunteer legal counsel" had cost him money over the past few years. "I was getting $15,000 for expenses," he noted. "I'm taking twenty-five trips a year. I never had a ballplayer buy me a meal; I picked up the checks. I paid the telephone bills, everything. At the end of the year it cost me $4,000, $5,000. I had to go to the bank a couple of times to borrow money."

So the deal fell apart. "I kept the job for a couple of weeks," Judge Cannon said. "I announced in Milwaukee I was quitting. Then Helen [Mrs. Cannon] and I went down to Baton Rouge [where he had a speaking engagement]. Joe Adcock met us at the airport. He said, 'I just heard on the radio you're quitting. Why?' 'Joe,' I said, 'it's a long story.'"

Other players asked him to reconsider, the judge recalled. And when he went to Pittsburgh to speak at the Dapper Dan Dinner, Dan Galbraith sent word that he wanted a private audience with him. "He said, 'I don't know what your reasons are for quitting,'" Judge Cannon stated, "'but if it's money you're after I'll have you in the players' pension fund within two years, and your salary will be, I don't know, a couple of hundred thousand dollars.'

"I looked at him and said, 'Mr. Galbraith, let me say one thing to you. All my life I've been a judge. I was the youngest judge ever elected in the history of the United States judiciary, twenty-seven years old. I came back from the South Pacific, ran against a sitting judge, and beat him. Since I've been in baseball all I've heard is money, money. I've got it up to here.' I said, 'I'm one Irishman. I was born naked, and I'm going out naked, and I'm going out of this place naked, too. I don't want any of baseball's money. I'm going back and have a good judicial career,' He said, 'Don't burn your bridges. The time will come maybe you will hurt yourself as far as your future in baseball by doing what you're doing today.' I said, 'If baseball is like that, I don't want any part of baseball.'"

The meeting with Galbraith, owner of the Pirates, demonstrates how anxious the management side was to have Judge Cannon, and not Marvin Miller, running the Players Association.

"I could have set this thing up in such a way it could have been great for everybody," Judge Cannon remarked, adding: "I was not that close to the owners in spite of what everybody thinks and says. . . . What Bunning said [about Cannon's wanting to be commissioner], that was the farthest thing from my mind. I never talked about the commissionership in any way. You see, it was a poisoning between Robin Roberts and Jim Bunning. I mean, there was a dislike there for me. They didn't come out and say, 'I hate you,' in any way, but . . ."

If the players had agreed to his demands for a pension, Judge Cannon commented, he would have stayed on. To this day, the judge becomes furious when anyone suggests that he "sold out" to the owners. "If I had my choice of the commissionership of baseball or [being] head of the players, I'd have taken the players because the commissioner would have to talk to me," he declared.

But the players were looking elsewhere. Despite the support of Roberts and Bunning, among others, Marvin Miller had to sell himself to the rank and file. He did it during spring training, going from camp to camp. Marvin got the job. Baseball ownership is still trying to recover.

"Marvin knew labor law better than any owners' representative that they hired," Bunning said. "Every time we got in negotiation with the owners they were behind the eight ball, and they hired some of the strangest people—John Gaherin, one of the biggest baseball fans I've ever met. Great guy, terrible negotiator. Marvin just tied him in little ribbons. I was in most every meeting.

"One thing I noticed Marvin never did was raise his voice. He never got into a confrontation. Just constantly monotone. He said, 'This is what we want, this is the way we're going to get there.' Every time one of the owners' people said something, he wrote it down. And next day if they changed their tune he had it written down. He was one of the most skilled negotiators I've ever seen. In fact, he *was* the most skilled. The reason they [the owners] hated him, they weren't ready far him."

With Judge Cannon, they were dealing with someone they considered a friend. Marvin Miller was the enemy, pure and simple.

"When we had Cannon represent us, we argued about mounds at Yankee Stadium," Bunning pointed out. "We worried about whether we were going to have a split doubleheader, all kinds of little, penny-ante stuff. As soon as Marvin took over we got into the meat of the thing. We had two basic things to negotiate—a pension agreement and a basic agreement.

"What Marvin did was to include in the basic agreement the Uniform Player Contract, which allowed an arbitrator to solve any dispute that was in the basic agreement. That's how the arbitrator threw out the reserve clause. The owners weren't smart enough to figure that out. They said, 'This is madness; we'll beat this in the courts.' Well, they went to the courts and the courts said, 'We don't have any jurisdiction over this. You signed an agreement with the players that the National Arbitration and Mediation Service will solve all these disputes.' Out it [the reserve clause] went. That was the Messersmith, McNally decision [that changed the business of baseball]."

It was, as Bunning indicated, a terribly one-sided fight. Slight, soft-spoken Marvin Miller won round after round, scored knockout after knockout. For his part in making Miller a part of the baseball world, Jim Bunning was no favorite with management types.

"I can remember being harassed and harangued," he said. "John Quinn just despised Marvin Miller. Bob Carpenter came to me and said, 'You don't need Marvin Miller.' I said, 'No, Bob, if you were the owner and I was the player rep we wouldn't need Marvin Miller. But you don't own all the other teams and I'm not the player rep on all the other teams. We're getting a lot of corporate ownership in here and we don't have a clue who's responsible and you don't have a clue who's responsible. So we need to be as firm as we could on what our rights are. If I had a dispute with you I wouldn't worry. I could come in and there wouldn't be a dispute; we'd solve it. Not everybody has that kind of relationship. If you go in to see CBS, who do you see?'"

It was a bitter pill for the Bob Carpenters and the Ruly Carpenters of baseball to swallow. Their relationship with the players had always been special. Now baseball was moving into a new era. It was all business: corporate America versus millionaire union men.

"Bob was a nonunion person; so was Ruly," Bunning said. "That's why they sold the club. But Ruly understood. John Quinn never would. I ran into Mr. Quinn when he was not capable of clear thought, where he cursed Marvin and the Players Association and things like that. But I excused that as alcohol speaking and not Mr. Quinn."

It is Bunning's view that in the days when he was a player rep and a pension rep Miller "always recommended and didn't dictate" where the union was going. "I'm not sure that's the case now," he noted, referring to current union leadership.

As big a part as Jim Bunning played in the early years of the Players Association, he was not—and is clearly still not—in agreement with everything that Miller and the current executive director, Donald Fehr, have done. The strike of 1981 upset Bunning, and Robin Roberts as well. The strike of '94, which resulted in cancellation of the World Series and brought about a widespread negative attitude toward baseball that still exists to some extent today, was strongly criticized by both of them.

Don't misunderstand. Bunning thinks a lot of Marvin Miller and all that he accomplished for the players. He continues to marvel at Miller's ability to negotiate without raising his voice or losing his temper.

"You know," Jim observed, "that rubbed off after a while in the way I used to deal with general managers. If anybody has ever dealt with John Quinn they know his forte was to get you mad. So I never got mad with John Quinn. If he got mad, I walked out. That's what Marvin used to do in negotiations all the time. He'd call us into a caucus, move the players group out. He never got mad. I said to him one time, 'Marvin, get mad. Get on their ass.' He said, 'No, I'm not going to do that. It accomplishes nothing.'"

Miller's many accomplishments led Bunning to declare: "I think his impact on the game is such that he will go down in baseball history as being more influential, his impact on the game will be more felt than any commissioner. A lot of people say he *was* the commissioner. He wasn't. He just was so much farther advanced in labor law and the intricacies of labor law than the owners group was at the time. It was a nice mismatch."

But there was nothing nice about the strikes and what they did to the game and to the public's perception of it. Bunning remains a strong supporter of players' rights. But he was critical of the way the strike vote was conducted in 1981; as usual, he was willing to express his feelings.

"I think the vote should have been a private vote," he said.

It wasn't. Taking no chances, Miller preferred a show of hands to a secret ballot.

"I think that's a ploy of the association leadership," Bunning said. "I don't think the way the association did it is the right way to do it. That's not the democratic way of doing things."

A secret ballot would have revealed how the players really felt about going out on strike in 1981, a walkout that lasted some seven weeks.

"If you don't like it, vote against it," said Bunning. "Get up and say, 'Damn it, men, if we strike, I'm going to lose two thousand dollars a day. I'm against it.'"

Using a show of hands created tremendous pressure to go along with the others. "Peer pressure," Bunning observed. "I've had peer pressure my whole life. Don't tell me you had nothing to do with it when you're on strike and you voted to strike."

In fact, the show of hands enabled the Players Association to announce 100 percent support. Had there been a secret ballot, Bunning guessed the vote would have been "damn close. . . . Marvin would argue and fight and scream and yell about that [opinion]. But see, that's what a smart negotiator does. He knows all the ploys to get the appearance of support. I would have objected strenuously to that type of ballot."

When Bunning made those remarks, he was quick to make it plain that he had not softened his position on baseball management.

"If you've dealt with the management of baseball very long," he said, "you find that they very seldom tell the truth. They are very deceptive people. They are not straight. So you deal with them on that basis. That's the truth."

At least, the truth as he saw it in the years after corporations replaced the Yawkeys and the Griffiths as owners. Even so, "The strike could be disastrous," he predicted. "I think it hurts both sides. A long strike will alienate those who pay the bills [the fans]. I've heard them already. 'The hell with both sides,' they're saying. They don't understand the issues. They don't give a damn about the issues."

He forecast—correctly, it developed—that the strike of 1981 would last "a minimum of six weeks."

"I would never have voted to strike," Bunning said. "Somehow, the tail is wagging the dog. When I was in, the players dictated policy to Marvin Miller. I think the vote indicated that he is in control of the players. I always thought two sides, at least two intelligent sides, could sit down and work something out."

As bad as it was for both sides—and, more important, for the game—in 1981, it was far worse in 1994, when a season loaded with memorable on-field exploits ground to a sudden and permanent halt. It was as if the persons involved in baseball had a death wish. Luckily for them, the game itself is too great to be killed, although the damage was considerable.

Bunning—and Robin Roberts, too—spoke out against the strike of 1994. Bunning felt there would have been no strike if major league baseball had a commissioner. A real commissioner, that is—or at least one who wasn't an owner in disguise. With Bud Selig, who controlled the Milwaukee Brewers, occupying the chair, baseball went through its darkest hour.

The owners paved the way for that disaster by firing Fay Vincent, who became commissioner upon Bart Giamatti's sudden death. Vincent hardly had a distinguished tenure, but Bunning believed he would have averted a strike if still in office. "I think he would have used the 'best interests of baseball' to intercede in some of their locked positions," Jim commented. "In other words he would have said, 'We're going to continue playing. We're going to negotiate. There will be no imposition of new work rules as long as we're negotiating,' which I thought is the way they should have done it."

But with no true commissioner to invoke the "best interests of baseball" power that existed before Vincent's firing, the owners and the players totally ignored the good of the game by doing the unthinkable—calling off a season in mid-August, and with it the playoffs and the World Series. Not even World War II had forced cancellation of the World Series, but the combination of greedy owners, greedy players, and a lack of leadership presented baseball fans with a season that had no conclusion, no champion. Jim Bunning reacted the way you'd expect anyone who loves the game to react.

"I was madder'n hell at [Don] Fehr and the Players Association," he recalled. Then he quickly added: "But they [the owners] drove them to that position. I just didn't think it should have got to that point. Somebody should have intervened prior to that. But it was set up [by putting an owner in the guise of a commissioner] so they wouldn't have that chance."

Jim Bunning may have been instrumental in making the baseball players union as strong as it is today, but that doesn't mean he has to agree with everything that Marvin Miller did or that Don Fehr, the current executive director, does. And he is not bashful about saying so—"I'm not for strikes."

And yet, on balance, he remains very much on the union's side in most of baseball's labor disputes. Clearly, the Players Association owes a lot to Jim Bunning, as demonstrated by Marvin Miller's presence at Bunning's induction into the Hall of Fame.

The Competitive Edge

Talk to men who faced Jim Bunning, who stood 60 feet, 6 inches away from him armed with nothing but a piece of wood, ask them to choose one word that best describes him, and the word that keeps popping up is "mean." If you were a lefthanded hitter, you'd better be prepared to have that sidearming righthander come in on you, try to muffle your power by jamming you so badly the bat just might wind up in pieces. If you were a right-handed batter, one of those guys who goes diving out over the plate, you would be well advised not to dive too far out or the next pitch might have you diving to the ground in self-defense.

Baseball was a different game when Bunning and Don Drysdale and Bob Gibson were pitching. Batters knew they couldn't take liberties with those guys. And if they didn't know, or had a temporary lapse of memory, they were quickly reminded. In today's game, a batter gets hit—or comes reasonably close to getting hit—and he's apt to go charging out toward the mound. In Bunning's time, hitters understood it was part of the game. Take too hard a swing, or take too long getting into the batter's box, and you'd better be prepared to duck.

Bunning's reputation as a pitcher who didn't hesitate to come inside on hitters grew fast. His first year in spring training with the Tigers, Jim faced the Brooklyn Dodgers in Miami. Dodger shortstop (and future Hall of Famer) Pee Wee Reese remembers it well.

"He hit me on the elbow," Reese recalled.

Blame that one on nerves, not an attempt to intimidate the opposition. Bunning was trying to prove himself then; starting against the Dodgers in an exhibition game was a golden opportunity, so presumably he was trying a little too hard.

"He [Reese] doesn't remember what happened next because it hurt so much," Bunning said. "But the next batter was [Don] Zimmer and the first pitch was right at his ear. The next pitch he hit over the left field wall."

That was a remarkable achievement on Zimmer's part. By all rights, the man who almost got hit in the head by a Jim Bunning fast ball in a spring training game should have been leery of digging in at the plate against the sidearming righthander. An outstanding prospect, Zimmer had been beaned in the minor leagues and nearly killed. His skull fractured, he remained unconscious in a Columbus, Ohio, hospital for almost two weeks.

"When I woke up it was crazy," recalled Zimmer, Joe Torre's bench coach on the world champion 1996 New York Yankees. "I looked over and I saw three of my wives, three of my moms, and three of my dads. I went to say something and I couldn't talk. I lost my speech for six weeks. I thought I woke up the next morning; it was the thirteenth day. I'd been operated on twice. I weighed 170-some pounds when I got hit, and when I got out of the hospital I weighed 128. I had to learn how to walk again."

Not only did Zimmer learn how to walk, he made it to the big leagues, where he's enjoyed a long career as a player, manager, and coach. He and Bunning played against each other as kids in the Cincinnati area. Although not close friends by any stretch of the imagination, there was always a mutual respect that endures to this day.

"Zim's a baseball guy," Bunning commented. "I mean, if there was ever a head and a face that fitted a baseball card, that's Zimmer. He's a dedicated guy. He'll kill for you. He's a good baseball man, a lot like Lee [Elia]. I'm glad he's back in baseball."

Jim didn't want to throw a spring training pitch at Don Zimmer's head that night in Miami. The ball simply got away from him. In light of what Zimmer had been through, for the little guy to jump up, dig in, and smash the next pitch over the fence spoke volumes for the man's courage.

"Any righthanded hitter watches Bunning pitch, he was intimidated," Zimmer recalled. "You know, as big as he was, a tall, lanky guy throwing sidearm with good stuff and people telling you, 'This guy's got a little mean spot in him.'"

To hear Zimmer tell it, he "was not a real good hitter" after he got hit in the head in the minors by a kid in the Cardinal organization named Jim Kirk. But you wouldn't have known it that night in Miami after Bunning knocked him down.

"I always felt if a sidearmed, tough righthander was pitching, one thing I was never going to do was run away," he said. "It's awfully easy to bail out and give. Even when I got traded from the Dodgers I told Drysdale, 'You might bury me at home plate, but I ain't giving an inch because if you give you're dead anyhow. So I probably tried to stick in there more against tough sidearmers like Bunning."

The story of Zimmer picking himself up, dusting himself off, and smacking Bunning's next pitch over the fence has been retold at countless banquets. Usually it's Bunning doing the telling.

"He's remembered that more than I have," Zimmer said. "He always brings that up."

In Zimmer's opinion, "Jim Bunning was in the class of Jackie Robinson and Drysdale and Gibson as competitors. You can't be a more fierce competitor than Bunning was. I always respected him as a pitcher, even though he has this little meanness in him. I respected him to the point, although I never really bummed around with him or nothing, that when he was inducted in the Hall of Fame I sent him a telegram. I was tickled to death he made it. He was his own man."

Coming from Don Zimmer, that's quite a compliment.

"I heard Campanis [former Dodger general manager Al Campanis] say, time after time, what a great player I'd have been if I never got hit in the head," Zimmer said. "Well, I got hit in the head, but I always say how lucky I am. I'm just lucky I'm still here in a uniform today. And to go and play twelve, thirteen years in the major leagues . . ."

Fortunately for all concerned, the pitch that got away from a young Jim Bunning in an exhibition game in Miami Stadium missed Don Zimmer's head.

As time went on, of course, Bunning hit a lot of batters, and, as long-time Phillies' coach John Vukovich pointed out "a lot of it was on purpose." Jim tied for the National League lead in hit batters with a dozen in 1965, and led the league outright with fourteen in 1964, nineteen in 1966, and thirteen in 1967. American League batters weren't spared, either.

"Baseball was still at that time where, if you took a big swing you had a chance to go on your ass the next pitch," said Vukovich, who was Bunning's teammate in Philadelphia at the end of Jim's pitching career.

When Bunning was wrapping things up as a Phillie, the Giants had a massive, young slugger named Dave Kingman, who was just starting his career. Vukovich was playing third one day when Kingman, facing a young Phillies pitcher, took a huge swing at a pitch, which was nothing unusual for the king-sized Giant. Bunning, who was scheduled to face the Giants the next day, didn't like it.

"I remember him getting on the top step of the dugout at the Vet and screaming at Kingman, 'If you swing like that tomorrow I'm going to knock you on your ass,'" Vukovich said. "I knew Kingman from the minor leagues. I knew he was a guy that would fight, and he was such a big, strong guy, and I saw this [nearly forty-year-old] guy telling him he was going to knock him on his ass. It tickled the hell out of me. Kingman knew only one way to swing, but Jim wasn't about to let him do that off him. Well, he might have done it once, but he would've hit him. I don't know what would have happened then."

Fortunately for Jim Bunning, his wife, their nine kids, their thirty-one grandkids, and Jim's constituents in the Fourth Congressional District of Kentucky, neither Vukovich nor anybody else ever found out. Kingman didn't say a word when Bunning screamed at him, and he wasn't in the Giants lineup the next day.

"Gibson and Drysdale and Bunning, those names are brought up a lot in today's [big league] dugouts when you see that big, hard swing, or that excessive styling that goes on," Vukovich pointed out. "If you did that to one of them, they'd hit you. And then they'd walk to the plate and pick the ball up. That's the way the game was played. I mean, if you looked at Bunning on a pitch that was inside when he was just trying to pitch in [and not trying to knock the batter down], he would hit you with the next pitch [as if to say], 'If you think that one's too far inside try this one.'"

For sheer intensity, a determination to do whatever had to be done to win a game, it would be hard to top Larry Bowa. But even Bowa, an All-Star shortstop with the Phillies, recognized Bunning as the man who raised intensity to a new level.

Bowa was a skinny kid, just starting his big league career, when Bunning was winding down his pitching days in Philadelphia. The Jim Bunning he saw didn't throw as hard as he once did, but he battled every bit as hard. Losing still ate him up inside.

"I remember one game in San Diego," Bowa said, "I made an error and he turned around [on the mound] and glared at me. I wanted to find a way to hide."

The Bunning glare could do that to people.

"Later he said to me, 'Larry, I didn't mean anything by that,'" Bowa recalled. "It's just that he was so intense. I mean this guy battled. When you see a guy like that when you're first coming up, it sets a foundation. That meant a lot to me.

"He said, 'Play the game all twenty-seven outs. Don't give anything away.' I always remembered that. And his work ethic. He worked harder than anybody and he was at the end of his career. You could see he had pride right to the end."

And he had that "killer instinct" on the mound, the "meanness" so many opposing batters still talk about. Bowa recalled a game in Montreal. Ron Hunt was leading off for the Expos, and Hunt was a master of getting hit by pitched balls to get on base.

"The second pitch, Jim threw this big, slow curve," Bowa remembered.

Hunt did his thing, artfully turning his shoulder just enough to get nicked by the pitch. Bowa, standing at shortstop, taking in the scene, saw Bunning walk over toward the Montreal infielder as Hunt trotted to first base. "He said, 'Ronnie, you want to get hit, I'll oblige you next time,'" Bowa said. "Next time up, Jim hit him with a fast ball right in the ribs."

"He was like Drysdale," remarked Joe Torre. "He gave you the same look as Drysdale—big, came a little sidewinding, and he was mean."

There's that word again. But pitchers like Bunning, Drysdale, and Gibson belong to another era. They've been legislated out of the game.

"They've taken that away from pitchers now," Joe Torre was saying. "You've got to come to the middle of the plate now. They won't let you come inside, and you don't get [borderline] strike calls. So they really neutralize the pitcher because they like those high-scoring games. That's just the way it is. Before, getting knocked on your ass was part of the game. My first at-bat against Jack Sanford, he threw one right at my head. I hit the ground."

Jim Bunning sent Torre and a number of others diving to the dirt. For a righthanded hitter, which Torre was, facing Bunning was a real test. The righthanded batter's box was no place for the faint of heart when Bunning was pitching.

"It was frightening," Torre said. "Damn, it was tough. You really had to have a meeting with yourself to stay in there."

But batting righthanded or lefthanded, facing Bunning was no picnic. He'd loosen you up, then toss a slow, tantalizing curve ball that seemed to take days to get to the plate. "He learned how to really take something off that 'slurve,'" the former Yankee general manager and manager Gene Michael commented. "He'd throw it with a real fast arm and batters would jump at it. My main recollection of facing Bunning is I couldn't hit him."

"He threw one curve ball I could never identify," Joe Torre remembered, "the one that just kept breaking and wouldn't get to the plate. I'd swing and miss at that son of a bitch every time. I knew it was coming and I still couldn't hit it."

But it was the "meanness," knowing that he'd knock you down if you looked too comfortable swinging against him, that made the Bunnings and the Drysdales and the Gibsons so effective. Jim Wright, the Phillies' top pitching prospect in the 1970s, recalled the time early in his career when Bunning, then the Triple A manager, walked up to him in spring training. "He'd say, 'Kid, how are you doing today?'" related Wright. "'How many guys did you walk? How many hits did you give up?' Then later he said, 'There's one thing I want you to learn. I want you to get hitters 0 and 2. When you get a hitter 0 and 2 you've got his balls in your hand. I want you to squeeze. I want you to knock him down with the next pitch. Not hit him, knock him down. Then the next pitch, throw a strike.'"

Wright, who was pitching in an "A" league that year, followed Bunning's instructions. "Early in the season when I tried to do that I hit six or seven out of nine guys," he said. "But because Jim Bunning told me to do it, I kept trying. About fifteen batters later, I had it down pat. I found out that hitters don't like to be knocked down. I learned how to move a hitter's feet, his waist, his upper body. I knew right then what Jim taught me worked."

Watching games now, Bunning sees how much baseball has changed. "I swear, I would never finish a game now," he declared. "I'd be thrown out of every game I started—not trying to hit somebody, but coming inside. The hitter would either have to get out of the way or get hit. The way [Jose] Canseco and these guys go into the ball, I'd be ringing it off their front wrist or something."

There is still an occasional pitcher who is able to establish command of the inner half of the plate, even today. "I watch [Roger] Clemens pitch," Bunning remarked, "and he comes inside as hard as anybody I've ever seen. Nobody dives in at the ball when he's pitching. So if you establish that as a pitcher, you don't have that problem. You can earn [the right to throw to] that area."

But Clemens is the exception. The age when big league pitchers controlled the inside corner, driving batters off the plate, dominating them by intimidating them is long gone.

"The biggest problem is the metal bats in college today," Bunning said. "There's no advantage to pitching inside. They can swing the bats faster and you can't jam people."

The Bunnings and the Drysdales and the Gibsons didn't have that problem on the way up. No hitter armed with a wooden bat could feel comfortable facing one of them. About a year before he died, Mickey Mantle told a story about the only time he came close to charging the mound. The pitcher who incurred Mantle's wrath was Jim Bunning.

The Tigers were playing the Yankees in Tiger Stadium, and Bob Turley, one of the premier Yankee starting pitchers of the era, was doing a stint as first base coach. Turley was adept at stealing signs, and it didn't take Bunning long to figure out that he was in his sign-stealing mode. Working to the first two Yankee batters, Bobby Richardson and Tony Kubek, Bunning realized that Turley was whistling each time Jim threw a fast ball. If it was a breaking ball, not a sound. Mantle was batting third, and by the time he came up Bunning was positive Turley was tipping off the Yankee hitters. Jim wasn't about to let that continue.

"I did a kind of semicircle, a quick U-turn [upon getting the ball from his catcher, Dick Brown]," Bunning said.

Instead of looking in toward the plate, Bunning looked at Turley in the coach's box and informed him, "If you whistle, I'm going to drill him." Then Jim walked to home plate and told Brown, "If he whistles we're going to drill him." All the while, of course, the "him" in question, Mr. Mantle, was standing there, taking it all in.

Bunning thought what he had done was enough to keep Turley

quiet the rest of the game. He was wrong. Brown signaled for a fast ball and Turley's shrill whistle caressed Bunning's ears. So Jim, a man of his word, did what he promised he would do.

"I drilled him," he said. "Drilled him hard. Hit him in the leg."

Pitching inside may have been part of the game in those days, but there was no doubt about this one. Mantle knew Bunning had hit him on purpose, and he started out to the mound. The Yankee slugger had muscles on top of muscles; the slender Tiger pitcher figured to have his hands full if Mickey made it.

"As he started out, Brown got in front of him and somehow, thank God, he got him to go to first base," remembered Bunning, who breathed a sigh of relief and prepared to face the next Yankee hitter, Yogi Berra.

"Berra happened to be hitting after Mantle that day," Jim said. "I don't know why, because [Roger] Maris usually did."

Berra dug in at the plate and Bunning went into his stretch, got the sign for another fast ball . . . and Turley whistled again. Bunning stepped off the mound and Berra stepped out of the batter's box and hollered out to him, "Hey, Jim, he's whistling, but I don't take 'em."

That was Yogi's way of telling Bunning that he didn't pay any attention to such helpful hints while batting.

"I thought it was because he was afraid I was going to hit him," said Bunning, who told the story at the impromptu roast the Hall of Famers have on induction weekend in Cooperstown. That's when Yogi set him straight, explaining that he didn't pay attention to Turley's whistling that day because he didn't need to know in advance what Bunning was throwing. "I could hit him without knowing," Berra explained. "It didn't make any difference."

Berra wasn't kidding. "Frank Lary [the Tigers' other ace righthander at the time] would go out on the mound and Yogi couldn't get a hit off him if his life depended on it," Bunning said. "But I could not figure out how to get him out. If I went outside, Yogi could still pull it, and if I went inside . . ."

Memories of those Berra home runs were still vivid in Bunning's memory.

"I could get two strikes on him really easy," he said. "Then I didn't know what to do with him."

But, as Mantle found out, Jim knew what to do when somebody tried to take advantage of him by stealing signs. Bunning also knew, as did many other pitchers of his era, how to get a little extra edge over the batters.

Gaylord Perry, Don Drysdale, Lew Burdette, Don Sutton, Tommy John, Whitey Ford . . . there's a practically endless list of All-Star-caliber pitchers who have doctored—or been accused of doctoring—baseballs. It goes on now; it went on then.

"If I had as good a greaseball as Drysdale at that time, I'd have had fifty-eight straight scoreless innings, too," Bunning said. "He had one of the best I've ever seen. Whoo-o-o.

"I started a game against Drysdale in that streak for Pittsburgh when he was shutting everybody out. You couldn't hit him. He had everything going, including control. He had great stuff, and he added this slippery pitch. The bottom fell out, and it was about 93-94 miles an hour. It was unhittable."

That, too, was generally accepted as part of the game.

Occasionally, though, a big fuss was raised—like the time, in 1962, that the Baltimore manager, Billy Hitchcock, accused Bunning of cutting baseballs with his belt buckle while beating the Orioles in Baltimore. Hitchcock collected the evidence—and got nowhere in his protest. Years later, Sparky Anderson, managing the Cincinnati Reds against the Dodgers, made a fuss over allegedly cut-up baseballs thrown by Don Sutton and Tommy John, keeping them in a desk drawer in his office to show to anyone interested in seeing them. Nothing happened then, either.

For a while, though, Hitchcock's complaint made lots of headlines and some lively reading. Bunning, naturally, laughed the whole thing off, explaining the plethora of sliced baseballs by saying, "Hoyt Wilhelm pitched against me. His fingernails were really sharp."

Hitchcock declared that Bunning's buckle was even sharper—sharp enough to slice American League baseballs through the leather, thereby making them do tricks on their speedy journey to the plate. As Bunning said later, "Hitchcock had come from Detroit as our third base coach, so he knew all the little ins and outs that we used when we pitched, and he made a big deal out of it. The league exonerated me completely. There was no proof I had done anything."

In fact, there's every reason to believe Bunning didn't do anything. Which is not to say that nothing was done.

"All I can say is that the shortstop, first baseman, third baseman, and various people handled the ball," Bunning pointed out.

Let the record show that they all had belt buckles, too.

Hitchcock undoubtedly knew what was going on, but he made a fuss anyway. The Orioles were pretty bad in those days; it gave the Baltimore sportswriters something to focus on other than how bad the team was. Reading the Baltimore papers that week provided a fair share of laughs.

"I had 15 [sliced baseballs]," Hitchcock was quoted as saying. "I gave four others to the umpires. I gave three to photographers who said they wanted to present them to either Ben Casey or Dr. Kildare so they could be stitched up before they died. The next day we had five fans call in who had caught foul balls in the stands. They said they had baseballs also neatly sliced."

The big story died in a hurry. Bunning helped bury it by pitching a three-hitter against the Orioles the next time he faced them. Joe Falls wrote in the *Detroit Free Press*: "Jim (Buckles) Bunning went up against his Baltimore accusers Monday night, and if Billy Hitchcock cared to, he could have complained about four things:

1. Bunning's fast ball.
2. Bunning's curve ball.
3. Bunning's slider.
4. Bunning's changeup.

All of them were working perfectly—cutting the corners, if Hitchcock will pardon the expression—and Bunning rode this baffling assortment of pitches to his most satisfying victory of the season."

Even Hitchcock surrendered without a fight after that one, saying, "All I saw Bunning do tonight was pitch a heckuva game."

Jim couldn't resist a little zinger, however, teasing his victims by turning around several times on the mound and flashing the baseball in front of his buckle.

Getting dubbed "Buckles Bunning" didn't upset him a bit. "I thought it was kind of funny, knowing all the things I know that pitchers and catchers and other people had done. . . . I think Whitey [Ford] had probably the best 'mud ball' other than Lew Burdette of any pitcher I've ever seen," Bunning said.

It was no secret that Bunning made good use of pine tar, as did quite a few pitchers. It helped them get a grip on the ball. At the time, however, opposing managers would scream about that, too. Herman Franks, then managing the Giants, made a big fuss over it after Bunning beat his team one day at Connie Mack Stadium. There was even a time, years later, when a pitcher, Dodgers reliever Jay Howell, was ejected from a playoff game because pine tar was found in his glove. Veteran ballplayers laughed at the absurdity of the punishment.

Said Jim Kaat, winner of 283 major league games: "I'm not boasting about the fact I used it, nor am I embarrassed by the fact I used it. The purpose was not to throw illegal pitches, but to get a grip to throw a breaking ball. Lots of pitchers use it. Jay Howell just didn't have it in the right place."

Bunning recalled that "one time [Cardinals manager] Red Schoendienst ran out of the dugout to smell me. Here's the opposing manager running to the mound. First of all, he went to the umpire and said, 'He's got this stuff.' They came out. I said, 'Here I am.' Red said he could smell the pine tar. They didn't find any pine tar anywhere on my person."

Did Bunning use the stuff? Of course. As Kaat and others pointed out, the practice was commonplace.

"It was so known I used pine tar," Bunning said, "that when I was traded to the Pirates [general manager] Joe L. Brown had a study done so that the pine tar we would possibly use in Pittsburgh was clear."

Brown figured it would be difficult to accuse somebody of using something you couldn't see. "I got a guy from Carnegie-Mellon to develop a pine tar that was white and had no smell," the retired general manager confirmed. "Jim wouldn't use it. He said, 'I'm doing all right with the black stuff.'"

Bunning's version of the Great Pittsburgh Pine Tar Experiment differed somewhat. "Unfortunately," he remarked, "I didn't stay in Pittsburgh long enough for them to develop it."

Farewell to Pitching

After three straight nineteen-win seasons, Jim Bunning signed for $70,000 in 1967. No agent represented him; Bunning represented himself. And John Quinn, a tough man with a buck, met his match. Seventy thousand may not sound like much today (it's less than half the big league minimum), but it was a lot in those days. Especially in Philadelphia.

"It was the most any player in Philadelphia had made in the history of the franchise," Bunning observed.

He showed up for his salary talks with the Phillies' general manager armed with facts and figures. There were times when Quinn wasn't in shape for those meetings; he drank a lot and could get belligerent when he overdid it. On such occasions Bunning would politely excuse himself, get up, and leave the office. They would meet another day, once Quinn was sober. Make no mistake, however. John Quinn, an old-school baseball man if ever there was one, was an excellent judge of talent, a terrific wheeler-dealer when it came to making trades. Bunning respected his considerable talents as a general manager. It's just that he belonged to another era, a time when management, not the players, held the upper hand.

After signing for that "record" salary in 1967, Bunning had a feeling that his Phillie days were numbered. "They knew they wouldn't be able to sign me again. That's why they traded me."

Besides, Bunning would be thirty-six by the time opening day '68 came around. He didn't figure to get better. Quinn, no dummy, chose to trade him while he was still among the league's elite pitchers. "He made a good trade," acknowledged Bunning, getting infielder Don Money, lefthanded pitcher Woodie Fryman, and two young pitchers, one of whom, lefty Bill Laxton, was considered a legitimate prospect.

The trade to the Pirates enabled Bunning to reach his high-water mark in salary—$110,000. His new club hoped to contend in 1968, and Jim was expected to play a key role. And not just on the days he pitched.

"I understood when I got to Pittsburgh what he [manager Larry Shepard] needed," Bunning recalled. "He needed somebody to go out and do the work and lead by example because Bob Veale wouldn't do it. Bob Veale was the best pitcher the Pirates had, and had way more talent than I did and anybody else did, but he wanted special treatment. He wouldn't go out, do the running and the work that was necessary."

Bunning did what was required—"and a little bit more." When the season began there was reason to believe the trade would be a big success for Bunning's new team.

"If I didn't break down, I think we are a contender," Jim said.

But he was at an age when even the hardest-working, best-conditioned athlete is liable to break down. He started off fast, won three of his first four decisions—and then it happened.

"I was pitching against [Dodger infielder] Jim Lefebvre," Bunning recalled. "I threw him a curve ball in the eighth inning in Pittsburgh, and I heard something go *pop!*"

It was Bunning's right groin. He had torn the muscle, and he couldn't walk, much less pitch. Still, he tried, throwing one more ball before realizing it was no use.

It was a warm night, not the sort of weather in which you'd expect this to happen. But happen it did, and although Bunning received credit for his third Pirate victory that night, his season—and to a great degree the team's—was ruined.

"I had a great spring," Bunning recalled, "and it all went in the tank after that."

He took cortisone shots, and he still couldn't pitch. The Pirates' orthopedic surgeon told him to go home. Bunning was ready to do exactly that, but he suspected that the Pirates weren't ready to see him go. They had too big an investment in him, and he meant too much to their chances.

"It was sad," Jim said, recalling his attempts to pitch when he was physically incapable of doing it. "It cost him [Shepard] his job. I said, 'Larry, if you can stand watching me pitch as bad as I am, I will go out and pitch. I cannot pivot on this leg. I can't run. I can't do anything.'"

Between the groin injury and an inflamed hip, he was a mess. Finally, there was a game against the Phillies. "Not only did I hurt my leg, but my right ankle went into a hole and I twisted it," he said. "Now I've got a sprained ankle on the same side I had the groin pull."

His season was over; even the Pirates had to admit that. They finally declared him disabled, the first time Jim Bunning had ever been on the disabled list.

Clearly, he should have been declared disabled immediately after injuring himself on that pitch to Lefebvre. But they asked him to pitch, and he was getting $110,000 to do it, and he felt obligated. "I was not smart enough to say, 'I am not going to pitch. I should be disabled,'" he recalled.

It was December before Jim was healthy again—or at least healthy enough to pitch with reasonable hope of success. As late as the following spring Bunning still felt a knot in his groin. And also, no doubt, in his stomach when he thought about what might have been, and what was: a 3-and-1 start that dissolved into a 4-and-14 finish because he had tried to do the impossible.

Bunning rebounded in 1969, won ten games for the Pirates, and then was traded to the Dodgers for cash, outfielder Ron Mitchell, and infielder Chuck Coggin in mid-August.

"I started nine games for them, was 3 and 1," Jim said. "I kept us in eight of the nine games."

So, with about two weeks left in the season, Bunning thought it would be a good idea to talk to Dodgers general manager Al Campanis and find out what plans, if any, the club had for him in 1970. If the Dodgers had merely grabbed him to finish the season, he needed to know.

Campanis assured him that wasn't the case. "He said, 'No, you're in our plans for 1970,'" Bunning recalled. "I said, 'That's good. I really appreciate that. I think I've done a pretty good job for you.'"

Just some pleasant small talk after that. Bunning left Campanis's office feeling pretty good about things. He would start the '70 season with the Dodgers. Not a bad way to wind down a career.

"I was home two days after the season, and I got a call," Bunning remembered.

It was somebody from the Dodgers. Jim isn't sure who it was, only who it wasn't. "It was from somebody other then Campanis," he said.

The message was short and not at all sweet. "We had an organizational meeting," the caller told him, "and we decided to release you."

As for what Campanis had told Bunning a couple of weeks earlier, the caller knew nothing about that.

"What are my options?" Bunning asked.

"You're a free agent," the caller said. "Do anything you want."

Bunning was shocked. "I had not dealt with a general manager who wasn't straight up," he said. "I had dealt with the Tigers and Rick Ferrell was as straight up as could be. John McHale was, too. And Jimmy Campbell and I got along really well. I didn't get any distortions or lies out of John Quinn. And when I went to the Pirates, Joe L. Brown didn't give me any. So when I went in to see Campanis I didn't expect any. I was dumbfounded that a person that high up in baseball wouldn't be straight up."

Maybe the lie was unintentional. Maybe on the day Bunning had his talk with the Dodgers' general manager, Campanis didn't know how his field people felt and was prompted to change his mind. In later years, when he thought back on the painful incident, Bunning tried to give Campanis the benefit of the doubt.

But the bottom line was, "He didn't tell me the truth at that meeting. That's an experience, at age thirty-seven, a lot of people go through [in professional baseball and other sports, as well], but I had just won thirteen games," Bunning pointed out.

There is nothing unusual about an organization lying to a player in baseball. It happens all the time. "But I don't deal with that very well," Jim observed.

It would have been so much better if Campanis had made that postseason call and told Bunning that there had been a change of heart, that in the best interests of the club the Dodgers had decided to give him his unconditional release. Or, better yet, if he had made the decision before Bunning went home. "Look me straight in the eye and say it," Jim declared. That he could have understood.

Coming off a pretty good year, Bunning wasn't ready to retire just yet. First thing he did was call his "home town team," the Cincinnati Reds. That's where he really wanted to close out his big league career.

The Reds didn't beat around the bush. "They were not interested and told me so right up front," Bunning recalled.

So Jim put Plan B into operation, sending telegrams to each of the other big league clubs—except the Dodgers, of course. The wire went something like this:

"I'm healthy. If you have any doubts, I just got done winning thirteen games in the National League this year. Ready to start. Ready to relieve."

"I was ready to do anything," he said. "I wanted to pitch."

John Quinn wasted no time responding to Bunning's telegram.

"What would it take to get you back to Philly?" he asked over the phone.

Bunning gave him a number in the $70,000 range. Quinn sent him a contract. No negotiating. No bickering. It was as fast, as simple as that.

"I didn't really explore [after Quinn's phone call]," Bunning recalled. "Since they met what I asked for and said, 'C'mon back,' I said, 'Let's go.'"

Jim Bunning had wanted to end his pitching career in Cincinnati, but ending it in Philadelphia, where he had spent four of his best seasons, was fine, too—even if the Phillies were in the early stages of a rebuilding program. "I was extremely glad to go back to Philly," he said.

Bunning's final two seasons with the Phillies couldn't compare to his four-year stay in the mid-1960s. He was thirty-eight when he returned to his old team, now managed by the delightful Frank Lucchesi, who had ascended to the big leagues, realizing a lifelong dream, after a lengthy career in the minors.

One of the young outfielders on that Phillie team was Scott Reid. Only twenty-three at the time, he couldn't help but be impressed by this veteran pitcher nearing the end of his active playing career.

"I met him in spring training," said Reid, who went on to become a successful big league scout for the Phillies, Cubs, and, currently, the Florida Marlins. "He was nice to me. I was just a young kid. He was an established big-name pitcher. The thing I remember about him as a player, the day he pitched you just stayed away from him."

Those "ground rules" were quickly explained to anyone new to the scene. You didn't engage in small talk, or any talk, with Jim Bunning on the day he was pitching.

"You just stayed out of his way," Reid commented. "You didn't even try to say hello to him. That was it. I was really impressed with his intensity, his approach."

Bunning won ten games and lost fifteen for the 1970 Phillies, a lightly regarded team that stayed in the race longer than anyone expected. On one memorable night at Connie Mack Stadium in late September he was ten outs away from another victory when the unthinkable happened: pitching with a one-run lead he got thrown out of the game. "The most ridiculous thing that ever happened to me," he called it.

Going into the sixth inning, Bunning was beating a New York Mets team that was still in the pennant race, 2-0. Bud Harrelson drew a leadoff walk and stole second. He stayed there as pinch hitter Dave Marshall hit a foul fly to left and Tommie Agee looked at a third strike. Then it all fell apart for Bunning.

Wayne Garrett socked a double to right center, scoring Harrelson with the first Mets' run. With the tying run on second and two out, Jim worked the count to 3 and 2 on the dangerous Cleon Jones.

"I threw a curve ball that was right down the middle," Bunning recalled. "The guy [plate umpire Stan Landes] said 'Ball.' I went 'Holy Christ!'"

Jim threw up his arms in frustration and the glove flew off his left hand. He didn't throw it; it came loose and went flying into the air. The umpire came to a quick decision: if the glove came down and hit the ground, its owner would be removed from the premises. Unluckily for Bunning, the law of gravity was in effect in North Philadelphia that night. His glove did, indeed, hit the ground.

"As soon as it did, he punched me out of the game," said Bunning. "I told him, 'You know, it came off accidentally.' He said, 'It doesn't make any difference. There's a rule you can't throw your glove.' I said, 'I didn't throw it.'"

Bunning's protests reached deaf ears. Jim was gone, fuming every step of the way. In a matter of minutes, the Phillies' lead was gone, too. Woodie Fryman, rushed into combat, gave up a walk and two singles. Before Billy Wilson retired the side, the Mets had a 5-2 lead and Lucchesi had been ejected. As if that wasn't bad enough, the Phillies rallied for four runs in the eighth to regain the lead, only to lose, 7-6 in the ninth on Agee's two-run single off relief ace Dick Selma.

It wasn't a happy bunch of Phillies who gathered in the clubhouse for the postgame snack.

"I didn't get fined," Bunning remembered, "but Selma did for what he said after the game."

The reporters were in the process of interviewing Selma, wisely steering clear of Bunning, when Jim overheard the relief pitcher make some rather strong comments.

"A few of us were sitting there, listening, and we're going, 'Holy ——,' because he's accusing the umpires of fixing the game," Bunning recalled.

And it all happened because the glove flew off Jim's hand.

This was a transitional period for the Phillies, whose 73 and 88 record in 1970 marked the only time between 1969 and 1973 that they failed to lose over ninety games. It was a stage when such promising youngsters as shortstop Larry Bowa and second baseman Denny Doyle were breaking into the big leagues. Bunning had just about come to the end of his career, but the ball club was moving to a new home — Veterans Stadium in South Philadelphia — and Jim wanted to be a part of that move.

"I told Frank Lucchesi at the end of the '70 season, 'Frank,' I said, 'if there's one thing I want you to let me do, it's pitch the first game in that new stadium.'"

Bunning reminded his manager of that request during spring training the next year. "I'll work my butt off," he told him. "I'll get in really good shape."

Jim lived up to his promise, and Lucchesi, a man of his word, gave him the opening-game assignment.

To Bunning, who saw the Phillies' move from Connie Mack Stadium to the Vet in historical perspective, it was the last truly memorable occasion of his major league pitching career.

Going to the Vet "changed the whole concept of the Phillies," he pointed out. "From the old, dirty, little stadium, they came into the modern era. A different crowd came to the park at the Vet and I wanted to be part of that transition. It was important for me to be part of it."

Lucchesi, he knew, could have given the opening-game start to any number of pitchers — to Grant Jackson or Woodie Fryman or Barry Lersch or Chris Short or Bunning. There was no clear-cut ace, no Robin Roberts or Steve Carlton or Bunning in his prime as the obvious choice. "So I asked," Jim said, "and I received."

Lucchesi wasn't about to turn down a request from Jim Bunning. He had the highest regard for him as a true professional and as a person. He thought so much of him, in fact, that one time during that season he asked Jim, on the spur of the moment, to go to the mound to offer advice to a struggling young pitcher. Bunning declined. The Phillies had a pitching coach to handle such duties and Jim wasn't about to infringe on his territory. Still, Lucchesi's request was indicative of the high esteem in which he held the veteran pitcher.

"He's one of the best competitors I ever managed," Lucchesi declared. "He was a jewel to manage. He never alibied. It was always, 'Just give me the ball . . .'"

Seldom did Bunning feel better about getting the ball than on the afternoon of April 10, 1971, the day the Phillies played their first game at Veterans Stadium. "It was a special day for me," Bunning said. "It was probably the only real special day I had in '71. I didn't have many good days."

But that day was very good. Montreal's Boots Day hit his first pitch right back to him, and Bunning remained in command most of the way. Ironically, the Expos manager was Jim's old Phillies skipper, Gene Mauch. The 4-1 victory Bunning recorded that day was one of only five, against twelve losses, in his farewell season. The fast ball had lost some of its zip, the slider some of its bite. At thirty-nine, after twenty-two years in professional baseball, he was ready to embark on another career.

Even so, there was something about Bunning that reminded observers of his past brilliance. Ex-Kansas City Royals manager Bob Boone, a twenty-three-year-old minor league catcher in the Phillies organization in 1971, still remembers the day in spring training that year when Bunning went to the minor league complex to get some work, pitching for the Triple A club in an exhibition game. Boone was catching, and he marveled at Bunning's ability to hit spots. "Best control of any pitcher I ever caught," Boone observed. "He didn't have much, but I'd put the glove here and he'd hit it."

Unfortunately, as the season wore along, opposing batters hit it, too.

Among the lasting memories of Jim's final big league season were some titanic home runs. Willie Stargell hit one at the Vet that soared into the upper deck in right field and down a runway. A star was placed there to mark the spot; it remains to this day.

Phillies coach John Vukovich remembered another one that looked like a Tiger Woods tee shot. Ken Singleton hit it off Bunning in New York. "Oh my God," said Vukovich by way of describing that blast years later.

The home runs that bothered Bunning the most weren't hit by the Stargells, Singletons, and other sluggers of the day. "I knew it was time to hang them up," he commented, "when Tito Fuentes, Roger Metzger, and David Concepcion hit home runs."

Bunning can still see those baseballs flying out of National League parks—Fuentes's homer in San Francisco, Metzger's in Houston, and Concepcion's in Cincinnati. But one of the homers he remembers so vividly never happened. Yes, Concepcion's only home ran in 327 at-bats in 1971 did come against Bunning. And yes, Fuentes hit one of his four home runs in 1971 (in 630 at-bats) off Bunning. But a check of the records shows that Metzger hit no homers in 1971. Further checking reveals that a backup Pittsburgh shortstop, Jackie Hernandez, hit three home runs in 203 at-bats that year, and one of them was hit against Bunning. Presumably, that's who Jim was thinking about when he gave the credit to Metzger. In any event, he gave up home runs to people who shouldn't have been able to hit them against him (although Concepcion, who added muscle in later years, wound up hitting 101 homers in his nineteen-year big league career).

What troubled Bunning most, it seemed, was that those home runs weren't hit off "mistake pitches."

"The pitches were all where I wanted them," he recalled. "They were sliders that slid, but they didn't have any pop on them. That told me I was embarrassed enough to go home. They [the Phillies] didn't have to tell me."

The fact is, John Quinn asked Bunning to came back as a short reliever in 1972. Jim said no thank you.

"I knew it was time," he said. "Maybe I would have [accepted Quinn's offer] if they were paying two and a half or three million."

Not then, they weren't. So Jim Bunning decided to go to work as a minor league manager for twenty-two thousand instead.

Back to the Minors

Think how Mary Bunning must have felt on the day her beloved Jim, his career as a major league pitcher over, walked into the house and announced that he wanted to return to the minor leagues to learn how to manage. For $22,000 a year.

The money wasn't a factor. Jim had deferred payments coming from the Pirates and the Phillies. It was the thought of enduring another minor league experience at this stage of their lives—and with nine children, no less. It was the idea of leaving their lovely home in Fort Thomas, Kentucky, and relocating for the summer in what surely would be far less spacious quarters in some minor league town. Plus all those road trips, all those times when Mary and the kids would be in one place and Jim in another. It was one thing when he was pitching in the big leagues; that made sense. But this seemed so unnecessary, so downright foolish. How many big league stars would consider doing it at the end of their playing careers? Darn few, that's how many.

Besides, you could argue that it wasn't imperative for a man who wanted to manage some day in the big leagues to learn the tricks of the trade in the minors. At least two men who are successful big league managers today—the Seattle Mariners' Lou Piniella and the Yankees' Joe Torre—started managing at the top, in the big leagues. Well, so maybe there were some growing pains, but each led teams to world championships—Piniella in Cincinnati, Torre in New York. So it wasn't *absolutely* necessary to start managing where Jim

Bunning started—in the Class Double A Eastern League. Or was it? In Jim's case, maybe it was. He was such a perfectionist, he expected so much from his players that he and the big leaguers of the day might have had a rough time coexisting, much as he and the minor leaguers of the day did.

"We all heard these horror stories his first year in Double A," recalled Scott Reid, who played briefly for Jim in Reading his first year, and then played for him in Eugene the following year. "Maybe it [managing in Double A] was too big a step down for a man of his stature."

Maybe so. But in his heart Jim Bunning knew that to be the best possible big league manager he needed to spend time in the minors, and that was the opening available to him in 1972. He believed in being prepared; this, he knew, was the best way—the only way—to prepare himself for what he hoped would be a second big league career.

"I wasn't so full of myself that I thought I knew everything about how to be a coach or a manager or whatever," he remembered. "I thought it was essential for me to do that [manage in the minors first]. I didn't say, 'Here, why not give me the [big league] job now?' I didn't say, 'I'm ready to manage your ball club.' I wasn't ready, and I sure wasn't ready to manage Reading when I got there, either. Not so much the strategy of the game and all that stuff, but the handling of the people."

Looking back on it now, you could make a strong argument that Mary Bunning would have been right in putting her foot down and asking him—pleading with him, if necessary—to stay with his stock brokering, or be a full-time players' agent, anything but what he had in mind. But Mary reacted the way Jim knew she would react.

"She said, 'If that's what you want to do, OK,'" Jim recalled. "She said that every time I did something."

All the while, of course, Mary was holding back an urge to clobber the light of her life, the breadwinner of the family, over his damn fool head. Or to cry out in anguish. But no, that wasn't Mary.

The Phillie farmhands who played for the Reading, Pennsylvania, ball club in 1972 wished she had put her foot down, said what she felt, and talked Jim out of it. Playing for the rookie manager was not a barrel of laughs. The perfect pitcher found himself stuck in a most imperfect world. Adjusting was not easy.

How could a man who spent seventeen years in the big leagues, a man who approached the game with total dedication and expected others to do the same, a man who accepted nothing less than perfection deal with the error-prone Reading Phillies of 1972?

Not very well.

Dallas Green, the Phillies' assistant farm director at the time, knew it wouldn't be easy for his friend. H also knew what kind of person Bunning was, and that Jim would give the job everything he had, which was how he approached every job. Having Dallas there was a major factor in Jim's decision to give it a try. He and Green were "about as close as you could get," Bunning declared. So when Dallas encouraged him to take the job, he listened. And the encouragement of Phillies' president Bob Carpenter, a man Bunning trusted and respected, didn't hurt, either.

But starting the great experiment at Reading? If Jim had his way he would have begun his managerial career at the Triple A level, the top of the minor league scale. But it was Double A or nothing, and even though he had less than fond memories of his early experiences as a Double A pitcher in the Detroit organization—the long bus rides and the subpar playing conditions and the crummy hotels—he took the job the Phillies offered him.

"I don't know if I have the patience to be a manager," he remarked. "I'd like to find out."

Patience was not his strong suit, and watching the Reading Phillies boot ground balls, butcher double plays, and go after pop flies as if they were live hand grenades pushed what patience he had to the limit. And beyond.

Early-season weather in Eastern League cities was notoriously bad, especially now that the league had expanded to Canada. You haven't lived until you have experienced an April night game in Sherbrooke or Three Rivers.

The day before the team known as the Little Phillies was scheduled to head for Three Rivers, a rainout loomed in Reading. It was a rotten day. A cold wind whipped across Reading Municipal Stadium, blowing straight out toward the scoreboard in left-center field that Greg Luzinski used as a target area two years before. The forecast called for heavy rains. At game time a light drizzle was falling. But Bunning felt his team needed to play this Monday night game, no matter how bad the weather, and he voiced his feelings to Reading's young general manager, Jimmy Bronson. So Bronson opened the gates and an announced crowd of 211 poured through. It could have been worse; a lot of people could have seen the Reading Phillies play that night. They made ten errors, five in the ninth inning. And, yes, they lost. Not exactly what the perfectionist Bunning had in mind. I can still remember the *Reading Eagle*'s Duke DeLuca, the official scorer, marveling at what he and the 211 paying customers had just witnessed: "You see ten errors, you figure the scorer must be mad at somebody. But I didn't have one tough decision. They were definite errors."

Bunning had a tough decision, though: after seeing that exhibition, he had to talk himself into getting on the bus for an all-night, eleven-hour trip to Three Rivers, Quebec, and an opportunity to see more of the same.

How could the Reading Phillies play that poorly? Their manager may have been partly to blame. Many of his players were in awe of the former big league star, and their awe, in many cases, turned into downright fear. One of the mistakes Jim made was to watch the game with a tape recorder handy. When a Reading player did something wrong—not an unusual occurrence—Jim would raise the tape recorder to his lips and begin talking into it. Nearby players could hear some of the words, and they weren't flattering. Those out of earshot could only imagine what he must be saying about them. And that was even less flattering.

The more uptight the players got, the more things Bunning had to say into his machine, which made the players even more uptight. It was not a good situation.

"I was always talking about things that we could improve ourselves in," Bunning said. "Finally I had [coach] Larry Rojas do the talking into the tape recorder instead of me. What I should have done was what the managers do now. They write it down."

Bunning, as one would expect, ran a tight ship. If he said there was a midnight curfew, it was a good idea to make it back to the room by midnight. If he said the team bus was leaving at 10 o'clock, he meant 10 o'clock, not 10:01.

"We left some people in Reading," he said, "They had to find their own way up [to Three Rivers, or wherever]. I was trying to train them to be major league players. What are you going to do if the airplane leaves at 10:30 [in the big leagues] and you're not there?"

Catch another plane to the major league city of your choice at your own expense, no doubt, which is easier than finding alternate transportation from Reading, Pennsylvania, to, say, Sherbrooke, Quebec. The direct flights from Reading to Sherbrooke are somewhat limited, and it takes a long time by dog sled. When Bunning taught his players a lesson, it was a beaut.

"[Infielder] Blas Santana got left, I can remember clearly," Bunning said of that first trip to the frozen north. "He eventually made it somehow, but it cost him a day's pay. He didn't get there the first night."

Which probably wasn't all bad from Santana's point of view. At least he was warmer than his teammates that first night. There was no such thing as a warm shower in Three Rivers. Or running water, for that matter.

"It was frozen," said Bunning. "Quebec, are you kidding? In Three Rivers it was dark all the time. It was so far north it never got light."

Making it even darker for the Reading Phillies, the Three Rivers club had Ken Griffey, Dan Driessen, and Joel Youngblood, future big leaguers all, on the roster.

Sherbrooke was worse. The ball park was so bad Bunning likened it to a Little League facility. If the Little League folks had seen the quote they probably would have sued him for slander.

The hotel? Don't ask. The joint was what passed for a hot spot in that town in those days. There was live entertainment downstairs. Hard rock. Bunning's room was directly over the steel guitar. When it vibrated, the room vibrated. When the room vibrated, Manager Bunning vibrated. Sleep was out of the question.

In the one move that earned the widespread endorsement of his players, Bunning pulled the Reading Phillies out of the place. They actually gave their fearless, if not exactly peerless leader a rousing round of applause. Then, fully rested in their new hotel, they went out the next day and lost a doubleheader, 12-1 and 8-0, committing half a dozen errors. In all, the perfectionist manager saw his troops commit forty-one errors in the first thirteen games. Even that wouldn't have been so bad if not for the promotional tape Bunning had made for a local radio station at the start of the season, in which he talked about his team's improved defense.

Jim can laugh about that now. He couldn't then. But if the errors, the early-season defeats, the road trips, the terrible weather, the bad playing fields, and the crummy hotels were getting him down, he tried not to show it.

"I wasn't going to let it bother me," he commented. "I expected the worst. It *was* the worst. . . . I knew that people watching me were going to say, 'That son of a bitch, he's been there [in the big leagues] for seventeen years now; why's he doing this?' I made up my mind I wasn't going to let them know it was bothering me."

But he knew, and that was bad enough. Asked to recall what it was like on that first road trip to Canada, Bunning thought a second or two and replied, "I said, 'What am I doing here?' I questioned my sanity. I said, 'Why did I want to do this?'"

And then he answered himself—"Because you are going to make one hell of a major league manager some day."

His immediate task, however, was to make himself a decent minor league manager. He knew how to run a game; he had to learn how to get the most out of his players. Having them quake in their boots whenever he opened his mouth wasn't the way. He wasn't about to be a surrogate father to them; he had enough children already. He wasn't going to baby them; it wasn't his style. "I treated them like men until they acted like boys," he said. "My first meeting with the club I told them, 'Hey, I got nine kids of my own. I don't want any other ones.'"

But sometimes he overdid it, to the extent that his coach, Larry Rojas, was on the verge of leaving the team in protest.

Rojas, a class act who has spent years managing, coaching, and scouting in the Phillies organization, was no pushover for the players. He was strict but fair. Above all, he was caring, and the players knew he cared. Among those he helped along the road to the major leagues was a onetime Phillies farmhand named Ryne Sandberg.

Bunning needed help to survive that first year of managing. "The errors—oh God! Unbelievable," he said. "And then they take the only two prospects away to the big leagues before they were ready."

Reading's two best pitchers, by far, were Mac Scarce, a lefthanded reliever with a nasty slider, and Dave Downs, a big righthander with outstanding stuff.

"Mac Scarce was blowing the league away," Bunning remembered, "but he needed to fail a few times [before he got to the majors]. I told them he wasn't ready for the big leagues. I told Paul [Owens] that. I said, 'He's just blowing the league away, but you should leave him alone. Or take him to Triple A. Don't take him to the big leagues.'"

Which, of course, is precisely what they did. It was, as Bunning expected, a bad move. Big league hitters didn't go fishing for Scarce's slider; when it broke away from the plate, they took it.

The mistake the Phillies made with Dave Downs was much worse. "They took him up and blew him out," Bunning declared. "God! Unbelievable! Rushing these kids, rushing . . ."

Downs's big league debut made him, and the Phillies, look good. He started in Atlanta—a tough ball park for pitchers in those days— and shut out the Braves. It looked like the start of a fine big league career, but the end came suddenly. Next time he pitched, he hurt his arm. Although he pitched briefly in the low miners after that, Downs never recovered. His career was ruined.

Nothing illustrates Bunning's ultraserious approach to managing that first year better than his reaction to the news that Max Patkin, the Clown Prince of Baseball, was going to appear at a Reading Phillies home game.

Patkin didn't perform before the game, or after the game, or between games of a doubleheader. He did his thing *during* the game. Dressed in a somewhat baggy baseball uniform with a big question mark where the number should have been, Patkin was an undeniably funny fellow. His pratfalls and mimicking and well-honed slapstick routines as he took over the coaching duties for the home team delighted the youngsters, and many of their elders, as well. Max was making minor league fans laugh years before anybody had heard of the San Diego Chicken or the Phillie Phanatic. And unlike those baseball comics, Max didn't need to dress up like a bird and wear something funny-looking over his head. Patkin's face was naturally funny.

Anybody who followed minor league baseball over the last half century knew Max Patkin's act. For him, the baseball season was a succession of one-night stands. It was hard work, and lonely work. Max loved it when he was "on"; the bad part was the traveling from one hick town to another, and the long hours staring at the walls in a motel room, waiting to go to the ball park.

Jim Bunning knew Max's routine only too well. He remembered pitching a game as a young pro in Williamsport, Pennsylvania, when Patkin was performing. It was not a pleasant memory. While Max mimicked the first baseman, and sprayed seemingly endless geysers of water out of his mouth, and flopped around in the coaching box, and made wisecracks, Bunning got clobbered. The fans may have thought it was funny; Bunning definitely didn't.

Twenty years had passed, but Jim never forgot. Nor forgave. Oh, sure, he and Max exchanged pleasantries at baseball dinners and such in the years that followed. Patkin, in fact, had come to consider Jim "a friend."

"I used to see him at banquets, at ball parks. I'd see him all the time," Max recalled.

But as Patkin would discover, it was one thing to hobnob with his "friend" Bunning away from the ballpark, quite another once the umpire cried "Play ball!"

"The worst thing in the world is a purist watching a clown or somebody doing something funny while the game is in progress," Patkin discovered.

Poor Max had lots of friends away from the ballpark who became enemies when he donned his working clothes. Eddie Stanky didn't go for his act. Neither did Gene Mauch. Nor Ralph Houk. "Clay Bryant and I were very close," noted Max. "He'd say, 'Max, I don't dig that shit.'"

Still, Patkin was "very unprepared" for Bunning's reaction. "My God, for close to fifteen years I'd go to the New York Baseball Writers dinner," Patkin said. "We'd be there with Ed Mosler [a wealthy businessman who loved baseball and was deeply involved in the U.S. Olympic program, as well]. We'd have a drink and we'd chat. Now Bunning becomes manager of the Reading Phillies and all of a sudden I get a call from [general manager] Jim Bronson."

"Max," Bronson said, "I'm going to have to cancel you. We can't bring you in."

Patkin was nonplussed. He'd been performing annually in Reading for many years—"I bet twenty-five in a row," he said.

"What's the reason you're canceling me?" he asked Bronson. "What'd I do wrong?"

"You didn't do anything wrong," the young general manager assured him. "Jim Bunning doesn't want you to perform. He doesn't want you in the ballpark."

Patkin couldn't believe it. His old buddy Jim? Nah, must be a mistake.

"I said, 'Are you kidding me?'" Max recalled.

"He said, 'No.'"

Patkin wasn't about to give up without a fight. He told Bronson he wanted to speak to Bunning. Bronson told him the Reading Phillies were in West Haven, Connecticut, and he gave Max the number of the motel.

"I called," Patkin remembered. "I got Jim Bunning on the phone. I said, 'Jim, I thought we were friends. What's the reason you canceled me out? I don't understand it.'

"He said, 'Max, do you remember when I was a young pitcher, pitching up in Williamsport?'

"I think I said, 'Vaguely. So what happened?'

"He said, 'Well, I was getting my ass beat that day and I said to myself after I got knocked out of the box I would never let you in my ballpark if I ever managed a ball club.'

"I said, 'Jim, that's cruel. I don't think that's right. I never missed a show in Reading.'"

"He said, 'Well, that's the way it's going to be.'"

But leave it to Max to get the last laugh.

"The funniest thing happened," he said. "I'm booked in Three Rivers for a doubleheader. I'm going to work the second game and Reading's there."

Bunning couldn't make them cancel Patkin in Three Rivers. They'd booked him, they'd advertised him, and they didn't really give a hoot that the visiting manager had bad memories from twenty years before in Williamsport.

"Bunning was burning," said Max, smiling as he recalled the incident. "He lost the first game and then I come out in the second game. He wouldn't talk to me. He wouldn't say hello even. The ballplayers came up to me later on and said, 'Boy, was he burning. When he saw you out on the coaching line and we blew that doubleheader, if he had a gun he would've shot you.' I'm telling you, the ballplayers were laughing inwardly. They hated him. As much as I thought of Bunning as a player, he was not a good manager. Maybe later—but he didn't understand how to handle young ballplayers."

And he certainly didn't know how to handle some guy in a baggy baseball uniform coaching for the opposition and taking pratfalls and mugging while his team was getting massacred. Bob Hope and Jack Benny combined couldn't have made Jim Bunning laugh at a time like that. Poor Max Patkin didn't have a chance.

"Bunning just stood there," recalled Patkin, "and he glared at me. Oh God, those eyes, those steely eyes. The fans were laughing like hell. The home team was winning both games. I felt good because I was going over so good, but when I looked at him . . ."

Max Patkin still laughs when he talks about that night in Three Rivers when he got even with the man who canceled him in Reading.

"It was like revenge in a way," the Clown Prince of Baseball remembered.

Bunning's hard-as-nails approach that first year bothered Larry Rojas, too. The Reading Phillies' coach understood where Bunning was coming from, but he didn't think that gave him license to say some of the things he said.

"He wasn't used to seeing players make those mistakes," Rojas knew. "Before, when he played Double A, you had to be a good ballplayer to get to Double A. Now it was different, but he told everybody they should play like they used to play in his time."

Rojas tried to tell Jim that wasn't possible. Most of these young men weren't capable of playing that well. Bunning didn't want to hear that. Rojas would see him grab that ever-present tape recorder and blast away while the players cringed.

"He would say, 'He can't play a lick!'" Rojas said. "He *couldn't* play, but don't say that in front of the others. Don't say that when seven kids are sitting behind you."

It was a learning experience for the players as well as for Bunning. "They never had a manager so involved in the game before in their lives," Jim said. "They never had anybody scream on the bench, 'Son of a bitch!' when a guy screwed up a ball. I wasn't mad at the guy; I was just upset that we screwed it up."

But the guy didn't know that. In Larry Rojas's view, Bunning went too far one night in West Haven.

"Something happened on the field and he said something I didn't like [to one of the players on the bench]," Rojas recalled. "He said something that was really out of line, I thought. I wasn't used to talking to players that way."

Rojas was so upset that he made up his mind to leave the Reading team and Jim Bunning. He asked the trainer, Ted Zipeto, who doubled as the team's traveling secretary, to get him a plane ticket, which Zipeto did.

"I was ready to go to the airport," Rojas declared. But first, he had to see Bunning and tell him why he was leaving.

"Next day, I went to his room," Rojas said, "and I told him, 'I'm leaving and I'll tell you why.' And we got into it."

Bunning understood. He and Rojas talked it out and the coach decided to stay.

"He wasn't the mean guy people made him to be," Rojas commented. "He was just very direct with his answers. He didn't go around the bushes like most people do. He tell you, 'This is way it is, son. If you do this, you no go to the big leagues.' They were so scared. I tell them, 'This man is a good man. He wants you to be a good ballplayer.' But they didn't want to believe it because he was [so critical] on the bench."

Rojas got an idea. Bunning had been coaching at third base, the way most minor league managers do. Maybe if he spent the entire game in the dugout he'd have an easier time running the game—and get to know some of his players a little better, too.

Rojas was very much like Bunning in one important way: he didn't beat around the bush, either.

"I say, 'Jim, let me coach third base,'" Rojas stated. "'You're a lousy third base coach.' We went to Quebec, I start to coach third base. Everything changes. Now he could teach instead of being at third base. He completely changed. He became a great, great handler of the game. He became what I call a real good manager, a handler of players. He still would take a shot at the kids, but not as much because now he was on the bench with them [when the Phillies were at bat]. He could talk to them when they come off the field. Once he realized they don't play the same way they used to, he became a great teacher, too."

Rojas would listen to Bunning when Jim worked with the pitchers in the bullpen. "I would be the catcher," he remembered, "and just listen to him talk." It was quite an education.

"I think we became very close [after the incident in West Haven]," Rojas said. "That's the thing with Jim. You got to confront him with the truth. Don't go on with no weak stuff. He'll run you out of the clubhouse."

Ask Larry Rojas about Jim Bunning today and he'll tell you, "I feel he should have been the manager for the Phillies." He meant the big Phillies, not the Little Phillies.

"Very few people I respect more than Jim," declared Rojas, who still scouts for the Phillies years after getting a heart transplant. "[Andy] Seminick, that's my idol. He's always going to be. Nobody is going to take his place. But Jim Bunning, I respected what he stood for. He don't want to go around the corner, dress up [the truth] or nothing. This is it. This is the way it is."

With Rojas's help, Bunning got through that first managerial year. He stopped using the tape recorder in the dugout. He toned down his critical remarks to a certain extent. The players responded, finishing a game over .500. By the time the season was over, they had learned quite a bit. So had he.

God's Country

Ideally, a major league baseball team wants to have its top minor league club as geographically close as possible. The advantages are great. Send a player down from the big club, or call one up, and he has a short trip. In addition, the fans in the nearby minor league town are familiar with the big club and likely root for it; they have a special interest in following the progress of the organization's minor league players. So where did the Philadelphia Phillies' Triple A farm club set up shop in 1973? In Eugene, Oregon.

Even if it wasn't a suburb of Philadelphia, it was a lovely place. Eugene was God's country—fresh air, lots of trees and grass, a pleasant college-town atmosphere. It should have been a delightful year for Jim Bunning. He was at the top of the minor league ladder, a manager in the Pacific Coast League (PCL). What's more, the Eugene Emeralds looked to be definite title contenders when they left their training camp in Clearwater, Florida, and jetted west. (One nice thing about Triple A, they *did* use planes for the longer trips. Come to think of it, they had to. The Hawaii Islanders were in the league at the time, and you couldn't go from Eugene to Honolulu by Greyhound.)

But Triple A, as Bunning was to discover, is a difficult place to manage. When the big league club needs help, it usually looks to its Triple A affiliate. And the 1973 Phillies needed plenty of help. They kept raiding Bunning's team until the potential contenders of early April became the dregs of June. Jim reacted the way one would expect—he got more and more upset, more and more frustrated. The daily reports minor league managers are required to file with the home office became more and more sarcastic. One late night, after a particularly grim outing by what now passed as a Triple A ball club, Bunning sent in a report that said, "If anybody cares if we win or lose would you please pick up the telephone."

Some of his reports must have been classics. "I wish I had the recordings [of the reports I called in every night]," he said. "One time, on a trip to Hawaii, I said, 'If there's anybody listening to this tape, *we are terrible*. Does anybody back there care?'"

Farm director Dallas Green cared enough to visit Bunning shortly thereafter to calm him down, try to make him understand the situation. The Phillies' brass didn't really appreciate Bunning's pleas for help. So Jim gritted his teeth and carried on. It wasn't easy. Maybe the bosses back in Philadelphia didn't care how many games the Eugene Emeralds won, but he cared. Managing an also-ran team in the PCL was no way to convince anybody he had what it takes to be a big league manager. Winning consistently was next to impossible when, week after week, the Phillies called up his most productive players. Mike Rogodzinski, a lefthanded-hitting outfielder who was leading the league in runs batted in, was yanked away. Then Bunning lost his closer, Darrell (Bucky) Brandon, and lefty Mike Wallace, who later put together an undefeated season with the Yankees. Righthanded reliever Dave Wallace (no relation), one of those rare souls who enjoyed playing for Bunning in that difficult, early stage of his managerial career, also got the call to join the struggling Phillies. It didn't leave much for the equally struggling Emeralds and their desperate manager.

At best, Triple A is a real challenge. "It's harder than the big leagues by yards because you've got guys coming down and you've got guys going up," Bunning learned. "You've got the constant conflict on the club of who's ready and who's not. When [the parent club] calls for a player, the manager has to make a recommendation."

The player he doesn't recommend is likely "to go in the tank for a month." So, as Bunning discovered, you not only lost the guy who went up but in effect you also lost the guy who's pouting because he didn't go up.

"They don't want an everyday player, they want a good bat," Bunning said of one such call. "So Mike Rogodzinski goes to the big leagues from the Eugene club. His going leaves a hole in the Eugene club you could drive a truck through. That's just the way Triple A is. You first get there, you don't realize that. You think you'd like to win. Rogo went up and did one hell of a job [as a Phillies pinch hitter]."

Bunning was glad for Rogodzinski, a player who always hustled, always did his best for Bunning. But Jim missed him and all the others who joined the Phillies in midseason, leaving the Eugene cupboard bare. The season that began with such promise deteriorated into an awful mess for the intense second-year manager. It was, he declared, "the total height of my frustration."

As painful as it was, Bunning did learn a few helpful lessons along the way. There was the day outfielder Scott Reid walked into the manager's office during a road trip and said his wife was about to have their first child and he'd like to go home to be with her.

Reid couldn't have been sure how his hard-nosed boss would react to that request. Jim needed his bat in the lineup. But Bunning, after all, knew what it was to be a father.

"I said, 'Listen, Scotty, you do what you have to do,'" Bunning recalled. "I said, 'I'm not going to tell you to stay with the club. You go to Eugene and be with her.' Well, the baby died, and I was so glad we had talked and he had made the decision to go and I hadn't prevented him from doing that. That would have been a horrible experience. So I learned a lot of things on the job."

"We were on the road in Albuquerque when I went to him and asked him if I could go home," Reid commented. "That was my last year as a player. Jim was very patient with me coming back. He said, 'When you're ready . . .'"

That, of course, was a special situation. Jim Bunning was still tough on his players. It didn't take Ted Zipeto, the trainer, long to find that out.

"We were in Albuquerque," he recalled. "I think we got beat. We always got beat. We're leaving in the morning and I was up at the desk, telling them to leave a call for everybody at 6:30 or 7 A.M., whatever it was, and he heard me. He said, 'What the hell are you doing?' I said, 'I was just leaving wakeup calls. . . .' He said, 'You want to run the club? Don't leave a wakeup call for anybody. They either make it or they don't make it.'"

On another occasion, Zipeto stood up in the front of the bus when it was about to leave the hotel in Spokane, Washington, for the ball park. "He said, 'What are you doing?'" Zipeto related. "'I'm counting heads,' I told him. 'Sit down,' he said. 'When it's 5 o'clock by my watch, we'll leave. You're on the bus. I'm on the bus. We'll leave."

Even so, Bunning was beginning to learn how to deal with his players. Slowly, surely he improved his relationship with most of them. There still would be growing pains in that area, but little by little he was mastering his job.

If there was one thing Bunning didn't need in the 1973 season it was another chance to watch his old friend Max Patkin at work. It was no longer necessary for Jim to go back twenty years for reasons; he merely had to think back to the previous summer in Three Rivers. But sure enough, Eugene's general manager, John Carbray, booked Patkin.

"Bunning heard that I was going to perform and he said he wasn't going to let me in the ball park," Patkin remembered. "The general manager called Dallas Green, who was the farm director by then. He said, 'Dallas, if Bunning doesn't let Max Patkin in my ball park I'm going to take all his clothes and I'm going to throw them out in the street.' True story. The general manager told me this, honest to God. Anyhow, Dallas had to get on the phone and talk to Bunning, and Bunning said all right. What could he do?"

One thing he could do was tell Patkin, who usually dressed with the home team, that he'd have to find somewhere else to change into that baggy uniform with the question mark on the back.

"He wouldn't let me in the clubhouse," Max pointed out. "He says, 'You ain't dressing in my clubhouse.' Jim actually chased me out. I dressed with the visiting team. It was one of the few times in my career that I ever dressed with the visiting club. I like to dress with the home team. My act is with them. I get friendly with them."

At least he attempts to get friendly with them. Now all Max had to do was walk up to Bunning before the game and make the necessary arrangements.

"I said, 'Jim, you know my act; I have to coach,'" Patkin recalled.

Jim knew his act all right. That was the trouble. But Max pressed on. And Bunning actually agreed to let Max coach for the two innings his act required. It was one of the biggest upsets of the Pacific Coast League season.

"There are certain managers who won't let me go to third," Patkin said. "Especially the purists."

Much to Max Patkin's surprise, James Paul Bunning, the purest of the pure, let him coach at third base that night.

If Max had waved one of Bunning's runners home on a suicide dash to the plate in a tight game, we can safely assume that he never would have been allowed to coach in a Jim Bunning–managed game for the rest of his life. Heck, he might not have made it out of the coaching box in one piece. But Max, who says in all modesty "I got to be a pretty good coach," came through the test with flying colors.

"It was a tight ball game, nothing to nothing," Max recalled. "Fourth inning, I go over to third base. There was a man on second base, and there was a line shot to the outfield. I'll be a son of a bitch if I don't send the guy in; I mean, there's one out. I got to hold the guy up because the outfielder gets it on one bounce. But I sent him in. He was safe at the plate; the throw was a little off line. They won the ball game, 1-0."

If they had a "coach of the game award" Max Patkin would have won it.

"After the game a photographer calls me over to the dugout and he says, 'Jim, will you pose with Max Patkin?'" Max said. "Jim says, 'Yeah, I'll do it.'"

The picture was taken. Bunning got a copy of it, had the thing framed, and kept it on the desk in his office for the rest of his managerial career. As he told Patkin, "Once in a while I look at that picture and I tell myself not to take myself so seriously."

Was Bunning getting soft in his old age? Not so some of his players could notice.

"A lot of guys were intimidated by him," noted Dave Wallace, who definitely was not intimidated by Bunning.

Dave, now the assistant to the general manager of the New York Mets after serving several years as pitching coach for the Los Angeles Dodgers, "loved playing for him" and credits much of his pitching expertise to the time he spent with Jim. Unlike most of his teammates, Dave was never afraid to tell Jim Bunning what was on his mind.

Dave remembers when the Eugene Emeralds were in Tucson, about to board the team bus for the ride to the ball park. "Bob Spence and Andy Thornton and Joe Lis were there, a whole bunch of veteran guys," said Dave, who was just in his second year of Triple A.

"It was 105 degrees, something like that. Guys are jabbering in the back of the bus," recalled Wallace. "They're going, 'You ask him.' 'No, you ask him.' I said, 'What are you guys talking about?' They said, 'It's so hot here, we wanted to know if we could wear sandals and shorts—change the dress code.'"

A reasonable request, given the conditions. And Dave had a reasonable suggestion.

"Why don't you just ask him?" he said.

Not one of those veterans was brave enough to do it, so Wallace hollered up to the front of the bus, "Hey, Jim, these guys want to know if we can wear shorts and sandals."

To which Bunning promptly responded, "Absolutely not."

"OK, thanks," said Dave, who scored major points with his teammates for sheer bravery, even if they didn't get to wear sandals and shorts.

There was another incident in Tucson that sticks in Wallace's mind. The Emeralds were clinging to a two-run lead. The home team had runners on second and third with two out. Dan Ford, a righthanded hitter, was facing the righthanded Wallace. There was a lefthanded batter on deck, so Bunning had lefty Mac Scarce throwing in the bullpen.

"I get Ford out, we win the ball game," Wallace said. "So I throw him a slider. I made a good pitch in my mind. He reaches out, hits a little bloop fly ball over the first baseman's head. It lands fair by a couple of feet, both runs score, and here goes Ford to second base. Jim comes out to the mound; he's going to bring in Mac Scarce. I said, 'Son of a bitch, I made a good pitch.' He goes, 'Good pitch, my ass. That's a two-run double, young man, in case you didn't realize it.' I said, 'OK, here's the ball,' and walked away. He was something."

Dave Wallace was something, too, frequently saying things to Bunning that no other player would dare say. As if things weren't bad enough for Bunning in 1973, that happened to be the year Bob Gibson of the St. Louis Cardinals passed him for the number-two spot, behind Walter Johnson, on the all-time career strikeout list.

The night it happened, Gibson's feat was the main topic of conversation in the Eugene clubhouse. Naturally, all talk ceased when Bunning came within earshot.

The following night, however, Wallace couldn't resist needling his favorite manager. "Well, Jim," he said in a solemn voice, "you're number three."

You could have heard a pin drop.

"What's wrong?" Dave asked his shocked teammates. "He's a human being, isn't he?"

From the looks on their faces, Wallace realized very few of them had considered that possibility.

In all honesty, some of the things Bunning did as a manager must have seemed inhuman to his players. Bed checks, for example. Bunning expected his players to get their beauty sleep on the road. No carousing until the wee hours, if he could help it. The fact is, he couldn't always help it. But he tried.

Bed checks were standard operating procedure during Jim Bunning's reign. Those who missed the curfew were fined $100, which Bunning sent to the Fred Hutchinson Cancer Fund. Players more charitably inclined, otherwise known as second-time offenders, had the privilege of donating $200 to the cancer fund. For some players, especially the younger ones, that was pretty stiff. But they couldn't say they weren't warned most of the time.

On a typical night when Bunning planned to check the rooms, he, or his coach, would say something like "Curfew is 1 A.M. and it would be a good idea to be in on time." To anybody paying attention, the meaning was clear.

The Emeralds were in Honolulu, and things were not going well. Which is to say, they weren't going well on the field. Off the field, Bunning suspected, they were going too well. Exactly what occurred on this particular night, following the latest Emeralds' loss, depends on who is telling the story. This much is certain: Bunning decided it was a good night to collect money for the cancer fund.

"We were eating, the three of us [Bunning, Coach Lee Elia, and the trainer, Ted Zipeto]," Zipeto said. "Jim always called Lee 'Coachie'; that ticked Lee off. Jim says, 'Coachie, how many guys do you think'll be out tonight?' 'Aw,' Lee says, 'they'll all be in.'"

It was a good try by Elia, but Bunning wasn't buying that argument.

"We're going to check," he said.

As Zipeto remembered it, Elia replied, "'Geez, you don't check in Hawaii.'"

Wrong.

Elia hated those bed-checking nights because he would have to make the rounds with Bunning, knocking on doors to see who was there, and who wasn't. "He'd hit one door and I'd hit the next," Elia said.

They decided to start at the top floor and work their way down, so at ten minutes past one Bunning and his coach took the elevator to the top floor. The elevator stopped, the door opened . . . and there was pitcher Larry Christenson. But let Elia tell it.

"He was all decked out, dressed like he was going out for the evening," recalled Lee. "Jim says, 'Where are you going, young man?' [Christenson] says, 'Well, I just got in about 15 minutes ago and the light on my phone was on. My laundry's downstairs. I'm going down to get it.' It was a great line."

Elia, you may derive from that statement, had a strong hunch Christenson was fibbing.

"Jim says, 'How much do you think your laundry's going to be?' 'LC' says, 'About $15.' Jim says, 'It's going to be $115.'"

To Elia, that was the funniest of the curfew episodes. The idea of Larry Christenson standing there, waiting for the elevator at 1:10 A.M., wearing his Sunday best, and claiming he was going down to get his laundry still makes him laugh. It doesn't matter that Bunning's memory of the incident is a little different. The way he recollects it, the young pitcher—a tall, good-looking bachelor at the time—was wearing swim trunks. Christenson, for his part, claimed he was "barefooted, wearing cutoffs, and a tank top shirt."

Elia insisted his version was correct; since it's the most amusing, let's accept it, giving Christenson full credit for thinking up that preposterous laundry story on the spur of the moment. In the interest of fairness, however, it should be noted that twenty-four years after the fact, when Christenson visited with Bunning in Cooperstown, just before the Hall of Fame induction ceremonies, he insisted his original story was correct. "Larry told me, 'I was really going to get my laundry,'" Bunning reported. "I said, 'Sure you were, Larry.'"

So Christenson never did get back that $100. Even so, the man who went on to become a solid big league pitcher—and a key member of the 1980 world championship Phillies—never let that $100 "laundry bill" color his opinion of Jim Bunning. Like so many of his former players, Christenson became a good friend, as evidenced by his decision to attend his former manager's induction.

Elia wasn't the only member of the Eugene Emeralds' peerless bed-checking duo to find some humor in the team's trials and tribulations. Even Bunning had to crack a smile once in a while.

Alan Bannister, an All-American shortstop from Arizona State who became the Phillies' number-one draft pick, loved to describe one play that perhaps best typified the plight of the Emeralds.

Fundamental mistakes were driving Bunning wild. When one of his outfielders missed the cutoff man one night, Jim had about all he could take. Next time it happens, he told his intrepid warriors, there will be an automatic $50 fine.

So the Ems took the field the next night determined not to miss another cutoff man. "There was a pop fly to short right field," Bannister recalled. "The second baseman, Rich Severson, ran back. The right fielder, Keith Lampard, ran in."

The ball dropped between them. It rolled to the wall with both men in hot pursuit. Lampard got there first in a near photo finish. He grabbed the ball and, with visions of that $50 fine dancing in his head, fired it to the cutoff man. Unfortunately, the cutoff man, Severson, was standing just a few feet away.

"[Lampard] threw it so hard he knocked him down," Alan Bannister recalled.

"Well," said Lampard upon returning to the dugout, "I didn't miss him."

According to Bannister, Bunning couldn't hold it in. "He almost fell down laughing," Alan said.

This was a club that needed all the laughs it could get. With that in mind, as well as a bit of revenge, a husky young man named Pete Koegel came up with a scheme to get even with Bunning after the manager nailed him for breaking curfew on the night the Fred Hutchinson Cancer Fund struck it rich in Hawaii.

"The toughest thing I ever did for Jim Bunning was collect the damn fine money," Lee Elia declared. And after the Honolulu "raid" there was a lot of collecting to do. Elia didn't need any more aggravation.

"Koegel came in," Lee remembered. "He had $200 in pennies. He was going to pour it on Jim's desk. I said, 'Don't do it. Please, don't do it. I'll be here all night picking them up.'"

One look at Elia's desperate face, his pleading eyes, and Koegel backed off, returned the pennies to the bank and agreed to pay his fine in the traditional way. We can only guess what Bunning would have done if Koegel had actually dumped 20,000 pennies on the manager's desk, and how long it would have taken Elia to pick them up after the leader of the Emeralds had sent them flying across the room.

The nice thing about being part of a bad minor league team—even one that finishes fifteen games under .500—is that there are always things to laugh about in later years. One incident that occurred in Honolulu in '73 was no laughing matter, however.

"It was the second trip to Hawaii," Bunning recalled, "the trip I collected $3,200 for the Fred Hutchinson Cancer Fund."

Elia and trainer Ted Zipeto had just sat down to eat lunch when catcher Harry Safewright came running over, shouting.

"He hollers to me, 'Chico's drowning, Chico's drowning,'" Zipeto said.

"Chico" was outfielder Chico Vaughns. A nice, relaxed lunch became a frenzied dash back to the hotel. When they arrived they saw Bunning walking out the door on the way to the hospital. Zipeto contacted Dr. Samuel Yee, the Hawaii Islanders' team doctor, who immediately dropped everything and went to the Queens Medical Center, where Vaughns had been taken. "I think he saved Chico's life by getting a pulmonary man as soon as they pumped him out," Zipeto said.

"I think Safewright was the guy who pulled him out of the water," Bunning said. "They were surfing and Chico fell off the board. A wave caught him and flipped him, and they couldn't find him. He never came up."

The way Zipeto heard it, "A bunch of Hawaiians pulled him out."

They knew the strong, tricky currents that had carried Vaughns a considerable distance underwater and were able to figure out approximately where he was. They pumped out his lungs on the beach, then took him to the hospital. It was touch-and-go for a while.

"This was like noon," Zipeto recalled. "Finally the doctor came and got me out of the dugout around the third or fourth inning. He said, 'I think he's going to make it.'"

The Ems left two days later for Salt Lake City. Vaughns remained in Hawaii far another ten days or so, his season over. Still, it could have been much worse, as Zipeto remembered one newspaper reporting.

"The *Portland Oregonian* had a headline, 'Eugene Emeralds Ballplayer Drowns on Waikiki,'" Zipeto noted. "They had him dead. So he was *that* close."

On a more pleasant note, 1973 will be remembered as the year Jim Bunning mellowed somewhat in his approach to managing. How else can you explain lefthander George Brunet breaking curfew one night and talking his way out of the $100 fine? Which is another story Lee Elia loves to tell.

Brunet was a rather portly veteran of many big league campaigns. He was nearing the end of the line when he joined Bunning's downtrodden Emeralds, where he quickly became one of Jim's most reliable pitchers.

Brunet was one of the players marked absent in the Great Hawaii Bed-Check Caper. When Elia banged on his door, there was no answer. Next day, when the fines were announced, Brunet protested vehemently, insisting he was in his room all the while, sound asleep, oblivious to Elia's knocking.

Elia, wise to such tricks, would have none of it. "Don't tell me that," he told the veteran pitcher. "I took the bed check myself, and I was pounding on your door."

Brunet had an explanation.

"How the hell do I tell Jim Bunning that I was blown away on margaritas and I was laying on my bed and I was paralyzed and I couldn't get to the door?" he asked Elia. "But I was in my room."

Finally, Elia weakened. It could have happened the way Brunet said it did. The coach told him he would see what he could do.

A man of his word, Elia headed for Bunning's room and proceeded to regale his boss with Brunet's tale of drunken woe.

"I said, 'Jim, the guy was in his room. He wouldn't lie to me. I've known him for a long time.'" Et cetera. Et cetera.

Bunning held firm for a couple of weeks, but Elia kept after him. The poor guy was just back from the Mexican League, Lee told him. He needed the money.

Finally, Bunning relented. "All right," he told Elia, "take the $100 out of the fund and give it back to him."

A very pleased Lee Elia returned the fine to George Brunet, who thanked him profusely. Elia, a most compassionate fellow, felt very good about his role in seeing that justice was served. Then came the final day of the 1973 Pacific Coast League season.

"We're leaving," Elia said. "Everybody's saying goodbye. Brunet gets in his car and he pulls away, and he calls out the window, 'Hey, Lee, I wasn't in my room. Screw Bunning.'"

For Jim Bunning, it was that kind of year.

Jim Bunning, Mud Hen

The man and the name didn't fit. Jim Bunning of the Detroit Tigers had a nice ring to it. Jim Bunning of the Philadelphia Phillies sounded just great. Jim Bunning of the American or National League All-Stars was terrific. But not Jim Bunning of the Toledo Mud Hens. Still, when a man is as determined as Bunning was to become a big league manager, he'll put up with just about anything—even two summers wearing a baseball uniform with the words "Mud Hens" plastered across the front. Pitcher Dick Ruthven felt so strongly about the name that he refused to tell anybody he was a Mud Hen. If someone, say, at a hotel or an airport asked Ruthven what team he played for, Dick would make up a name or deny he was a baseball player, anything to spare him from telling the awful truth. "I'll be damned if I'm going to admit I'm a Mud Hen," he would say after such incidents.

Bunning didn't go that far. If pressed, he would admit the sobering truth; yes, he was a Mud Hen, through and through. As such, he spent a good deal of time at the Lucas County Recreation Center in Maumee, Ohio, where the Toledo club played its home games in front of a select gathering of curiosity seekers. The ball park was a short distance from the Ohio Turnpike and a fairly long distance from downtown Toledo, which probably explained, in part, why so few Toledo residents bothered to make the trip. From downtown Toledo it was almost as easy to drive to Tiger Stadium in Detroit.

One night the Mud Hens had a big promotion scheduled. Naturally, the rain clouds moved in. With no word from the front office, the Toledo players turned on the clubhouse radio for the latest weather report. Was the game still on, or was it off? The station that carried the Mud Hen games figured to be the first to know, so the players fiddled around with the radio, trying to pick it up. That wasn't as easy as it sounds. The station kept fading out. Apparently its signal barely reached Maumee.

"That's what the minor leagues are all about," Dick Ruthven said. "You have to find out on the radio whether the game's rained out or not, but you've got to be out of town to hear the station."

Adding to Bunning's woes in Toledo was a general manager he couldn't stand, and who couldn't stand him. Charley Senger and Jim Bunning clashed from the start, and it kept getting worse. "I just ignored him," said Jim. "That's what made him so upset." Finally, Senger informed the local media that he planned to fire the manager at the end of the season. Since Jim was known nationally, the story hit the wires and went coast to coast. Senger may have *thought* he was going to give Bunning the boot, but it was up to the parent organization in Philadelphia to make that decision, and the Phillies stood behind their embattled Triple A manager.

"He [Senger] called and asked for me," remembered Paul Owens, who had taken over the general manager's job with the Phillies by then. "Dallas [farm director Dallas Green] was around, but he wanted to talk to me."

Owens was annoyed. Green was in charge of the minor league operation. If Senger had something on his mind, Green was the man he should call. But Owens returned the call with the intention of making that perfectly clear to this minor league general manager he barely knew.

"He said, 'I don't know how you people operate,'" Owens recalled. "He told me, 'I could call [Tigers' general manager] Jim Campbell direct' and blah-blah-blah."

Owens listened, getting more and more annoyed.

"Finally he said, 'I want to talk to you about the manager. I'm not happy with the manager.' I said, 'You're not? You might be very fortunate. You might have a future Hall of Famer.' 'Well,' he said, 'that may be so, but my board and I . . .'"

About there, Owens said, he cut him off. "I told him, 'Dallas Green is in his office. Why don't you go through him first? We don't operate that way in Philadelphia.' 'Well,' he said, 'I thought I'd go right to the top.' 'You have,' I said, 'and you've got a hell of a manager and as far as I'm concerned there aren't going to be any changes.'"

Senger's complaints were mostly "little stuff," Owens said. "He told me Bunning wasn't cooperative. I said, 'Is he happy with you?' He said, 'I don't believe so.' 'Well,' I said, 'there'll be no change as far as I'm concerned, and I'm sure Mr. Green will tell you the same thing.'"

According to Paul Owens, that's how the conversation ended. Charley Senger wasn't about to tell the Phillies whom to hire as their Triple A manager. After two years in Toledo, the Phillies would solve the problem by moving their number-one minor league team from Toledo to Oklahoma City, from the International League to the American Association. For now, Bunning would manage the Toledo Mud Hens and Charley Senger be damned.

"It got tense with the general manager to the point he wasn't even allowed in the clubhouse," recalled Scott Reid, Bunning's coach his second season in Toledo.

Bunning had phoned Reid over the winter to tell Scott he wanted him to be his Triple A coach. Reid readily agreed. It was a bumpy ride for the young coach, but overall a worthwhile experience.

They lockered in the same room in the Toledo clubhouse at home, and they got along just fine. On the road, they'd usually eat together, and often wind up in a hotel room discussing that night's game.

"We had sessions," Reid said. "I remember one that went well into the night, just the two of us. 'Scott,' he'd say, 'what do you think? What's going on?'"

Reid would pull no punches. "I had no trouble talking to him," he said.

Scott couldn't accept the way some of the players—especially the older ones—were acting. But he couldn't accept some of the things Bunning was doing, either.

"I said, 'Jim, there are times you're very intimidating with some of the actions that you do,' and he would agree. But he'd never say, 'I'm going to change.' I could see that he'd listen to me, though, and he'd understand it. He was working very hard at becoming a manager.

"I'd walk out of these sessions with a pretty good feeling. I thought, 'Well, maybe he's going to try something different,' And I'll be damned, the next day he was—Boom!—just the same.

"He would do so many good things [in his relations with the players]. He really did care for the guys. He tried to make them better within his expertise. And then all of a sudden he'd do one thing—just the way he'd react, or treat them or stare at them or make a sarcastic remark—and that would destroy everything he'd done, all the good things. I'd hear it and go, 'Oh shit, why did he do that?'

"I left there and told people I felt he would have been a better manager at the big league level. Later on, as I was scouting, that's when I heard players were having less problems with him. Maybe he mellowed. I know this: he's a guy I'm glad I had the experience of being around for a part of my life. There was a very good man there. It's turned out better that he didn't become a big league manager. [Some players] weren't ready to make the adjustment to Jim Bunning, and he definitely wasn't ready to make the adjustment to them."

The International League left a lot to be desired in the early 1970s. Some of the ball parks weren't Triple A caliber. The traveling was often less than first-rate.

"When I was in the International League as a player we never rode a bus," Bunning said.

Now there were frequent bus trips. It was like being in the Eastern League all over again. The trip from Rochester to Toledo was a dilly. Pawtucket, Rhode Island, to Toledo was no bargain. Only when the Mud Hens took the southern tour, playing in Tidewater (Norfolk, Va.) and Richmond, did they take to the air. The International League has several fine ball parks now. Not then. During Bunning's two-year managerial stay in Toledo, it was far and away the worst of the Triple A leagues. McCoy Stadium in Pawtucket, the home of the Red Sox's top farm club, was a disaster area then. Now that the stadium has been significantly upgraded, it's a good place to watch a ball game.

When Bunning's Mud Hens played there the visiting clubhouse was a disgrace. It was small and it was borderline filthy, the odor being enough to send a person outside, gasping for fresh air. On Bunning's first trip, a man, nicely dressed in slacks and a sports jacket, walked into the Toledo dugout while the game was in progress. Jim stared at him—the same withering stare that melted the toughest of veteran Triple A players—but the guy ignored him, going over to the water cooler and examining it for a while. Then he abruptly did an about-face and headed for the visiting clubhouse. Bunning couldn't believe his eyes.

He dispatched a member of the traveling party to follow this character into the clubhouse and make certain he didn't walk off with anything. It turned out that the man was from the local board of health. There had been complaints—all completely justified, no doubt—about the visiting clubhouse at McCoy Stadium. He was on the scene to conduct an investigation. The mere fact that a baseball game was in progress didn't deter our friend from his appointed rounds.

McCoy Stadium definitely wasn't Bunning's favorite ball park. Even at what should have been the best of times, things had a way of going wrong. For example, the Mud Hens had the bases loaded one cold, damp evening. Shortstop Ron Clark sent a long fly ball down the left field line. If it stayed fair, the Mud Hens would have four badly needed runs. If it hooked foul, they'd have nothing except a strike on the batter.

As luck would have it, Bunning was coaching at third that inning. At the crack of the bat, he turned and watched Clark's drive head toward the fence, and the foul pole. Jim twisted and turned, edging forward in an attempt to supply the body English that might make the difference. And, believe it or not, the ball stayed fair, soaring over the fence for a grand slam. Bunning thrust out his arms in jubilation, and then let out a bloodcurdling yell.

Mike Rogodzinski, who was on second base, had also been watching the flight of Clark's home run. He was just rounding third as the ball vanished into the night, and, his attention on the left field fence, Rogodzinski ran into Bunning, spiking him in the foot.

As much as Bunning liked Rogodzinski and the way he played, he had to fear for his safety whether Mike was running the bases or at the plate. One night in Toledo, Bunning was feeding baseballs into the pitching machine and Rogodzinski was taking batting practice. The lefthanded hitter drove a scorcher right back to the mound, where a protective screen was set up to protect Bunning. Some protection! The ball shot through the mesh and nailed Bunning in the chest. "He kind of waddled back and went, 'Uh-h-h,'" Rogodzinski recalled. But he recovered.

"One time in Syracuse, I lined a ball in the dugout," Rogodzinski said. "Jim ducked, put his arm up, and the ball hit his watch and broke his watch band. I stood there watching it slide down his arm."

Such were the adventures of Jim Bunning, Mud Hen manager. That he kept going told you how determined he was to make himself into a big league manager. He was driven to be the best manager he could be, just as he had been driven to be the best pitcher he could be.

"I've committed myself to it," he said during that first season in Toledo, explaining why he had no intention of quitting. "I'm going to be a big league manager. Dallas [Green] has given me a chance to manage. Somebody else has to believe I can manage. When somebody else does, I'll get my chance."

The truth was, a lot of people were beginning to believe that Jim Bunning could manage. Elia believed it. To this day, he thinks Bunning would have made an outstanding major league manager. A growing number of players were starting to believe it, too. High on that list was reliever Dave Wallace, who appreciated Bunning's tell-it-like-it-is approach.

"I was kind of buried in a Triple A situation," Wallace recalled. "Jim sat me down in his room and he said, 'Young man, you know how I feel about you. We're trying to trade you, but nobody wants you.' He says, 'You're a marginal player. You can pitch in the major leagues, but they [the Phillies] are going to ask for a top-flight player for you, and, of course, nobody's going to give one to them . . . so I'm just telling you up front, that's what's going on.'"

Some players would have resented a manager who told them, "Nobody wants you." Dave Wallace was glad that Bunning leveled with him.

"No," he remembered, "I didn't resent it, at all, because somebody finally spoke the truth. So much bull goes on in the game, especially when you're talking to players. I think, with players, you can look them in the eye and say, 'Hey, this is what we feel. You have a chance to be a pitcher, but these are your shortcomings. Once they learn that you are candid, they respect you more."

The way Wallace respected—and still respects—Jim Bunning.

"I believe this," Dave said, "I would not be where I am today without having played four years for Jim Bunning. There's no doubt in my mind."

Wallace cherished his relationship with Bunning and his ability to talk to him and kid with him. "Guys would say, 'How the hell can you talk to him that way?'" Dave remembered.

One day the Mud Hens flew to Tidewater, and the team was in the baggage claim area waiting for their luggage to arrive. As fate would have it, Bunning and Wallace were the last two left. The Norfolk airport had just been remodeled. Luggage was now being delivered on a conveyer belt, something new at the time.

Finally, the last two bags showed up. As they were coming around on the conveyer belt, Bunning turned to Wallace and remarked about the newfangled invention and what a good idea it was.

"He goes, 'This is pretty inventive . . . uh, invent . . . uh,'" Wallace said, "and I go, 'You mean innovative, Jim?' and I grabbed my bag and I walked away. And I thought, 'I got him.' And I looked back and he gave me that look of his."

In retrospect, you wonder how Bunning kept his sanity during some of those minor league games. "There was a runner on third base in Rochester one time," Wallace remembered. "Kniff [lefty Chuck Kniffin] was pitching. You know Kniff; he's nervous, anyway."

Doubly so when Jim Bunning was in the dugout, watching every move, every pitch.

"Anyway, their best hitter is up," said Wallace, "and Bunning gives the order to put this guy on base."

Kniffin made sure the batter couldn't reach the first intentional ball. He heaved it up against the screen. The runner at third trotted home.

Jim was direct with everybody, not just Dave Wallace. Ed Molush another righthanded reliever with the Mud Hens, remembers the day Jim Bunning, his idol as a kid, watched him throw in spring training.

"I thought I had a decent slider coming out of college," Molush said. "Then he stood behind me one day and he said, 'Kid, that's a pretty good slider you've got.' I was beaming. I didn't know the kind of sarcasm Jim Bunning had in him. His next comment was, 'You want to get out of 'A' ball?' I said, 'Sure.'"

And with that, Bunning showed Molush how to throw a *real* slider. He showed him a lot of things.

"He taught me about counts, how to think about where the hitter was in the lineup," Molush said. "He told me, 'You ought to be able to estimate by how he swings on any one pitch what kind of swing the guy has. Is he a big-swinging guy? Is he going to hit an inside pitch?' He always said, 'If you don't pitch inside you're as good today as you're ever going to be.'"

"I teach my college players the same thing," added Molush, who uses much of what Jim Bunning taught him in his capacity as head baseball coach at Haverford College in Pennsylvania.

"I loved playing for him," he said. "I think the guys that were really honest about themselves and didn't want to blame somebody else for something that didn't go their way were the kind of guys that liked Jim. He was tough. He was hard-nosed. He always used to say, 'I'm not your father, so don't expect me to be that way.' He could be kind of nasty with people, but I didn't mind it. I think he respected me because he knew I was a competitor. I think those kinds of guys were the guys he really liked. He liked Dave Wallace. He liked Alan Bannister. He liked [lefthander] Larry Kiser. I was never afraid of him. I always wanted to be closer to him, and I couldn't get there. Dave got real close. I was always a little jealous of Dave's relationship with him. I'd see the two of them talking . . ."

There was plenty to talk about in the Toledo years. And, yes, there were plenty of bed checks. That never changed.

Ted Zipeto, Jim's trainer throughout his five minor league managerial seasons and a big Bunning booster, remembers a night when Jim decided to check up on his merry band of warriors in Syracuse. The timing threatened to spoil things for Bunning's trainer and coach, who had made postgame plans.

Zipeto, who lived in Syracuse, invited Lee Elia to spend the night at his home, meet some of his friends, and have a nice, home-cooked breakfast the next morning. News of the bed check was not welcome. But in this business, a man learns to adjust.

"The game's over about a quarter after ten," Elia noted. "I went with [Zipeto], met a few of his buddies, and we came back to the hotel about a quarter to one. I met Jim in the lobby and we took our bed check. No problems. Everybody was in. About 1:30 I told Jim I was going back over to [Zipeto's] house."

Elia went downstairs and hopped in the trainer's waiting car. Zipeto just sat there. "What are you doing?" wondered Elia. "Let's go."

"Just wait a minute," the trainer said. "Just wait and look."

So they sat there for a few minutes and then, one by one, the players appeared. Curfew check completed, they felt safe in going out. "About seven or eight of them," said Elia, who had the decency not to break the news to Jim.

Among the veterans who came down from the big leagues to pitch for Bunning's Mud Hens was George Culver, who once pitched a no-hitter against the Phillies in Connie Mack Stadium. Culver enjoyed having a good time and wasn't about to let Bunning's curfews spoil that. He and Ron Clark were rooming together.

"Both single, both ex-big leaguers, we'd go out quite a bit," Culver said.

So they decided to do the town one night after a game in Syracuse.

"We met these two girls," Culver recalled. "We told them we had a curfew, but if they'd go back to the room with us we'd go out after 1:00."

They went back to the hotel with Culver and Clark as the one o'clock curfew approached, making it with a couple of minutes to spare.

"We waited and waited," said Culver. "He never knocked on the door. About 1:30, we go out."

Next day, Bunning had a team meeting, at which he reeled off the names of the Mud Hens who missed the 1 A.M. curfew. Culver and Clark made the $100 list. Naturally, they protested, swearing they were in the room at the appointed time. Their cries of anguish fell on deaf ears.

"Bunning told us, 'I'm on the same floor. I started early with you guys.'"

Jim's conscience was clear. He may have given them a raw deal by checking on them at 12:50 instead of 1:00, but he must have had a pretty good idea that they'd pulled a fast one or two in the course of the summer. Besides, as former big leaguers they could afford to donate $100 apiece to a worthy cause.

"We fooled him a few times," Culver readily admitted. "We had girls hiding behind shower curtains, in closets. As many times as I was out after curfew, that was just the second time I was caught—and I was in when I was supposed to be!"

One player who wasn't about to let Jim Bunning intimidate him was John Stearns, sometimes known as "Bad Dude" because of his football-playing heroics at the University of Colorado. A catcher who became an All-Star with the Mets, Stearns was a number-one Phillies' draft choice who never quite forgave the club for trading him. He and Bunning had some differences of opinion at times, but Jim loved the way Stearns played the game and was positive, almost from the day he first saw him, that John was headed for big league stardom.

When Stearns joined Bunning's Mud Hens he was fresh out of 'A' ball. He was simply too good for the league, so the Phillies jumped him to Triple A.

"We're in Rochester," recalled Dave Wallace, "and he's catching as only Dude can do. Now he's in the on-deck circle; the leadoff hitter is up there. The count's two balls and one strike. Jim's in the dugout and I'm standing next to him. Stearns turns around and he goes, 'Hey, Bunsie, if he gets on, will I hit-and-run?' Jim just goes, 'I'll let you know.'"

Not even Dave Wallace called Jim Bunning "Bunsie." But that was John Stearns. If you were playing a ball game, or fighting a war, you wanted him on your side.

Stearns didn't pick a very good day to arrive in Toledo. Mud Hen first baseman Dane Iorg had been fighting a slump, and Bunning made a comment to a reporter that became headlines in the local paper. "Iorg," he remarked, "was sinking faster than the *Titanic*."

Iorg was a soft-spoken young man whose manner may have led Bunning to believe he lacked the motivation to become a productive big leaguer. If so, Bunning was wrong. Iorg was a fine hitter, and he went on to help the Cardinals, and then the Royals, win World Series by delivering key hits.

In his early years in the Phillies' farm system, however, Iorg had a rough time dealing with Bunning. He came to dislike him so intensely for a while that he wrote a letter to the Phillies at the close of Bunning's second season in Toledo, stating that he could never play for Bunning again. After a lot of thought, however, Iorg made up his mind to return the following season, and he enjoyed an outstanding year. By the time it ended, Iorg was solidly in Bunning's corner.

But the day Jim made the crack about "the *Titanic*," Iorg was understandably hurt. That's when outfielder Jay Johnstone, a specialist in hitting line drives and dreaming up practical jokes, decided to have some fun.

"He dressed up in a wet suit, got a bat, came out, straddled the [rolled up] tarp, and used his bat like an oar while we were stretching [before the game]," Stearns remembered. "He's got his baseball cap turned around and he's 'rowing,' going, 'Dane . . . Dane . . .'"

For Stearns, it was quite an introduction to baseball, Triple A style.

"I thought, 'You've got to be kidding me,'" he said. "It was the funniest thing I'd ever seen. But Jim was not laughing."

Bunning was not a very good audience for Jay Johnstone's high jinks. He'd learned to coexist with Max Patkin when necessary, but he didn't appreciate having one of his players doubling as a clown, too. It was inevitable that Jay and Jim would have a major clash.

"Paul Owens signed me and he said, 'We don't have any room for you on the [big league] roster right now; why don't you go to Toledo?'" Johnstone recalled. "I had never met Jim Bunning before. I'd heard about him. Obviously, I knew about his abilities as a pitcher. But I didn't know anything about the man."

It didn't take long for Johnstone to find out.

"Our personalities are different," he pointed out in one of the year's great understatements. "So it was an exciting experience."

Jay liked to have a few laughs before a game, loosen people up. Bunning preferred a serious approach.

"I was pretty much thrust upon him by the Phillies just as the season was about to start and he already had his lineup pretty much set," Johnstone said. "All of a sudden here comes this guy, and we've got to play him until we can use him in Philadelphia. So Jim wasn't very happy. I think we kind of got off to a rotten start that way."

And it quickly deteriorated as Jay took it upon himself to bring some laughs into the lives of the Toledo Mud Hens.

"I mentioned to Lee [Elia], 'I've been in the big leagues. You've got to loosen these guys up. You got to have some fun,'" Johnstone said. "I told him, 'Bunning's got these guys all scared. He's got 'em too tense and too tight.' Lee Elia was always the buffer between Jim Bunning and myself."

The manager came to resent Johnstone's attempts to inject levity into the serious business of developing players and molding a winning team.

"He wanted all these young guys to have the same mentality, the same work habits, the same mental approach to the game as he did," said Jay. "So I would go around after he gave one of those stern lectures, and I'd talk to them and say, 'Look, he's the manager, but take it easy . . .'"

Bunning didn't want them to "take it easy." And he didn't want Jay Johnstone to tell his players one thing after he had told them another.

"He thought I was trying to undermine him as a manager," Johnstone realized. "Actually I wasn't. I was just trying to help him out . . . trying to boost their confidence. One time he called me in, told me he didn't appreciate me talking to them, no matter what I said. I couldn't explain to him because he wouldn't listen at the time and I didn't want a confrontation myself."

For a guy who didn't want a confrontation, Johnstone had a way of pushing Bunning to the limit. Said Elia, "He was a typical, happy-go-lucky, at times a pain-in-the-ass kind of guy. He'd always have his little pranks; that was just his makeup."

Jay loved to needle Bunning. "He had some Jim Bunning bubble-gum cards," Elia recalled, "and he tacked them up in his locker. Just another little way of throwing a dig in."

The blowup occurred in the second game of a doubleheader at home. The way Johnstone remembered it, he'd had a big first game and was listed to bat cleanup in the nightcap. As Toledo's designated hitter, he didn't have to take the field in the top of the first, which was just as well because he was in the bathroom at the time.

"I mean, you talk about being in there a long time," remarked Dave Wallace, recalling that historic evening. "Our leadoff guy hits. Our second guy hits. Now it's the third hitter."

But Johnstone wasn't in the on-deck circle.

"Jim says, 'Where's Jay?'" Wallace remembered. "He tells Jerry Martin to hit for him."

"I got back in time to hit," Johnstone insisted, "and he had another guy in the on-deck circle. I said, 'What's that guy doing in the on-deck circle?' Bunning said, 'Well, you weren't here on time.'"

Wallace's recollection is a bit different. "Jerry Martin's up there hitting and Jay still hasn't come out," Dave said. "He finally comes out and the inning's over. We're running out on the field and here comes Jay. Jim says, 'You're fined $100 [or whatever] and suspended until further notice. Get the hell out of here and go in the clubhouse.'"

The real fireworks started after the game. "Jim challenged him, face to face," Elia said. "'I had enough of this,' he said, and he went right after him. He even told him, 'You take all those pictures of me off your locker; I don't think it's funny.' They went at it good. In fact, it got to the point where I thought maybe if Jay would've tapped him or pushed him, Jim would have cold-cocked him. So I grabbed Jim, kind of got him away. . . ."

"We're all sitting at our lockers," Wallace said, "and Jay says in front of the whole team, 'What was that all about?' And Jim says something like, 'I'll tell you what. I'm in charge here.' And Jay says, 'Well, I think that was horseshit.' And Jim says, 'You son of a bitch, if you have something to say, we can settle the score right now.'

"Jay says, 'Yeah, you'd love for me to hit you.' And Jim says, 'You bet I would.' And then they both came to their senses. They were face to face. I'll never forget it. That was incredible."

"He wanted me to hit him," Johnstone said. "I was sitting down and he was yelling, screaming and hollering behind me. I stood up and turned around. There was a long bench between us, and he was yelling, 'Go ahead, hit me, hit me, hit me.' It was one of those things where you really want to, but you know you can't."

Johnstone had succeeded in pushing his manager past the breaking point. Bunning's irritation with all the little things—the bubblegum cards, the times Jay went on the field wearing the funny "umbrella hat" he employed for comic relief, the kidding-around, behind-the-back catches he'd make in the outfield before the game—had been building up. "I did things to make people laugh, but it would aggravate him because he thought it was taking away from the intensity he wanted in the game," Johnstone said.

Fortunately, he didn't accept Bunning's challenge to hit him that night, and things settled down in the Mud Hen clubhouse. The players showered and dressed and went home, leaving Bunning and Elia to mull over the events of the night. What happened next says a lot about Jim Bunning.

"We shared the same office," Elia recalled, "and no sooner did we get in there, the phone rang. Somebody had gotten hurt in Philadelphia and they needed an outfielder. They said, 'Who's the best choice you have to help our ball club right now?' Jerry Martin was on our club and doing well, remember. Jim said, 'The best hitter I've got'—and he's still huffing and puffing and sweating—'is Jay Johnstone. He's the guy that I would recommend.'

"I think that tells you something about his character. I mean, he had an opinion to make about somebody, and he didn't let his personal feelings enter into it. I don't know if I would have done that."

"That was typical of Jim," Dave Wallace remarked. "He's so damn honest."

But then, it never took his players long to find that out.

"He lined us up one day in Toledo and told us, one by one, what he thought about us," Jerry Martin recalled.

As clubhouse meetings go, this was a dilly. The players sat there, awaiting their turn, wondering what Jim would have to say about them.

"He told George Culver, 'If that's all you got you might as well go home,'" Martin said. "He was really tough on those pitchers."

Which is not to say he spoke in kinder, gentler terms to the men who played every day.

"He told me, 'You can't hit a curve ball; you'll never be in the big leagues,'" said Martin, who went on to prove that prediction wrong.

Bunning may have been all business most of the time, but there were occasions when his players saw him in a more easygoing mode. "On one of our bus trips—I think to Charleston, West Virginia, from Toledo—we had a day off," Wallace remembered. "Jim had us stop off at his home [in Fort Thomas, Kentucky]. He said, 'Hey, this is a day for you guys. Everybody come over. Bring your bathing suits. We're going to have fun.'"

And they did.

"We went swimming in the pool," said Wallace. "We were downstairs in his play room. There was a barbeque . . ."

They had a chance to look at all the pictures and trophies and, best of all, to spend a day with Jim Bunning when he was relaxed. No ball game to manage. No decisions to make. No reports to file.

One time Lee Elia was invited over to Bunning's house for dinner; he remembers it still.

"He had so many kids," Lee commented, "that every night at dinner they had seat assignments. He would stand there and Mary would say, 'It's time for dinner,' and the kids would all stand, waiting to get a seat assignment. He had to mix them up so they wouldn't argue during the meal."

Whatever he had to do, he did. And whatever he did worked just fine. The Bunning kids, all of whom went to college, flourished under Jim's tight rein. His players and coaches learned a few things, too.

"I'll never forget we were in Richmond—me, 'Red' Zipeto, and him," Elia said. "He always had a way, a little remark or an innuendo that let you know he was a quality guy. Well, we're in this little bar after an afternoon game. We were going to have a cocktail before dinner. The waitress asked us what we wanted. 'Red' had his little shot and a beer. I had VO and water. She said to Jim, 'What would you care for?' He said, 'I'll have a gin and tonic.' She said, 'Any particular kind of gin?' He said, 'Boodles gin.'"

Zipeto and Elia exchanged glances.

"We heard of Gilbert gin," Lee said. "We heard of Fleischman's and Calvert's. But Boodles?"

That little bar in Richmond didn't have any Boodles on hand. Jim had to settle for a lesser brand.

"Next day we went to the park and we were busting his chops," Elia said.

"Boodles?" they kept saying. "You had to order Boodles?"

Who else but Jim Bunning would order Boodles gin in a little bar in Richmond, Virginia, during a minor league road trip? Nobody else on that traveling squad; of that they were certain.

"He was just a class act all the way around," Elia declared.

Bunning's coach was in the unenviable position of being the buffer between the intense manager and his fun-loving players. Jay Johnstone fondly recalled the night Elia came to him and said, "Jim's on a tear. You better tell all the guys."

In other words, it was bed-checking night and you'd better be in.

"I said, 'We're going to have a little fun,'" Johnstone recalled. "So we set him up."

Jay and Harry Safewright were in their room at the magic hour. They were sitting on the bed playing cards. But the lights were low, and they went to great pains to remain quiet. From the corridor outside, no busybody bed-checker would ever dream the roam was occupied.

"He couldn't believe we were there," Johnstone said. "He thought he had us. He didn't even bother to knock."

Jim opened the door and did a double-take. There were his two players wearing the most innocent of looks.

"I said, 'How ya doing, Skip?'" remembered Johnstone, "and he threw the keys at us and stormed out. Next day he says, 'You did that on purpose.' 'Who me?' I said. You've got to have some fun in the game. He never laughed the entire time I was there. He never found anything I did funny."

One of the hardest things about managing in the minor leagues is that sometimes winning a game becomes secondary to the task of developing players and answering questions about them for the front office. One such occasion had Lee Elia temporarily baffled. The Mud Hens were in Richmond, engaged in a high-scoring, back-and-forth struggle with the Braves.

"We went ahead in the top of the ninth," said Elia, "and he's going to go to the bullpen in the bottom of the ninth."

Lurking on the Richmond bench was a dangerous righthanded slugger named Wayne Nordhagen. Available in the Toledo bullpen were two good righthanded relief pitchers, Dave Wallace and Bucky Brandon.

"We're figuring, this is a given," said Elia. "He's going to bring in Bucky or Wally."

To their surprise, Bunning brought in a lefthander, Steve Cates, to start the bottom of the ninth, even though Richmond's first batter was righthanded and Nordhagen was at the bat rack, ready to pinch-hit for the second batter.

"What's he doing?" Elia wondered.

The leadoff man blooped a single and Nordhagen came striding up to the plate. No way Cates would face him.

But he did, and Nordhagen hit a two-run homer to win the game.

"Jim walked in the clubhouse and he had that way of glaring," Elia said. "He propped his chair up right by the doorway where the players come in, and as they came in he just looked at Wally."

All very strange. The Mud Hens showered and departed. Whenever Bunning was angry, he'd say, "What are you doing tonight, Coachie?" Which is what he said to Elia on this night.

"I don't know what I'm doing tonight," Elia told him.

"Well, do you want to stop up in the room real quick?"

"So I went up to his room," said Elia, "and he said, 'You seem upset.' I said, 'Yeah. I'm not second-guessing you, but this isn't you.' He said, 'I know it's not me, but I just got a phone call the other day. They wanted to see if Cates could get righthanders out because I'd been putting in my reports he can get lefthanders out.'

"I said, 'Why did you have to do it tonight? Couldn't you wait another night? These guys busted their ass to go ahead.' He said, 'Well, I kind of thought about that. But it seemed like tonight would be the real, true test to see if he could do it. If it was 8-1 or something, I might never know. I know I made a sacrifice for the team, but I answered the question, and that's what they wanted.'

"I don't know if that says anything about him," Elia said, "but in some way I think it does because other guys in this day and age would have gone for the win and the hell with answering the question for Philadelphia."

If there had been serious doubts about Bunning's ability to handle players that first year in Reading, they were all but gone by the time he closed out his two-year stay in Toledo. He had mellowed somewhat. His relationship with the players had improved. Maybe Jay Johnstone couldn't make him laugh, but Max Patkin could. At least, he succeeded one night in Tidewater.

The Mud Hens were getting pounded. It had been a long, hard, losing road trip. Jim Bunning was not in a good mood. So, of course, the Clown Prince of Baseball showed up to bedevil him.

Max was in his second inning of work, coaching at third base, which happened to be where the visiting dugout was located. He was in the midst of one of his routines. The crowd was laughing. Bunning? He was standing in the front of the dugout, arms folded across his chest, glaring at Patkin.

Poor Max was knocking himself out. Anything for a laugh. And still the visiting manager stood there, glaring his nastiest glare. Suddenly Max caught Bunning's eye and, turning to face him, he said in a voice loud enough to be heard in the stands, "The trouble with you, Bunning, you don't take this game seriously enough."

Even Jim Bunning had to laugh.

The 89ers

In 1976 Jim Bunning completed the baseball version of a "hat trick." He managed in his third Triple A league, the American Association. His "education" was complete. He was ready to manage in the big leagues. Unfortunately, the big leagues weren't ready for him.

Even Jay Johnstone had become a Bunning supporter by then. "They asked my opinion," he remembered. "I told them I thought he'd be a hell of a manager."

Johnstone and Bunning buried the hatchet during spring training in Florida. "Ruben Amaro got us together," said Jay, who had played with Amaro on the California Angels. "Ruben kept telling me how great Jim was, so we went out to dinner and actually became real good friends. I called him after he made the 'Hall,' left a message in his office congratulating him."

Johnstone even invested some money with Bunning during Jim's stock brokering days.

The 1976 Oklahoma City 89ers were, by far, Bunning's best minor league team. Dane Iorg, who almost quit rather than face another season with Jim Bunning earlier in his career, had an outstanding season. "He's been super this year," Iorg said of his manager. "I'm sure a lot of managers would have buried me for the way I played for Jim in the past, but he didn't do that. He let me go out and play. It was like he forgot anything had ever happened. That's a big man."

Iorg was equally big. When the season ended he went out of his way to thank Bunning for all he had done.

The man whose mere presence turned his players into quivering, error-prone incompetents a few years before had them singing his praises now.

"Jim Bunning can take an individual, evaluate his talent, and utilize it to the fullest," declared the catcher and utility man Jack Bastable, a former University of Missouri football star. "I really wanted to play for Jim," Bastable said. "I had a high school basketball coach, a similar type individual. He was 100 percent at all times. Everything he did was to help you become a better player and to help him become a better coach. I just hadn't come across an individual like that in baseball—until I played for Jim. I said, 'Gosh, this is the kind of manager I really want to play for.'"

So many of them felt that way: Iorg, Bastable, outfielder Rick Bosetti, infielder Jim Morrison, lefthanded pitchers Quency Hill and Randy Lerch, righthanders Danny Boitano and Dave Wallace. The list kept growing. It hadn't been easy, but Jim Bunning had learned how to get through to these young men, and they had learned what he was all about. The majority of them understood that underneath that hard-as-nails exterior he cared about them and was trying to help them become big league ballplayers. And they knew when he said something—good or bad—he meant it.

"He tried to train pitchers to pitch in Philadelphia in front of 55,000 or 60,000 people to win a championship," Lee Elia pointed out. "He didn't teach them to be pitching in the big leagues on a second division club. He'd tell them, 'My job is to teach you how to pitch for the Philadelphia Phillies to win a world championship, and if that can't happen then it's to pitch for some other ball club in the major leagues to win a championship.' That's the way he approached it, and that's why you had to admire him. He was really no different than Dallas [Green]. Dallas was the same way."

"Any time anybody asks me what kind of manager I am, I say, 'Please, go ask the guys I manage,'" Bunning commented. "That's what a manager has to do: get the most out of his players."

And that's what he was doing now. "I'm not strict," he would say. "I'm fair. You've got to have a minimum amount of discipline on a club. I expect a guy getting $2,000 or $3,000 a month to show up on time."

He expected them to run out ground balls, to go all-out for the two and a half or three hours a night they were on the field. Not an unreasonable request.

"He'll tell us, 'You're here to play in the big leagues, I'm here to manage in the big leagues,'" Dave Wallace recalled. "He told me, 'The time may come when I have to chew you.' I said, 'Chew me out all you want if it helps me become a better pitcher.'"

Jim Bunning and his players—at least most of them on that Oklahoma City ball club—were on the same wavelength. The 89ers did not finish nine games over .500 by accident. And their record would have been considerably better than that if the Phillies hadn't decided to trade Wayne Nordhagen, Oklahoma City's top slugger, late in the season.

There were problems along the way, of course. One of the biggest occurred on what should have been a banner evening at the Oklahoma City All-Sports Stadium. It was August 24, 1976, and, as storm clouds gathered over the ball park, a crowd of more than twenty-four hundred turned out to honor the home team on Awards Night. They had plenty of people to honor, too. Dane Iorg wound up hitting .326 and put together a twenty-four-game hitting streak. Jim Morrison smacked eighteen homers, drove in seventy-one runs, and hit .289 after making a big jump from the Class A Carolina League. Rick Bosetti, in his first Triple A season, hit .306 and excelled in the outfield. And then there was Lonnie Smith.

Like Morrison, he was just up from "A" ball. Also like Morrison, he had a fine season, hitting .308 and leading the American Association with ninety-three runs scored. Surely, he would be one of the honorees on this night.

One by one, the awards were handed out. Most valuable and most popular and most improved and top rookie; all the usual ones. Lonnie kept waiting to hear his name. And waiting. And waiting. It never happened.

He was just twenty years old, an African American who had never spent much time around white people until signing a pro baseball contract. He felt left out, unappreciated. Worse than that, he felt he was a victim of discrimination.

A very sensitive young man, Lonnie Smith took it hard. "All the white guys got awards," he observed. "They had beauty queens there, and all the white guys got to escort them."

By the time the pregame festivities were over, Lonnie didn't feel at all like playing a baseball game for these people who apparently didn't give a hoot about him. "I expected something," he recalled. "When I didn't get it, I felt pretty bad."

He left the 89ers' dugout, went into the clubhouse, and began to remove his uniform. Jim Bunning had to go after him and, with considerable effort, talk him into changing his mind, putting his uniform back on, and playing the game. Reluctantly, Smith agreed. The game began and he was in center field, batting third, but his heart wasn't in it.

That became evident in the top of the third inning. Wichita's Tony Franklin hit a fly ball to center, a routine play for Lonnie Smith. He trotted in and then, instead of catching the ball on the fly, he let it drop in front of him and fielded it on a hop. It was obvious he hadn't made the catch to the reporters in the press box, and to the fans in the stands, not to mention the manager in the Oklahoma City dugout. But Joe West, who was umpiring on the bases, blew the call. Apparently taking it for granted that the easy fly ball had been caught, he signaled "out." An incredible argument ensued. Smith, credited with a catch he hadn't made, charged the umpire to protest the call. Before Bunning could intervene, West threw Lonnie out of the game, which was exactly what Lonnie wanted.

Bunning had a long, heart-to-heart talk with the confused, unhappy player after the skies opened up and the game was rained out. Lonnie listened to what his manager said; a few nights later in Denver's Mile High Stadium he singled, tripled, and doubled his first three times up to spark an 89er victory. The incident in Oklahoma City on Awards Night and the closed-door talk that followed led to a close relationship between the two men, one that endured for years. When Lonnie Smith decided he needed an agent, he chose Bunning. When Jim was looking for an African American to go with him into a black neighborhood during a political campaign years later, he asked Lonnie, who readily agreed.

With his fifth managerial season nearly over, Bunning had a visitor from Philadelphia. Howie Bedell, his one-time coach, was now the assistant farm director of the Phillies, working under Dallas Green. Joining the 89ers on their final road trip of the season, he met with Bunning over dinner after one of the games. As expected, they discussed plans for the following season. The reached an agreement that Bunning would return to Oklahoma City if he didn't get a big league job.

I saw Jim later that night. "We're all set for next year," he told me, hitting the highlights of their meeting. Nothing surprising about that. Bunning was closing out what had been by far his best managerial season. Of course the Phillies wanted him back.

Or so you would have thought.

The Firing

Jim Bunning lived the life of a minor league baseball manager in Reading, Eugene, Toledo, and Oklahoma City with one thought in mind. He wanted to become a big league manager. No secret about that. The Phillies knew it. Everybody knew it. And there were times his prospects looked extremely bright.

One such moment came at the close of the 1972 season. Jim didn't exactly wow them at Reading, but he survived the season, improving as he went along. The Phillies were looking for a manager and he was a candidate.

"I didn't think I had the job," he said, 'but I thought I was being seriously considered."

He met Ruly Carpenter, the owner; Paul Owens, the general manager; and Dallas Green, the director of the farm system. They asked him what he thought had to be done to make the Phillies competitive, and he told them.

"They asked me, 'Would you trade [Steve] Carlton?' I said, 'You bet—if I could get enough players for him that would make it worth our while because if he wins twenty-five games every year and we finish sixth, what good will it do?'"

As usual, Jim didn't beat around the bush.

The meeting seemed to go well. At least Bunning thought so. Time passed. Nothing happened. Rumors swirled. Dave Bristol, the former Reds' manager, was being touted as the front-runner. No matter. Bunning's hopes remained high. "You're *this* close to being manager of the Phillies," Paul Owens told him.

How close was he?

"That's a good question," Owens told me over lunch in a South Jersey diner. "He was one of only six I talked to. There was Dave Bristol and Danny Ozark and Richie [Ashburn] and . . . I don't even remember all of them, to be honest with you.

"See, I wasn't after a 'name.' I was after someone who had played and had minor league experience, someone who was low key and patient. I didn't care about the big name. I wanted someone who would go along with the program. I had to have somebody who wouldn't fight me."

The Reds were in the World Series that year, and, Owens confirmed, he and Bunning got together during the Series. Although he told Jim he was close to getting the job, Bunning obviously didn't fit the description of a man who was "low key and patient" and "would go along with the program" without an occasional dissenting word. Also, Owens pointed out that day in South Jersey over lunch, both Bunning and Ashburn had been star players, and that concerned him.

"Sometimes when you're a star you don't realize the repetition needed, especially with a young ball club," Owens explained. "That bothered me more than anything else. It wasn't the individual. Jim Bunning, to me, is a class man and a dogged man who had learned his trade the hard way. He was perfect. Ashburn I liked. I brought that thing down to six, seven guys, and he was right there. I could have hired any of them. I remember I said, 'Jim, with your qualities and what I know about you . . .'"

So Bunning thought he had a good chance for the job. So did Bristol. And Ashburn. "In fact," said Owens, "Ashburn asked me about that a dozen times. 'I really thought I might get that job,' he said. I told him, 'You were number one or two, you and Bunning. And Dave Bristol. Bunning had a hell of a shot at it. That's the way I felt. I felt the same about Ashburn."

Even while praising Bunning, however, and saying how close he came to picking him for the Phillies' job, Paul Owens sprinkled hints about why he chose Danny Ozark instead.

"Jim was the kind of guy—you always felt like he was aloof," Owens said. "I mean, that was the impression."

At one point he added that Jim Bunning was great "if you ever wanted a true, lifelong friend. You and him might argue and argue, but you'd find out how honest the man is."

Paul Owens was looking for a manager, however, not a lifelong friend. And he wasn't looking for any arguments. So Bunning went to Triple A, not to the Phillies. But he was the heir apparent as the next Phillies' field general. Which probably explains why the club was so anxious to get rid of him at the close of his finest season as a minor league manager.

While Jim was enjoying a successful season in Oklahoma City the Phillies were doing even better. Owens and Green had built a solid contender the best possible way—through the farm system. And now their day in the sun had arrived. Led by such homegrown products as shortstop Larry Bowa, third baseman Mike Schmidt, left fielder Greg Luzinski, and catcher Bob Boone, the Phillies won their first division title. The town was jumping with excitement. It was an ideal time to unload Jim Bunning. Who would notice?

Bunning, of course, had no idea what was coming. Howie Bedell, the assistant farm director, had assured him the Phillies wanted him back in Oklahoma City.

"Everything was all set," recalled Bunning. "I was going to manage there the next year."

Add to that the statement Ruly Carpenter made to Bunning in 1974 when Jim asked him how he stood with the organization. Ruly replied, "If Danny Ozark crossed the street and got run over by a car you would be our manager in Philadelphia."

In short, as the National League championship series between the Reds and the Phillies approached in the fall of 1976, getting fired was the last thing on Jim Bunning's mind. He had planned to fly to Philadelphia for the first two games of the best-of-five series, then return to Cincinnati for the conclusion. The tickets he had ordered from the Phillies for the games in Cincinnati hadn't arrived, so he phoned to make sure they were on their way. Bedell told him not to worry; they would be sent.

The following Tuesday, Jim got a message to call Bedell in Philadelphia. Thinking it had to do with the playoff tickets, he phoned. What he heard floored him.

"I made some decisions," Bedell told him. "You're not going to be retained next year as manager of Oklahoma City."

Bunning couldn't believe his ears. This was the same Howie Bedell who, a few weeks before in Denver, assured him everything was set. Now he was telling him the Phillies had decided to fire him. Or, even more ludicrous, that the assistant farm director had decided to fire him.

"It was my understanding we agreed I'd be back," Bunning told him.

"It wasn't mine," Jim said Bedell replied.

Bunning thought back to that night in Denver, to their conversation over dinner that continued in Jim's hotel room. They had talked about next season, hadn't they?

"Did you or did you not offer me the job?" Bunning inquired over the phone.

Bedell said he had not. End of conversation. End of Jim Bunning, manager of the future.

The entire business was incredible. Why hadn't Jim's long-time friend Dallas Green, the farm director, called? Why would he have Bedell do the dirty work? And how about Bedell telling him that the decision was his? Did he really think anybody would believe that the decision to fire Jim Bunning would be made by an assistant farm director? And why did the Phillies wait until a week before he was scheduled to leave for a winter-ball managing job in the Dominican Republic to lower the boom?

Contradictions and absurdities abound. If we are to believe the party line, the same people who came within a hair of offering Bunning the big league managing job before the 1973 season, after he had completed a most unsuccessful season as a Double A manager, fired him four years later at the close of a successful season as a Triple A manager, in which the majority of his players not only respected him but enjoyed playing for him.

Although he was deeply hurt that Dallas Green, his long-time friend, hadn't delivered the news himself instead of having an assistant do it over the phone, Bunning never believed for a minute that Green was behind the firing. From the day it happened he was convinced that Paul Owens had made the decision, choosing a time when the Phillies were riding high to ease Bunning out of the organization. Jim was too hard to control. If he disagreed, he wouldn't be afraid to speak up. Had he remained as a Triple A manager, it would have been difficult *not* to give him the Phillies job when it opened up; so Owens seized on this opportunity to get rid of him. The more he thought about it, the more certain Bunning was.

The reasons Bedell gave him over the phone made no sense. He wasn't "offensive-minded enough" as a manager, the assistant farm director remarked. He was entitled to his opinion, but the facts didn't support it. And Bedell used the old standby: he didn't communicate well with the players. Early in his managing career, that charge would have made sense. Not now.

Then there was the reason to top all reasons. Bedell suggested that Bunning's desire to get a big league managing job was a negative factor in evaluating his performance. Be serious. Did they really think he had spent these last five seasons bouncing around the minor leagues, enduring those long trips, those miserable clubhouses and second-rate hotels with the intention of making minor league managing a long-term career? The idea had always been for Jim to go down there to learn how to be a manager, to find out if he liked it and could do it. They knew that from day one.

Bunning had good reason to be hurt. And he was plenty hurt. With the playoffs approaching, I flew into Cincinnati to attend a Reds workout. Jim met me at the airport, which is just across the river in Kentucky.

"You won't believe what I'm going to tell you," he said for openers.

"What do you mean? What happened?"

"I'll tell you after you get your luggage and we get in the car," he replied. "You'd better be sitting down."

He knew I'd been with the Oklahoma City 89ers in Denver when Bedell arrived to talk about next year, and that I'd be as shocked as he was over the sudden about-face.

"I don't have the answer," he told me. "I wish I knew the answer. I suppose a lot of people resent me. They resent the fact that I was a successful player who decided to go down [to the minor leagues] and do my thing and learn my job to get back to the major leagues. 'How can he do that?' they want to know. 'Why doesn't he go home and count his money? Why doesn't he get the hell out of it?' Not all people obviously, just some people. I feel used. It's as if they [the Phillies] said, 'We've picked his brain for everything he can do. Now let him get out of here.' That's the way I feel."

Whatever the reasons, they wanted him gone. To Bunning, the man behind it had to be Owens, not Green. That's the only way it made any sense. And perhaps it provided an explanation, however weak, for Dallas Green permitting someone else to make the phone call.

"The thing about the firing that bothered me the most was the fact that the guy who hired me didn't have enough guts to do it himself," Bunning said.

It not only bothered him and his wife, it mystified them. If there was one thing Dallas Green had in large supply, it was guts. He was very much like Bunning—only too willing to tell the truth, even if it hurt. What's more, Jim and Mary Bunning had been very close to Dallas and Sylvia Green. That's what hurt the most. Mary was so upset she wrote Dallas a letter without telling Jim. The answer came in longhand, but it didn't do much to clear the air.

Writing it could not have been a pleasant task for Dallas, who had high regard for Jim, and does to this day.

"I still hold I was right on this judgment," Green wrote, "but do realize the hurt he felt because I did not tell him."

Dallas told Mary Bunning how he and Bedell had "wrestled" with the decision "as to the direction to take that was best for Jim Bunning and for the organization." He emphasized that "both of us feel strongly that Jim Bunning can manage in the major leagues and I've told Ruly and Paul I feel (and still do) this way."

Although calling the change necessary "for the best of the organization," Dallas made it clear that he felt it was for Jim's good as well. "Mary," he wrote, "I told Jim he was stagnant in our organization and was being billed to the outside world as a 'Phillies man' and this made it tougher for him to get a major league job. . . ."

"Mary," he concluded, "I value your friendship and that of your family's a great deal. When friends are in positions like this it never is pleasant for anyone. . . . May I ask your understanding and your prayers as always."

After mulling that over, Jim and Mary felt more confused than enlightened. The explanation given to Jim by Ruly Carpenter several months later, when the onetime manager stopped off to see the president of the Phillies, did little to clear things up in Jim's mind. According to Bunning, Ruly told him, "It's just, we don't think you can manage. . . . My field guys tell me you can't manage."

Jim Bunning remained convinced he knew who wanted to get rid of him. And at least one man close to the scene at the time says he was right.

Hugh Alexander, one of baseball's top scouts for an incredible sixty years, was a key member of the decision-making team Paul Owens put together in the 1970s when he turned the long-moribund Phillies into one of the game's finest organizations. Owens and Alexander— he was known fondly as "Uncle Hughie"—conferred on all the big trades, all the important moves. Along with Dallas Green, they were primarily responsible for the Phillies winning three successive division titles (1976-78) and topping it off by going all the way for the first, and only, time in franchise history in 1980. Ironically, the manager of that championship team, the one Jim Bunning dreamed of managing, was Dallas Green.

Alexander knew everything that went on with the organization in those heady years. I saw him at Legends Field in Tampa in the spring of 1997, and the conversation got around to the firing of Jim Bunning.

"Jim thinks to this day that Paul Owens was responsible for his firing," I commented.

"He was," replied Uncle Hughie, a man with a remarkable memory. "I was there. 'Pope' [Paul Owens] said, 'Get rid of him. I don't want him around. I don't care how many no-hitters he pitched. Get rid of him.'" According to Alexander, one of Bunning's "faults"—as seen through Owens's eyes—was his refusal to go out drinking with the boys from the front office when they came to visit. "'Pope' liked to take the manager out after the game," Alexander said. "They'd drink to three or four in the morning. Bunning wouldn't go."

Nor would he take part in those long drinking sessions during the winter meetings in New Orleans the year John Stearns was traded to the Mets (over Bunning's vociferous protests). "I wouldn't drink with them," Jim declared. That wasn't his style. But to Owens it meant he didn't fit in. Or, as Alexander remembered him saying, "He's not one of my people."

Ironically, the man who was responsible for Bunning leaving the Phillies organization, and ultimately leaving baseball, also played a role in bringing him to Philadelphia in the first place. "I was one of the two people who recommended Jim in my reports [before the trade with the Tigers]," noted Owens, who was scouting for the Phillies then. "I was covering the American League when they [the Angels] were still playing in Dodger Stadium. I saw Bunning in about three ball games. Tony Lucadello and I both had good reports on him. Tony saw him a lot; I didn't know if they used my report until two or three years later. Al Cartwright [a Wilmington, Delaware, columnist] did a story on Bunning. He went in and went through the files and he found out they used it. I really loved Bunning because he was such a competitor. A lot of people don't realize Jim Bunning pitched so long in the minor leagues before he ever got a shot. That's the way it was in those days. Today, these guys get one hundred innings and they're in the big leagues. Anyway, I liked the way he approached the game. He was tough. He was a battler. I didn't know him as a person; I just liked what I saw."

But the man who became the Phillies general manager and the man who aspired to be the Phillies field manager simply were not cut from the same cloth. Owens didn't feel comfortable with Bunning, and a general manager needs to feel comfortable with his manager. If that means exchanging ideas in the wee hours over a bottle or two, so be it.

"If Bunning had gone out with us, he'd probably [have] been manager of the Phillies," Alexander observed during that lunch at Legends Field in Tampa. "I think he'd have been a good manager, too. Look at the players who played for him who got to the big leagues."

"They let me go for a specific reason, and I know that," Bunning said recently. "They [the Phillies] were riding very high. Paul saw it as an opportunity to get rid of somebody who wasn't a 'yes' person in the organization. I understand that."

And the fact that Owens still refutes that?

"He shouldn't," remarked Bunning. "It was the right time. I understand it. I'm not bitter at all. I was a little mad at the time the way it was handled. Everything was all set [for the next year]. Dallas had sent his underling [Bedell] to talk to me. I said, 'What about next year?' He said, 'Everything's OK.' I don't care what Bedell said later. I'm telling you the truth. He said, 'Yes, you are the manager of the Triple A club next year,' and somewhere between that and when they went back for their own meeting, which I wasn't invited to, they decided to fire me.

"Dallas should have come and said, 'Hey, we've gone far enough. We can't go any farther. Bedell was not free to tell you that you were hired for another year. I made a decision that we cannot use you next year.' End of story. But Dallas didn't have the guts to tell me. I thought we had a great relationship. Dallas and I go back to when he was a player rep with the Phillies and I was a rep with Detroit. When Dallas couldn't make the last train to Delaware [where he lived], he stayed with me. . . . He should have taken the bull by the horns and done what he had to do. Better to look a guy in the eye and tell him."

Making the situation even worse, Bunning had already committed to managing that winter in the Dominican Republic, where he would be in charge of several Phillie farmhands. That was supposed to be a stepping-stone to the big leagues, another chance to hone his managerial skills before rabid, demanding fans in the pressure cooker that is Dominican baseball. Instead, it was Jim's farewell to managing.

Time heals, at least to a certain extent. Looking back now, the Bunnings have come to see that Jim's firing wasn't so bad. In fact, it might have been the best thing that could have happened to him, clearing the way for a different, far more important career. Besides, who knows if a big league managing job ever would have come in an era when front-office types prefer field managers they can control? The Phillies weren't the only big league team that feared hiring someone with a mind of his own for such a visible job.

"I think Mary was the happiest person in the world when Howie Bedell phoned and said, 'You are no longer associated with the Phillies,'" Jim said.

Not really, but his point is well taken. Mary had let her husband go back to the minor leagues without a fight because she wanted him to get the baseball managing bug out of his system. Bedell's phone call accomplished that.

But even if the Bunnings are extremely happy that he is out of baseball, there remains a lingering disappointment over the failure of their old friend, Dallas Green, to meet the issue head-on.

They had struck up a friendship almost immediately when Bunning became a Phillie in 1964. Jim was already an established big league star. Dallas was, in his own words, "a young, rookie kind of guy really struggling to keep my head above water at the big league level."

They had met, however briefly, through the Players Association. Green was a player rep and therefore attended meetings.

"Back in those days it wasn't all the pension and the salaries and the things that are paramount today," Green recalled. "It was playing conditions and travel and parking for your family, little things that were itches and scratches. The Robin Robertses and the Jim Bunnings, those were the guys that got into the pension stuff real heavy and realized early on that that was something that they really needed to take care of. A lot of us were just guys that wanted to do things just a littler bit better for the team—you know, for the guys."

The established star and the struggling "rookie kind of guy" were drawn together almost from day one in spring training. Green admired what Jim had accomplished and, above all, the way he went about playing the game.

"When Jim came to the Phillies we all knew his reputation and we knew his toughness and competitiveness," Green remembered, "and he brought that to the locker room right away. That's really what we needed because we had an awful lot of young people who were really getting started and needed the strength that he brought to the club-house. We had some older guys, but they didn't have Jim's strength.

"Right from spring training we started playing bridge together, Mary and Jim and Sylvia and I. We would go to the old Clearwater Convention Center right in the middle of town and play duplicate bridge and spend the evenings together. We got to know the families. We just kind of hit it off."

When the season began Bunning and Green would kill time on the plane rides by teaming up against Gene Mauch and relief pitcher Ed Roebuck in bridge games. "Jim still swears because we beat them all the time that's the reason I always got sent out [to the minor leagues by Phillies' manager Mauch]," Dallas said. "That wasn't true, but it was interesting. Nobody was more competitive than Gene other than Jim."

The friendship blossomed. Although Green, his chances for stardom ruined by a sore arm early in his career, won only twenty games spread over parts of eight big league seasons, the two had much in common. Both were strong-willed men with a genuine feeling for the game and a belief in hard work and what it can accomplish.

"We really became good friends," noted Dallas. "I mean we buddied around, and we'd go to dinner, that kind of stuff."

Consider the irony. The superstar pitcher who wanted to manage the Phillies—or some big league club—never got the opportunity. The struggling, sore-armed pitcher went on to manage the Phillies to their only world championship in 1980, then put together a Cubs team that ended a long postseason drought on Chicago's north side, and then served as manager of both New York teams. Their close friendship may have ended the day Dallas let Howie Bedell handle Jim's firing, but Green's opinion of Bunning remains as high as ever.

"A special guy," Dallas observed. "I'll tell you, I learned a lot from him. He brought a tremendous work ethic to the ball club. He's so intense. That intensity, we all say we have it, but his was really special.

"The work ethic was something that hit me right away. I mean, I was a work-ethic guy anyway because I felt that was the only way I was going to survive in baseball. But I watched Jim work and I watched him go about his pitching. There was nobody, *nobody* that was better prepared, nobody that was more intense and more competitive. Robbie [Robin Roberts] was a guy I looked to basically for the same kinds of things. Robbie was a workhorse, loved to throw and pitch. Jim did it differently. His work was running and preparing his body. Robbie had that work ethic, loved the game, was very, very competitive, loved to have more fun at the game than Jim did. Jim really made baseball the business of his life. There is no question about that. Fun to him was winning. I learned that from him because I say it all the time: you never hear losers saying, 'Well, I had a lot of fun this year.' It's always the winners. And Jim brought that to us."

It is Green's belief that Bunning's approach rubbed off on the '64 Phillies, helping them overachieve for the first 150 games.

"When he came to the clubhouse everybody had to be ready to play," Dallas said. "There wasn't a heck of a lot of joking around. It was time for Jim to pitch and it was time for you to strap it on and get after it, too."

But Dallas Green saw a different aspect of Jim Bunning. Only a comparative few get that opportunity.

"A lot of guys never saw the other side of Jim like I did," Dallas commented. "When we went to Cincinnati we'd slip over to his home with the family."

Dallas would go, and so would catcher Gus Triandos, a good friend of Bunning's during their days together in Detroit and Philadelphia.

"Jim loved to be with the guys and be with his family, and he never minded sharing," Green recalled. "He was just a lot of fun then. But he was amazing in that he could turn that off to become the Jim Bunning that's the only Jim Bunning a lot of people see—the glaring, mean-minded, miserable son of a bitch that he can be at times, and he's not really that way."

If he liked you, if he trusted you, if he came to feel comfortable with you, you got to see the warm side of Jim Bunning. If not, he could be very tough.

"There's guys didn't like him," Green said. "Most of them were opposing hitters."

But some, remarked Green, were teammates. "He was so single-minded that I think a lot of guys had trouble warming up to him. Some of the younger guys were kind of in awe of him at first. He would never let you get real close to him unless he chose to do that, and he chose to do that with me. Why, I'm not sure."

Whatever the reasons, their friendship was such that what happened in 1976, when Bedell, Green's second in command, lowered the boom on Bunning's managerial aspirations, was especially difficult for Jim to understand. After all, if not for Dallas, he likely would have left base-ball at the end of his playing career in 1971.

"Jim wanted to stay in baseball and I knew that," Green said. "I could never figure out whether he wanted to go into top management or whether he wanted to stay on the field, and I don't think he knew. I just felt he would be really special as a manager because of that intensity. I knew he'd bring that to the table. He'd never lose that. Unfortunately, it hurt him as much as it helped him. It was really at the beginning of [the time when] kids didn't have the same drive and intensity about baseball that some of the older guys had, and Jim couldn't stand that. He had a hell of a time understanding why kids, when they made the decision to play the game, didn't play it with their heart and soul like he did. And yet I still respected him for it because that's what we really wanted to bring to the Phillies. That's what we kept talking about—de-veloping players in a winning atmosphere, learning how to play cham-pionship type baseball, learning how to be the best you possibly could be. That's why I wanted Jim to be a part of it."

Fine. But why, after Bunning had become a pretty darn good man-ager at the Triple A level, did his good friend, the man in charge of the farm system, preside over his sudden firing?

Even after more than two decades, it was not an easy question for Dallas Green to attempt to answer. But he tried.

"It just got to the point he wasn't going to be able to survive at the minor league level," he said. "He was going to either have to go to the big leagues real quick or move into the executive end of it, and he wasn't prepared to do that."

But Bunning *was* surviving at the minor league level. In his fifth managerial season, he had the majority of the players on his side, many of them eager to play hard for him. And he was fully prepared to enter yet another minor league season as a Triple A manager. Even if Dallas Green thought it was time for Bunning to move on, why was the firing handled in such a terrible, slipshod way? How could he let somebody else make the phone call? Furthermore, why didn't he argue with Paul Owens when the general manager apparently decided the time was right to ease Bunning out of the organization?

"I wouldn't blame it on Paul," Green argued. "I just don't think that's right. I think, if anything, it would have been a collective decision."

But Hugh Alexander, whose memory for details is nothing short of remarkable, distinctly recalled Owens delivering an order to fire Bunning.

"I don't remember it being that way," Green said. "But that part of it is a little fuzzy. Truthfully, I was really concentrating on the scouting end of it so much then. Howie [Bedell] and I had a great working relationship. I had a great trust in guys that I hired. I tried not to interfere.

"Pope [Paul Owens] never told us to fire anybody. You know how Pope was. 'Get rid of that son of a bitch,' [he'd say]. If I went back and said, 'I don't think that's right,' he'd back off. So that's why I can't blame it on Pope. I have to take that responsibility, and yet I didn't think it was right for me to pick up the phone and call Jim because I wasn't the guy in charge of that program at that particular time. I mean, I was and yet I wasn't."

Dallas Green is not the type of person to beat around the bush, but on this day, and on this subject, he was giving the bush a terrible beating. "The only reason I'm skirting this," he said at one point, "is I'm not real clear on it."

According to Dallas, to the best of his recollection, he let Bedell make the decision to fire Jim Bunning. He did nothing to stop him. And he let his assistant deliver the message a few weeks after Bedell had met with Bunning and apparently sealed an agreement with him to manage the Phillies' Triple A farm team the following season.

Asked if he was aware of Bedell's late-season meeting with Bunning in Denver in August of '76, Green replied, "No, I can't say I was." And Bedell denied it ever happened.

"Those kinds of things kept coming back about Howie," Dallas pointed out. "They kept building up, these stories that he would say something and ten days later it was something different."

Despite Bedell's version, Green has no doubt about what actually happened. "Put it this way," he remarked. "I know Jim's not a liar."

The bottom line is that firing anybody—especially in a business as public as professional baseball—is never easy to do. Green said he found that out when Paul Owens, as Phillies' general manager, decided he had to fire Frank Lucchesi as field manager in 1972. "I knew Paul loved Frank," Green said. "I mean they grew up together. They were best buddies. Paul and I had a hell of a time telling Frank. Paul said, 'Dallas, sometimes you've got to do what your gut tells you is right.'"

Later, as the man in charge of the Chicago Cubs, Dallas Green fired his good friend Lee Elia as manager. That, too, was difficult. And, although he apparently stood aside and let an underling do the dirty work, he fired his friend Jim Bunning as well.

It is evident that Green now wishes he had handled it differently—if not stopping Bedell from making that phone call, at the very least delivering the news of the firing himself, as painful as it would have been.

"I have no excuse for it," Dallas Green said. "No excuse."

The old baseball teammates and bridge partners have gone their separate ways. They have not been close since the day that botched-up firing occurred.

"I don't know that I blame him for the way he feels," Dallas commented.

They met, rather briefly, at a reunion of the '64 Phillies. The Bunnings and the Greens "kind of got together," Dallas said. "We had breakfast together, and the next day we kind of just touched base."

The closeness had vanished. When Bunning was elected to the Baseball Hall of Fame, Green tried to call him twice in Kentucky, twice in Washington, D.C. "Always the same thing," Dallas said. "'He's in a meeting.'"

Green left messages, but never got a return call. He knows both Jim and Mary were, and still are, upset over what happened. And he understands.

"I've never lost respect for Jim Bunning one iota," Dallas Green said. "I learned a lot from him. Jim was Jim. He was not afraid to say what was on his mind. I respected him for that. He was a fighter, boy, an in-fighter. He was into that pension stuff. He wouldn't let them get away with anything. He wasn't afraid to go to that [front] office or pop off, at all. I never lost respect for what he brought to me. I didn't give him much. He gave me more than I gave him by a long shot, and I never forgot that."

Jim and Mary Bunning—especially Mary—have never quite forgotten the hurt they felt when Dallas failed to tell them in person about Jim's firing.

"Mary trusted us and we didn't honor that trust, was her feeling, I'm sure," Green said.

"I felt sorry for Jim," Mary Bunning says now. "Yet I knew in my heart why he wasn't going to make it [as a baseball manager]. He was too tough. Things were changing. You had to be more of a counselor to your ballplayers and put a Band-Aid on things instead of telling it like it was. Jim has never been that way.

"I thought, 'Five years wasted with your earning power.' That was my problem with it."

For a time Jim also felt that he had wasted those five years. "But as it turned out, just the opposite happened," he said. "I had learned how to deal with people. That was the most rewarding thing coming out of those five years—learning to deal with young adults, some older."

In the end, many of them thought so much of Bunning they asked him to represent them in their contract negotiations, which he did, serving as agent for as many as thirty players at one time. "Why, if they [supposedly] disliked me so much, would they trust me to represent them in the most critical area?" he asked.

Among those he represented in the years between managing in the minor leagues and tackling big league politics in Kentucky were a number of players who made it to the majors: pitchers Randy Lerch, Dick Ruthven, and Jim Wright; outfielders Lonnie Smith, Jim Dwyer, and Rick Bosetti; third baseman Jim Morrison; catcher–third baseman Keith Moreland; and first baseman John Poff.

Jim Bunning had covered a lot of bases in professional baseball by the time he and the game parted. He had been a minor league ballplayer and would be a major league Hall of Famer. He had been a leader in the Players Association, a manager in one Double A league, three Triple A leagues, and winter leagues in Puerto Rico and the Dominican Republic. And, finally, he had been a players' agent.

Still, some goals eluded him. He tried and failed to become part of baseball ownership, making an unsuccessful attempt to put together a group to buy the Houston Astros in 1976 after the Phillies fired him. Working with Harry Valentine, owner of the Oklahoma City 89ers, the group raised $18 million in a bid "not only to buy the Houston franchise in the National League, but all the operation of the Astrodome, Astrohall, and all the facilities down there," Bunning recalled. "We couldn't raise enough money; they wanted $19.5 or $20 million; I guess that was a lot of money in 1976. Now I would not have trouble raising that because I know a lot more people with a lot more money."

Bunning's group engaged in "serious talks" with the Astros, but the $1.5 or $2 million they fell short killed their chances. Had the deal gone through, Jim likely would be club president Bunning today, not Congressman Bunning. "None of this [the political career] would have happened," he mused.

Nor would it have happened if Bunning had satisfied his ambition to become a big league manager. And eventually, perhaps, a general manager.

"As I got in deeper and deeper into baseball as a player and as a manager in the minor leagues, I didn't think my ultimate goal was as a manager in the major leagues," he said. "I would rather have had the opportunity, like Dallas did, to build a ball club and see if I could build a winner, and see if my ideas on how to build a ball club—mine and Lee Elia's and Ruben Amaro's—worked. We plotted on how to do it, but we didn't get the opportunity. Tough luck, I had to move on with my life."

Had the opportunity been there, baseball might have a different look today. Surely, Bunning's team would have had a different look.

"The reason I didn't have any arm trouble, I threw a lot, was trained to pitch nine innings, was trained to start every fourth day," he said. "It wasn't, 'Give me five or six good innings.'"

Five-man pitching rotations are the norm now. Complete games are practically extinct. As the head of a big league organization, Jim Bunning would have done his best to change that, get the game—at least the pitching end of the game—back to where it was. It is his contention that pitching more often, and for a longer time, makes for sounder arms. The great number of injuries sustained by today's pitchers would seem to back up his theory.

It's an accepted practice now to pitch every fifth day," he remarked. "That's the way you're trained. They resist [pitching on three days' rest] because of the potential of arm injury. They ought to go back and do a little history study. Cincinnati always had a five-man rotation and they always broke down—the Gary Nolans, the Jim Maloneys, the Donnie Gulletts, all those great young arms."

Bunning's approach would be different. "I would tell my minor league system I wanted starting pitchers to go every fourth day," he said. "I'd say, 'Here are the reasons. If you look at history in baseball, people who pitch on the fourth day are a lot sounder than people who pitch on the fifth day, and you can make a heck of a lot more money pitching on the fourth day. You're going to get forty starts instead of thirty-two. And it won't shorten your career.'

"All I can tell you is, the game has changed because baseball has changed it. Baseball *management*. Minor league people who didn't have to pitch on the fourth day, people who are running major league teams with no major league experience. . . . Somebody came up with the idea, if you pitch a pitcher less there's less strain on his arm; he'll be sounder. It doesn't work. Like the designated hitter, I hate it."

But as a congressman, Jim Bunning has had more serious matters to consider. It would have been interesting to see what he would have done as a big league manager or general manager or owner, but looking back on it now he is extremely grateful that he didn't get the chance to find out.

The Winter Game II

(The Manager)

ired by the Phillies, his major league managerial aspirations spoiled, Jim Bunning had to play "skipper"
one more time. Before the firing he had agreed to
manage the Escogido Leones in the Dominican Winter
League. So off to Santo Domingo he and Mary went for a
final taste of baseball life. For them, this last managerial trip
brought back memories—good and bad—of the colorful,
often wacky, sometimes frightening world of winter baseball.

Jim, in his effort to learn all he could about managing,
had spent one full season and part of another leading the
Caguas team in Puerto Rico. Actually, Bunning hadn't in-
tended to manage Caguas in 1974. He went there to scout
Phillie pitchers who were on the club, which was managed
by his old teammate Bobby Wine. While Jim was there,
Wine and the owner of the team had a falling out. Bobby
went home and Jim was asked to take over with a few games
remaining in the regular season.

"I told him I'd manage under one condition, that I get to
come back next year and manage the team," Bunning recalled. "I wasn't going to manage ten games, lose the playoffs maybe, and never be invited back."

The deal was struck. Caguas won the first round of the
playoffs, then lost a seven-game series in round two. Among
Bunning's players were Willie Montanez, Felix Millan,
Jerry Morales, Sixto Lezcano, Wayne Simpson, Eddie Fi-

gueroa, Larry Christenson, Dick Ruthven, and John Stearns, all of whom made their mark in the big leagues.

Bunning loved Stearns's attitude, his gung-ho, football-type mentality. John was, to put it mildly, a piece of work, one of the most dedicated and motivated players you'll ever find in any pro league. There were times, though, when he would get a little too hot under the collar. One such moment occurred in Puerto Rico.

"Jim was acting mad because we were getting beat [in the playoffs]," Stearns said. "He was really pissed off. I thought I detected him calling me 'a pussy' or something like that."

Rest assured, Stearns was hearing things. There is no way Bunning, or anyone else, would think of calling John Stearns "a pussy." The guy was a tiger, through and through, every bit as competitive as Bunning was in his heyday. It didn't take much to get John riled up.

"I went in after the game," Stearns recalled. "I went right into his office, threw down my stuff, and I said, 'Let's fight right now.'"

Bunning had no idea what he was so upset about, and Stearns calmed down. "I challenged him to fight. We didn't fight," John said. "I didn't press it. He didn't come around the desk. After that everything was cool. I liked him. There was something about him. He got to a level in baseball that very few players reach and he got there basically on intangibles—being a competitor and working harder and wanting it more and doing all the things you have to do to be better. I would have liked for him to be [managing] in the big leagues some day and played for him. He never bothered me—aside from that one time that I thought he was saying something to me. Maybe I was wrong. . . . Bunning loved me because Bunning and I are a lot alike. We're both red asses."

Back in Puerto Rico for a full season of managing, Bunning's club—with seven Puerto Ricans plus Stearns playing every day—closed with a rush to win the pennant after a terrible start. The irrepressible Stearns celebrated the clinching by dousing his favorite manager with a bucket of water. "He came into the manager's office," Bunning remembered, "and dumped the water all over the room and all over me."

Once again, Caguas came up short in the playoffs. The way they lost was a killer, precipitating an incident that very nearly got out of control.

"I think it was against Bayamon," Bunning said. "We're behind 1-0 or 2-1. It's the seventh inning, or maybe the eighth. Yeah, it was the eighth."

Caguas was fighting for its playoff life. A defeat and it was over.

"Felix Millan is the hitter with two on for us. Bottom of the inning, first and second, one out, and Millan hits this screaming ball down the third base line. The umpire calls it fair. We get two runs. We're ahead. And then the guy out in left field [umpire Greg Kosc] comes running in waving like this . . ."

Kosc was waving his arms back and forth, signaling no play.

"He said he'd called time out. Nobody in the ball park had seen him call time out."

Instead of Caguas being ahead by a run, Bayamon had a reprieve. Manager Bunning had a fit.

"I go absolutely bonkers, out of my gourd," he said.

Because of that phantom time out, the two runners had to go back, and Millan had to bat all over again. "By then," said Bunning, "I'm gone."

It was one of those situations where a manager has to get ejected. No way he can sit there and take something like that in stride. But Jim, having exhausted his vocabulary in the offending umpire's ear, wasn't about to leave the scene as ordered.

"We lose this game, we're out of the playoffs," he reiterated. "Let me tell you what I did. I went in [the dugout] and I sat on the bench and I will not leave. I said, 'I'm not going to leave.'"

And he stayed there, still fuming, while the crowd grew increasingly ugly.

"They had to call the troops out," Jim said. "The head of police came down and begged me to leave before they had a riot."

And still he sat, daring them to throw him out on the heels of that terrible miscarriage of justice.

Finally, the plate umpire, Durwood Merrill—"a very happy-go-lucky, nice guy to be an umpire," Bunning pointed out—started walking over to the dugout.

"I'll never forget this," Jim said. "I'm sitting in the dugout and he's coming over and somebody takes a paper cup of beer and hits him right in the face before he gets to the dugout. He says, 'Jim, you got to leave.' I said, 'What are you going to do if I don't leave?' And I said, 'An umpire can't be the one to win or lose the game.' The other umpires all realized this guy [the left field umpire] had made a big blunder.

"Finally, the head of police, or security, whatever he was, convinced me to go into the clubhouse."

Merrill's calm demeanor under bad circumstances helped to defuse the situation, as well. So Bunning left . . . and Millan couldn't duplicate the clutch double he hit on the pitch that didn't count. The runners were stranded. Caguas lost the game, and the series.

"I was very unreasonable and should have realized there could have been somebody hurt," Jim said. "I was so angry I probably wanted to get the umpire out in left field hurt."

Winter baseball in the Dominican Republic could be rough, too. Just getting there could be an adventure, as outfielder Rick Bosetti found out the year he played for Bunning's Escogido Leones in Santo Domingo. Bosetti's Dominican Airways flight out of Miami was scheduled to leave at 2:30 P.M. "I go to the desk at 12 to check in," Rick said, "and they say, 'No flight.' I go, 'What d'ya mean, no flight?'"

It turned out what they meant was that the plane had been damaged by a cement truck that was doing repair work on the runway. So Bosetti had to fly to Santo Domingo on a Spanish airline that stopped there twice a week on the way to Madrid.

"Here's my first taste of baseball in the Dominican [Republic] and before I even got there I knew what it was going to be like," he said.

A few months later I waited at that same Dominican Airways counter in Miami. And waited. And waited. Why the delay? Because the president of the country was using the plane to fly his wife to the dentist, the woman behind the counter cheerfully explained.

Watching a baseball game at the government-owned Estadio Quisqueya, where two of the four Dominican teams play, bore very little resemblance to watching a game at, say, Veterans Stadium. If you think Philadelphia fans are tough, you should spend a few hours with the fanatics in Santo Domingo. At least in Philadelphia they don't peddle bottles of rum and scotch in the stands the way vendors do Cokes in the States. Little wonder the Dominican fans get a bit unruly at times.

Jim Bunning's Escogido team lost a playoff game to Licey in the stadium they share, and the fans who had rooted for the losing Leones—and probably bet on them—were not happy. The losers showered in the cold water provided for them, dressed in the smelly wooden clubhouse that third baseman Jim Morrison called "our castle," and piled into a limousine outside the gate. There were forty or fifty fans waiting for them, and they didn't want autographs.

"They were yelling things at us—'Yankees go home! Get out of here!'—things like that," Morrison remembered. "The police had to come and clear them away."

But not before some of those fans got their hands on the limousine and rocked it, with the players inside.

Horror stories abound. Bob (Buck) Rodgers, the Licey manager, was arrested for going ten miles over the speed limit and spent forty-five minutes in a jail cell before Manny Mota—"a friend of the president," Rodgers later explained—arranged to get him out.

Actually, Santo Domingo is on the mild side compared to Santiago, according to eyewitness accounts.

"The people in Santiago are so crazy none of the umpires will ever make a call against the home club there," Bosetti declared. "Those guys are scared to death."

There was the night Bunning's team was leading Santiago by three runs. The home club had two runners on base. Bosetti faded back for a long, high fly ball.

"I go back to the fence and the ball's coming straight down," Bosetti said. "I know I've got it, but I'm going to have to jump."

He jumped, but the ball never reached his glove. Fans reaching over the railing got their grubby paws on it first. And all this time you thought such things only happened at Yankee Stadium.

"This little umpire, he's nowhere near the play and he starts saying, 'Home run, home run,'" Bosetti said. "Jim [Bunning] got thrown out. It was just a big mess."

Nevertheless, many players will tell you that, given a choice of winter league destinations, they'd choose the Dominican Republic. The Jaragua Hotel, where Jim and Mary stayed, was pleasant enough. If you got bored, there was a gambling casino on the premises with talented blackjack dealers who had an uncanny knack of drawing to twenty-one.

There weren't many dull moments during that Dominican winter. In one of the liveliest, a huge glass partition in the lounge of the Jaragua was shattered when a member of the Leones went hurtling through it. The stories told by eyewitnesses vary, as usual, but Rick Bosetti's version seems to carry the most weight, since he was the guy who went through the partition.

Jim Morrison, Bosetti, catcher Gary Alexander, and pitcher Wayne Simpson were having a few drinks when it happened.

"Mo [Morrison] stands up and says, 'I'm going to the bathroom,'"

Bosetti recalled. "I got up and said, 'Yeah, I'm going, too.' Simpson goes, 'Sit down, you'll get him [Morrison] into more trouble,' and he pushed me back. I stumbled and I went through the glass. Wayne and Mo left. It was just me and Gary Alexander sitting there. This guy comes around and starts hollering at me in Spanish, and he pulls a gun."

Fortunately, he didn't pull the trigger. There were no serious injuries, although Bunning, who heard about the incident secondhand, referred to it as "a riot."

"They tore up, I mean literally tore up, the lounge," he said. "They didn't think I knew about it, but [trainer] Mac Havard told me everything that went on."

All in all, it was a winter to remember. According to Bunning, "It was an interesting experience for me because we won [made the playoffs] in spite of all that because Felipe Alou [who coached for Bunning] was such a steadying influence on the team."

Jim Bunning's baseball career ended in late January 1977 in Estadio Quisqueya, where the Escogido Leones lost in the semifinals. It wasn't exactly the way his managerial career was supposed to end; not what he had in mind when he decided to devote all that time and effort to learning the managing end of baseball.

Certainly, he deserved a better farewell to the game that meant and means so much to him. The setting was all wrong. Even the "45" on the back of his uniform was wrong. Jim had always worn "14" but the Escogido jersey bearing that number didn't fit him.

The last game of his last season over, Bunning removed his red baseball cap and tossed it into a faded old Phillies' equipment bag on the floor of his locker. "I might as well add it to my collection," he said. Then he pulled off his jersey and took a last, long look around the clubhouse.

"The first time I sat down on the toilet in here," he reminisced, "the seat fell off and I went with it."

Jim Bunning tried very hard that night to exit laughing. But he knew he had managed his final baseball game. After all the effort he put into the last five years, and his twenty-two seasons in pro baseball before that, it was a sad moment. No way he could hide that.

"How long have you been writing?" Jim asked. Then, without waiting for an answer, he added, "that's what makes it so difficult to stop."

The Political Game

When Dick Ruthven heard that his old minor league manager Jim Bunning was turning to politics, he laughed. And the more he thought about it, the louder he laughed. Jim Bunning in politics? Jim Bunning campaigning, knocking on doors, making small talk at PTA meetings and bridge clubs? Jim Bunning kissing babies and shaking hands with total strangers and smiling through the entire ordeal? Jim Bunning giving patient, serious answers to silly questions? No way. Not the Jim Bunning that Dick Ruthven knew.

"I didn't think he could smile enough," Ruthven commented. "I could just hear him say to the first guy who said something he didn't like, 'Get lost.' What I'm trying to say is, our similar personalities led me to believe he wouldn't be a very good politician."

If Jim Bunning had overheard Dick Ruthven express that opinion, he probably would have nodded in agreement. Even Jim's biggest rooter, his wife, Mary, would have found it difficult to dispute Ruthven's analysis.

What Ruthven said "is very true," Mary Bunning acknowledged. "Jim is not a people person. In fact he is—that is, he was—an anti-people person."

He wasn't the hand-shaking, small-talking, hail-fellow-well-met type. Besides that, he had this lifelong habit of saying what he thought. Jim Bunning simply was not a political animal. And yet, through the cooperation of the Phillies, who fired him as a minor league manager, and his failure to become part owner of the Houston Astros baseball team, this most unlikely occurrence became reality.

"The fact of the matter was, I was not going to get into politics ever," Jim said. "I never had any desire to be in politics."

All that changed in the late 1970s. His managing aspirations buried, his bid for baseball ownership thwarted, Bunning went home to Fort Thomas and resumed working in the brokerage business. In addition, he opened his own "little agency" for representing ballplayers. The first year, he had "fifteen or so" under contract; the second year, the number doubled. "All young kids," Jim recalled, "mostly Triple A players who were trying to get to the major leagues."

He got infielder Jim Morrison a three-year contract. And he got outfielder Lonnie Smith a three-year contract. "These were guys who never spent a day in the big leagues and they're making $75,000 in Triple A," Bunning declared. Things were moving along very nicely when this most unlikely political candidate was visited by three of his Fort Thomas neighbors.

"I thought they were coming to talk to me about investments," Bunning said.

He thought wrong. Fred Erschell (a funeral director who was running for mayor), Jack Steinman, and Jack Cook were there to ask him if he would consider running for city council.

Bunning's initial reaction was not promising. "I told them, 'No, I don't really think I want to do that,'" he recalled. "I had just gotten out of the frying pan; what did I want to get into that for?"

They asked him to think it over, not make a hasty decision. Jim agreed to at least talk it over with Mary.

This was a whole new world, a very public world for a very private man. Jim's only political activity had been in Richard Nixon's first presidential campaign, as a member of Athletes for Nixon, and in Gerald Ford's 1976 campaign for the presidency. But those were just one-time involvements; he had never been active at the local level.

"Mary and I talked about it," he remembered. "We talked about what a great city Fort Thomas was, how it was so nice to raise our family there because we didn't worry about crime, didn't worry about anything."

They had grown to love this town of sixteen thousand and their lives there. The more they talked, the more they came to believe that they should give something back to Fort Thomas. "We said, 'OK, we'll do it,'" Bunning said.

So it was that in June of 1977 Jim Bunning did what Dick Ruthven, and countless other friends and acquaintances, thought he could never do: he became a candidate for public office. The man who "never thought about running for anything" was about to take the first small step in what was to become an exciting new career.

"I'd been in the public eye for twenty-seven years," he said. "I had no idea I'd ever want to get back into the public eye."

That first campaign didn't match Bunning against the real test of his political career: the hand-shaking, small-talking part of running for office. He was one of six candidates running on what they called the "People's Ticket." They had eight thousand postcards printed with a message that read, "Dear Friend, We would like you to vote for the People's Ticket." And each card was signed by one of the candidates.

"Everybody was supposed to send cards to the people they recognized," Bunning recalled. "The five other people went in and took about half of them. There were about four thousand cards left, and I took them all."

Then came the hardest part: he had to sign them. "And I put a little personal note on the back," he said. "I'd say, 'Dear Joe and Irma . . .' I had nothing else to do."

This was far more time-consuming than autographing baseballs in the big leagues, but Bunning kept at it. "It took me every spare moment I had," he said. "I wrote and wrote."

The hard work paid off. According to Jim, "I got the most votes of anybody because I did more work than anybody."

Making the accomplishment more noteworthy was that he was the last of thirteen candidates listed on the ballot. In Fort Thomas, at least, Jim Bunning's name recognition was very high.

He served one year on the Fort Thomas City Council. While Jim was in office, Don Johnson, his state senator for fifteen years, switched from the Republican Party to the Democratic Party. Bunning had always supported Johnson; the switch in parties bothered him.

"I talked to Jack Cook," Jim said. "I told him, 'I don't think what he [Johnson] did was very good. I think he should be challenged for the state senate seat.'"

And so, in 1979, Jim Bunning took the next, much bigger step along the political trail. He went up against the man who switched parties.

This was a whole new ball game. No longer was it enough to sign postcards and wait for the votes to pour in. This was the political game

Much of the fire was out of Bunning's fast ball by the time he returned to the Phillies in 1970. But Jim still had enough left to pitch—and win—the first game played at Veterans Stadium in 1971. Here, he's pitching against the Cincinnati Reds later in the season. *(Photo courtesy of Jim and Mary Bunning)*

There are times when even a Hall of Fame pitcher doesn't have things come out the way he planned. Here, judging from the expression on Jim Bunning's face at Connie Mack Stadium, is one of those times. *(Photo courtesy of Charles H. McGowen)*

Jim Bunning didn't always laugh at the antics of Max Patkin, the Clown Prince of Baseball; to Jim, baseball was a most serious business. But he and Max became friends, as evidenced by this picture Patkin presented to Jim as a peace offering. *(Photo courtesy of* Eugene Register-Guard/*Wayne Eastburn)*

Jim Bunning sits in the stands behind home plate in Connie Mack Stadium. No, he's not charting pitches before his next start; Jim always did that in the dugout. So what's he doing there? Just having his picture taken, apparently. *(Photo courtesy of Fred Comegys)*

Jack Kemp greets the Bunnings at a 1986 fundraiser that began in Crescent Springs, Kentucky, with a reception at the home of a supporter and was followed by a dinner at the Drawbridge Inn in Fort Mitchell. *(Photos this page courtesy of Jim and Mary Bunning)*

A smiling George Bush with the Bunnings in Louisville in November 1986. The occasion was a fundraiser held before the Republican primary during Jim's first bid for a seat in the House of Representatives.

that Dick Ruthven, among others, thought was beyond Jim Bunning's capabilities.

Jim was forty-seven by now and a grandfather. The competitive instincts were still there; the trick was to channel them in a new direction. In mid-March, with the television cameras zeroing in for close-ups, Jim Bunning made his announcement.

"I do not yet believe, I am not yet convinced, that the executive and legislative branches of the Commonwealth of Kentucky are doing all they can do for our people," he declared. "Because of that, and because I believe I can serve capably, I am announcing my candidacy for the office of state senator from Kentucky's Eleventh District. I will not only work for you, I will work with you. I will be an effective, vocal, active legislator. That is my commitment to you, and those who know me know I do not take my commitments lightly."

A week earlier, Bunning had been on the west coast of Florida, rushing between baseball training camps—the Phillies, the Mets, the Reds, the Blue Jays, the White Sox—negotiating contracts for the forty-six players he now represented. His agency business was flourishing; three years after getting fired by the Phillies he represented nearly twenty of the team's players, including seven of the fifteen pitchers on their big league roster. It was Bunning who negotiated Dick Ruthven's five-year contract, worth more than $1.5 million. But as rewarding as the agency business could be, he was itching to get more deeply involved in politics, to have some say in furthering the conservative causes he so deeply believed in. And if that meant shaking hands and talking to strangers and making speeches—well, Mary would help him get over that hurdle.

"Politics would be one of those things that she's probably better at than I am," Jim acknowledged years later. "She was always better than I was." The best thing about politics was that, unlike baseball, they could do it together. "We said, 'If that's the case, then we really like it,'" Jim noted.

They would learn the business together, walk the precincts together, do whatever the job required. It wouldn't be easy; Jim understood that. He had to prove to Dick Ruthven—and maybe to himself, as well—that he could develop a new personality, a politician's personality. Or at least a reasonable facsimile.

"I'm not a politician," he said the week he declared candidacy. "Just so they don't think I'm some dumb jock who's going to run just to run.

I owe no allegiance to anybody. The Republican Party hasn't said, 'You've got to do this, this, this, or this.'"

He had been his own man in baseball, which ultimately ended his hopes of managing the Phillies. Friends told him his independence, his unwillingness to follow the "party line" if he didn't think it was right, could work against him in politics, too.

His answer was typical Bunning. "That's just too damn bad," he responded. "If they don't want those kind of people in office, then I'm not going to be the right person. At least they'll say, 'Hey, we know where he stands.'"

His bitterness and anger over being fired by the Phillies, and the crude way it was handled, was gone. He had come to realize that, if anything, the club did him a favor by forcing him to seek out a new career. "They made the right decision," Jim commented. "I had to get out of there. The more I think about it, Paul Owens made the right decision."

It was a decision that had led to a lucrative agency business, and now to a run for the state senate.

"I'm not entering the campaign to lose," the candidate remarked. "If it means doing some things I'm not really good at—like meeting three hundred people and shaking their hands—I'm going to do it. My feeling is this: if people feel you're honest and you're trying as hard as you can to do what you feel is right, they'll vote for you. If you don't try to manipulate the truth, I think more people will be for you than against you."

If successful, then what? he was asked. The U.S. Senate perhaps?

"Yes," he replied. "Definitely. *Definitely.*"

And if not successful it would be an interesting experiment—like the five years he spent in the minor leagues trying to learn how to be a manager.

On the day he announced his decision to run, a television reporter asked Bunning why he thought he could do a better job as state senator than anyone else. "I don't know if I can," Jim replied with his customary candor, "but I'd like the chance to try."

To earn that chance, Bunning began "walking precincts" in July of 1979. Facing Ted Williams with the bases loaded and the game tied in the ninth inning would have been easier. If Mary wasn't there to walk with him, Jim wouldn't have gone. But there she was, walking one side of the street while Jim walked the other.

"I wasn't very good at it," he said. "Mary was a lot better at walking precincts and knocking on doors than I was, as you can imagine. It's just a matter of doing it and getting used to doing it and asking somebody to vote for you and having a pattern to follow about six hours a day."

To Jim, those were excruciatingly long hours. "He wouldn't do it without me," Mary confirmed. They started in the morning, went up and down the streets in forty-five targeted precincts, took half an hour off for lunch, then resumed walking. The young set of twins, David and Amy, were still living at home, so Mary's mother would come over and do the cooking for the kids while Jim and Mary walked. And walked.

Then came a glitch. Their daughter Bridget was about to get married, and there was to be a bridesmaids' luncheon while her parents were on the campaign trail. On the day it was held, Mary and Jim started out on their walk as usual; then Mary broke the news. "I said, 'You know, Jim, I've got to leave at a certain time,' and he said, 'I'll never be able to do this alone.' And I said, 'You will be fine.'"

And with that, Mary left.

Poor Jim. He must have felt as if he were pitching without any fielders behind him. Somehow, he forced himself to keep going, to knock on more doors, to introduce himself to more strangers, to ask for their votes.

Mary got home late that afternoon. No Jim. She waited anxiously. Still no Jim.

"Gosh," she remembered, "it got to be seven o'clock that night and he didn't come home."

Tension mounted. And then, finally, there he was, a big smile on his face.

"I did it," he told his wife.

Perhaps that was the moment Jim Bunning proved that he could, indeed, be a successful politician. Still, to this day, he prefers having his wife at his side. "He's funny," Mary said. "He really likes me to go with him. He says I'm his security blanket."

Jim was "terrible" at doing these things that politicians have to do when he first hit the campaign trail, according to his wife. The improvement has been considerable, but he's no Bill Clinton.

"The thing that bothers me," Mary declared, "and I've told him this. . . . He has a very keen mind and he has the capability of talking to you and doing the computer and opening mail and doing three things at one time. When I talk to somebody I like to look at them. A lot of times he'll be thinking of something and he'll look beyond, and see, I hate that. I tell him that. When we go to some of these things, you watch him. He'll not really look at the people, but that's the way he is. Still, he's come around 150 percent."

The Jim Bunning who won a sixth term as a United States congressman in 1996 and was inducted into the Baseball Hall of Fame the same year had indeed come a long way in that regard from the rather shy, very private man who ran for state senator in 1979. It was a difficult learning process, but a necessary one.

"Especially since the Hall of Fame, people want to shake his hand, and he's sort of shy like that," Mary observed. "What I do when I'm with him, I will shake their hands and I think it embarrasses him or something and he knows he has to, too. That's how I handle that. He's just never been that open. He's a private person. That's all right, except when you're in a political life. Then you better stick your hand out there."

Jim, with Mary's considerable moral support, shook lots of hands in the summer and early fall of 1979. He was waging an uphill battle against a popular, longtime incumbent who was considered a shoo-in when the campaign began. His opponent, Bunning recalled, didn't take Jim very seriously until the last few weeks of the campaign, when the polls began to show the race tightening significantly.

If learning to walk those precincts and shake those hands was difficult, so was election night. It was so close that the outcome couldn't be determined until the results from the last of the eighty-five precincts came in. The wait was excruciating. Bunning led by a few hundred votes, but the machines had broken down in the last precinct, and it would take a couple of hours to fix them. About five hundred votes were at stake, enough to turn a spectacular upset victory into a tough, extra-inning defeat.

The final wait, in a house filled with people eager to celebrate, was especially difficult for Mary Bunning. "It reminded me of the '64 season," she noted. "There we were again, so close to winning. I thought, 'This is terrible. All these people here waiting to celebrate and we can't celebrate yet because the final results aren't in.'"

In 1964, the final results were heartbreaking; the Phillies lost by a game. In 1979, the final results were exhilarating; Jim Bunning won by 398 votes out of more than 21,000 cast.

"When we were going through this," Mary remembered, "I felt like I was going through the perfect game all over again."

To Jim, when the final tally was in, it was tantamount to getting that final strike against the Mets at Shea Stadium fifteen years before. He had done what so many thought he could never do. He went out and campaigned the way a man has to campaign to win an important public office, and he won a race he wasn't supposed to win.

"I've never been involved in anything that was so consuming," he said as he and Mary prepared for a short vacation in Guadalajara. "It's a very personal and satisfying thing."

Particularly satisfying was the fact he had stayed under his $30,000 campaign budget while his opponent was spending $84,000.

"We knocked on 14,250 doors," Bunning said. "And Mary walked every precinct with me. We went to the people."

And they wrote to the people. Mary signed a letter to every registered woman voter, a total of about nineteen thousand. Twelve thousand letters were sent to senior citizens. But what counted most was that daily, door-to-door, person-to-person campaigning.

"I lost twelve pounds in my campaign," Bunning remarked. "I'm down to 208. I'm in pitching shape. I'm telling you, it's a tough racket. It's like managing. You're dependent on an awful lot of people. At times you get the same feeling of hopelessness or helplessness."

At other times you get a great feeling of accomplishment, a sense of unabashed exhilaration, the kind of deep satisfaction that, Jim Bunning suspected, managing the Phillies never would have brought.

In the final analysis, Jim's popularity in his home town made the difference. Fort Thomas voters favored him two-to-one, although his opponent also lived there. Beating Don Johnson gave Jim instant political credibility in Frankfort, the state capital, where the defeated incumbent was known as an aggressive state senator as well as a popular one. After serving two years of his four-year term, Bunning became the floor leader for the Republicans, who held just nine of the thirty-eight seats in the upper house. It was a rare honor for a state senator serving his first term. But there were bigger challenges ahead.

The Republicans were looking for somebody to run for governor in Kentucky, obviously a thankless chore in a state that had elected only two Republican governors since 1907. Jim Bunning was helping with the search, calling on potential candidates, trying to persuade them to accept the challenge. He had already filed for re-election to the state senate; running for governor as the longest of long shots in this strongly Democratic commonwealth was not high on his list of priorities, although the topic came up repeatedly when the Bunnings and Jack and Edie Cook went to the British Virgin Islands for a vacation that Jim called "the best we ever had."

"We had talked and talked about running for governor," Bunning recalled. "'No, Jack, no,' I told him. 'We're not going to do it.'"

Jack Cook understood only too well. He, better than most, knew the pitfalls that confronted a Republican running statewide in Kentucky, and he spelled them out to Bunning. So it was decided: Jim was not going to run. They would have to go on looking for somebody else, some other sacrificial lamb to throw at the Democrats.

That was in January of 1983. When the Bunnings and the Cooks returned from their vacation the pressure mounted. There was still no Republican nominee.

"We had no credible candidate," Bunning said. "You always have fringe people; that's what we were going to wind up with. None of our congressmen would run. Both U.S. senators were Democrats."

As minority leader in the state senate, Jim was the GOP's highest elected state official. The filing deadline was March 28, which happened to be Mary's birthday. Maybe there was a message in that. At any rate, Bunning began to weaken as various Republicans tried to talk him into running and promised to help if he did. Jim Host, who had been on the screening committee with Bunning, promised to be his campaign chairman and to help him raise money if only he'd say yes.

Money. That was going to be a problem. Martha Layne Collins had raised approximately $3 million already in her bid for the governorship—and the Republicans hadn't even found somebody to run against her. How could an opponent start this far behind and hope to make a race of it?

"I didn't even think about that," Bunning recalled. "It didn't enter my mind that we couldn't overcome anything if we worked hard enough. That's the way I'd always been."

So he finally said yes about a week before the deadline.

"I was totally not ready to run for statewide office," he pointed out, "but I ran anyway."

There's a big difference between running in 120 counties and running in one county. "It was a real learning experience," Jim Bunning said. "I never did catch up to the curve."

It wasn't for lack of trying. Slowly, steadily Jim was improving his campaigning technique. As Jack Cook explained late in the race, "When Jim began he'd sit there. He wouldn't move. Now he plunges into a room. You wouldn't believe it's the same person."

Billboards popped up around the state. Jim Bunning, looking ever so serious, stared out at the would-be voters—with the same unyielding stare that once terrified his players in the minor leagues. Next to his face, one word in big, bold letters: Leadership. There was one problem, though. Kentucky had 1,276,150 registered Democrats and 521,494 registered Republicans. Jim had better odds than that when he was pitching for the Phillies. The early polls showed him thirty-some points behind.

There were some good days along the campaign trail, and quite a few bad ones. Flying around the state in small planes, and occasionally helicopters, wasn't much fun on days when the fog rolled in and the rain poured down. One day Bunning took off from northern Kentucky and headed south for Lexington. "It was a very heavy rainstorm," he remembered. "We came out of the clouds and the runway was over there and we were landing here. I mean, we were landing in a field."

They got down safely, but it was hard on the nerves. "I would never do those things anymore," Bunning declared.

A helicopter trip to the Shelbyville Village Plaza Shopping Center, where fifty people waited in the rain, was equally breathtaking. Once again, fog was the problem. The pilot announced he would have to make an emergency landing; he could hardly see a thing. He hovered, squinting into the soup, and finally found a possible landing area in the parking lot of a big mall. "We'll be OK," he informed Jim and his traveling companion, "as long as we don't hit any wires."

The copter descended. The passengers—and no doubt the pilot— held their collective breath. No wires were hit. All lived to tell the tale. And write about it.

It's unlikely Martha Layne Collins encountered such problems. In Kentucky gubernatorial races, the fog generally lifts for Democratic candidates, or so it seems. A former beauty contest winner (she was chosen Kentucky Derby Festival queen in 1959) the lieutenant governor, then forty-six, had a lot going for her in this campaign. Some of those things, the Republicans charged, were highly unethical. Or downright illegal.

Dirty tricks were very much a part of this race; the Democrats, with the arrogance that comes from long-time domination, pulled out all the stops. A Bunning press conference would be scheduled, and then reporters would receive a call saying it had been canceled. Except it hadn't been canceled. "Bunning for Governor" signs posted along the road would be torn down as fast as they were put up. Lots of penny-ante stunts like that. But not everything was penny-ante. Before this election was over, the Republicans would accuse the Democrats of literally buying votes—handing out $10 and $20 bills in small towns to make sure that their supporters would vote, or that Bunning's supporters wouldn't. Most of the money apparently was spent in the Fifth District, a Republican stronghold that Bunning had to carry by a wide margin to have any chance to win the election.

"Buying votes," Jim muttered when it was over, "it never ends. If nobody does anything about it, they're going to keep getting away with it."

Bunning and his people were warned what to expect early in the campaign when a woman who had worked for Harvey Sloane, who had opposed Collins in the Democratic primary, came over to work for Jim.

"She was in the Sloane suite the night the primary was going on," Bunning observed. "She told me this story: [an election official] called the Sloane campaign about four o'clock in the afternoon and said, 'If you want the right numbers out of here we need that $25,000,' and the Sloane campaign was so convinced they were going to win they said, 'No, we don't need your votes.' As the night progressed, Sloane saw he was going to lose. So they made a phone call from that suite in the hotel to the county-court clerk in either Floyd or Perry County, I'm not sure which, and said, 'Is that deal still available?' They said, 'No, it's been taken care of; you're too late.' I don't think Martha Layne had a clue [what was going on], but somebody did."

Any way you look at it, the race was a long, uphill fight for the Bunnings. But Jim, who loved to compete, couldn't wait to get started. And Mary was the eternal optimist.

"A lot of people think that running for governor is an ego trip," she told the *Campbell County Recorder*. "That's not it. Jim and I don't need that. If people could only realize it, we're doing it for all the people in Kentucky."

Mary fervently believed that, and so did her husband. They saw the long-ruling Democrats as corrupt, and some of the things their people spotted the enemy doing did little to change their minds.

Once of the biggest plusses Jim Bunning had going for him was his wife. Mary was a terrific campaigner—so terrific that Bunning's strategists decided to let her go out on her own by July. "They figured I could handle it," Mary said. "I'm a very happy person and I love people."

And people, with very few exceptions, loved her. Mary was on the go bright and early, doing her exercises by 6:30 in the morning, then rushing off to check her campaign schedule for the day. "One time I didn't get my schedule until [9:10]," she said, "and it said, 'Leave at 8:45.'"

Such minor snafus didn't bother her. She didn't even appear to get upset the day someone mistook her for Martha Layne Collins. Mary handled the case of mistaken identity with a smile. And if she ran into Collins supporters, as she often did, that didn't faze her either. In fact, she seemed to enjoy it. "Just to see the look of surprise on their faces to see that I'd go into the lion's den with my head high and say, 'Hi, I'm Mary Bunning,' was worth it," she said.

As the campaign progressed, the polls showed the race tightening. Bunning still trailed, but it no longer seemed hopeless.

When you're a politician, you can't allow yourself to think it's hopeless, and you certainly can't show it to the outside world. With Bunning, it wasn't an act. He never went into a baseball game thinking he had no chance to win, and he wasn't about to concede this race to Martha Layne Collins and the hated Democrats.

The last two weeks were hectic. Jim was getting daily tracking polls now, and a glimmer of light began to show as the numbers grew closer. On Monday, October 31, he flew from the Greater Cincinnati Airport to Lexington, where he was to check with his precinct leaders. Joe Cowley, a big, happy-go-lucky guy who was a major league pitcher and a Bunning client, was Jim's driver during the campaign. Cowley met him at the airport, still bubbling with excitement over the rock and roll concert he had attended the night before at a sold-out Rupp Arena. The group, Cowley explained, was called The Police.

"I went backstage and saw them," he told the candidate. "I had a drink with them at the Hyatt. What do you think of that?"

"I'm not going to tell you what I think," Bunning told him in a rare display of diplomacy.

There simply wasn't much time for small talk. Election day was rapidly approaching. At times tempers grew short. "The only reason you want me around, you want somebody to yell at," Mary told him, and the candidate quickly calmed down.

There was a big round of applause as the Bunnings entered their Lexington headquarters, giving each other a hug as the applause grew louder. A television reporter asked Jim why he hadn't agreed to run in January, waiting until March instead. "Do you really want to be governor?" the guy asked. Jim assured him he wanted it very much, explaining that he had waited until he was convinced there was a chance to win.

It was pleasant being in campaign headquarters, surrounded by his people. Somehow, the outlook seemed rosier that afternoon — until Bunning learned shortly before 2 P.M. that yet another mystery caller had notified news organizations that Jim was holding a 2 P.M. press conference on the steps of the courthouse. No such press conference was scheduled. Another one of those penny-ante dirty tricks. "We're dealing with some bad people," Bunning commented before resuming his calls to backers around the state.

"Hello, congressman, this is Jim Bunning. Jefferson County is coming around. If northern Kentucky and the Fifth come through, this is going to be a barnburner. She's starting negative commercials on the radio this afternoon, the same ones she used for Harvey Sloane [Collins's opponent in the Democratic primary]. Only the name's changed."

One call after another, always expressing optimism, doing everything possible to keep his troops pepped up and working.

"OK, keep it going," he was telling a county chairman. "And get those damn door hangers up."

Always there were problems, big and small. A photographer who took color stills for national television had taken the wrong type, Jim was informed. Did he have time to pose for new ones?

"No, I don't," he said. "What I'm doing is more important than those pictures."

And then back to the phone. "Hello, this is Jim Bunning. Keep it going. Don't let 'em steal it from us. It's a barnburner, let me tell you."

Somebody let him know that Beechwood High School had taken a vote of the students. They favored Jim 224-64. Better yet, Woodford County High School, in Martha Layne Collins's home district, went for Bunning 164-157. If only high school kids could vote in the real election.

All the while, Mary never stopped campaigning. At lunch in a restaurant with Jack Cook's wife, Mary asked the owner if he'd mind her going around from table to table and introducing herself to the patrons. He told her to go ahead. Edie Cook was impressed with Mary's easy campaigning style. "If someone says, 'No way I would vote for him,' it doesn't disturb her," she said. "Mary just smiles and says, 'It was nice to see you, anyway.'"

It was Tuesday, November 1, one week before election day. Bunning came out of a midmorning strategy session wearing a long face. The latest poll showed him 12 points behind. "Mary'll be upset when she hears that," he said.

Jim was upset, too, of course, but that didn't stop him from putting away a patty melt with everything on it, a bowl of chili, and a piece of chocolate cream pie for lunch at a local eatery. Three men at a corner table spotted the gubernatorial candidate and struck up a conversation.

"You've got these three votes, anyway," one man told him.

"Don't you have any friends?" Bunning asked.

"Yeah, they're going to vote for you, too," said the man, "but they don't think you can win."

Suddenly, the chocolate cream pie didn't taste quite so sweet.

Bunning was still fuming over the latest reports of dirty tricks. In one area his posters had been torn down and burned. And there were more of those phony calls telling the media that scheduled events had been called off. Tough game, politics.

The next day Jim was off and running again. On the steps of the annex to the capitol he said, "I've come to assure the people that state employees have nothing to fear from a Bunning administration. When they go in the voting booth they can vote their conscience. . . ."

A reporter asked him about the latest polls.

"Ask her [Collins]," Bunning snapped. "It's her turn to release a poll. We did the last time."

"What if the polls show her ahead?" the reporter pressed on.

"That's fine," Jim replied. "That's her poll. I wouldn't pay good money for her pollster."

"How would you assess your chances?" somebody inquired.

"Even money," answered Bunning, calling the campaign and the uphill battle he was waging "the most rewarding experience of my life."

Then it was off to a shopping center. There, standing on the back of a fire truck, he renewed his attack on the Democrats. "Six days to go," he noted. "The race is dead even. We do not want to go back to what we had, the old group paying off this person and that person."

Except, of course, the race wasn't "dead even." Not yet at least. Jim was convinced a lot could happen in six days. He had done things no Republican gubernatorial candidate in Kentucky had done before, and he wasn't about to quit now. He had gone into a black neighborhood on the west side of Louisville to campaign and Lonnie Smith had gone with him. Maybe the people who lived in that tough area couldn't relate to Jim Bunning, but they surely could relate to this black baseball player who had made it back to the big leagues after asking for help to combat a serious drug problem. Lonnie spoke openly and passionately about his difficulties, and about how his former minor league manager and current agent had helped him. For three days and two nights, the young man, who had been so shy when Jim first knew him, campaigned with Bunning. It took a lot of nerve on Lonnie's part to do it, and it underscored the way he felt about Jim.

Recalling that experience, Lonnie Smith said: "I was scared, nervous. I wasn't used to doing anything like that. We went to a little college where girls and boys were learning to become nurses and things like that. I did all right there because most of the kids were around my age. I felt a lot more comfortable.

"I just explained who I was, why I was with him, helping him with his campaign, the type of person he was, why I trusted him and believed in him, and how they could do the same because he was an honest person who worked real hard to help the people. I told them a little bit about my background, my drug problem and everything. I did real well there. . . . It was an experience; I enjoyed it.

"The thing I couldn't get used to was constantly going from one place to another, driving from one town to another. You've got to be dedicated to do that, there's so much work involved."

Lonnie Smith even helped out at Jim's campaign office. "That was where I had most of my fun," he recalled. "I got to meet the people helping him. But God, I don't think I could ever run for office."

Bunning was grateful for Lonnie's help, but would it do any good? After all, those neighborhoods were Democratic strongholds. They wouldn't be voting for Lonnie Smith; Bunning's name was on the ballot.

Jim had to be asking himself that question and more as he raced here and there, back and forth, in the final week of campaigning, memories of the last several months tumbling through his head. So much work. So many people willing to help. But would it add up to victory?

"[Martha Layne Collins] spent one million dollars the last three weeks on TV," he was telling the people from the back of a flatbed truck. "We're going to spend a total of 1.5 million dollars for the entire campaign on everything. Touch as many people as you can. Come November 8 we'll all have a big celebration."

He kept pushing the idea that the race was up for grabs, that anything could happen on election day.

At Bunning headquarters in Danville, home of the Centre College Praying Colonels, whose football team had beaten Harvard in a monumental upset sixty years before, Bunning told his supporters, "When you're even in the ninth the last three outs are the most important. Please take part in the last six days of this campaign. It's been an uphill battle from the start. Now's the time to put on the coals."

Then off he went on a walk down Main Street, stopping in a crowded pool hall. "I just want to say hello," he told the somewhat startled clientele, shaking hands and smiling. Dick Ruthven wouldn't have believed it.

Next stop was a bank, where a man told him about a remark allegedly made by a "big Democrat." It was, he said, something to the effect, "What scares me most about this campaign, one of them might win."

Hmmm. Maybe Democrats were having second thoughts about Collins.

It was a seemingly endless grind, this last-ditch round of campaigning. Now a shopping center in Shelbyville. Later a school cafeteria in Louisville, where a bingo game was in progress. Not all the bingo players were happy to see him. A gray-haired man with a cast on his left arm, obviously a Democrat, glared at the intruder and said, "If he stays much longer we'll have to ask him to buy an entrance card."

Someone asked Bunning about his views on gay rights.

"That's not my bag," Jim replied without hesitation. "I've got problems with that. . . ." And then he added, "Well, I guess I just blew the gay vote."

Off to the Knights of Columbus Blessed Mother Council No. 4089 he rushed. Two reporters were waiting outside when Bunning arrived. They had been told they couldn't come in.

They missed hearing Bunning say that being governor "takes decisive leadership, someone who's not afraid of the job we've got to do.

. . . I can't imagine someone directing our state for four years saying, 'Maybe,' or, 'I'll study the issue.'"

No doubt about it. The contrast between the candidates in that regard was about as clear-cut as you can get. Martha Layne Collins did a lot of hedging. Jim Bunning did not—except for the time a red-headed kid with glasses at the University of Louisville asked him, "Who do you like better, Louisville or the University of Kentucky?" Jim wisely ducked that one.

Through it all, a candidate and his supporters were hard-pressed to maintain a sense of humor. But they tried. A cartoon prominently displayed on the wall in Jim's Louisville headquarters had this caption: "Drive carefully. The life you save may be a Republican and we can't afford to lose a single vote."

Martha Layne Collins's campaign slogan, "Democrats Together," also came in for some not-so-gentle ribbing. Mary Bunning, an accomplished artist, did an oil painting of pigs at a trough. "We call it *Democrats Together*," her husband explained.

Thursday, November 3, dawned with an article on Jim in the *Louisville Courier-Journal* that didn't receive high marks at Bunning headquarters.

"He came from a family of Democrats and was a union leader in the entertainment industry, but wound up a conservative Republican," it began.

"Bunning, who relatives recall was a bit withdrawn as a boy and uneasy with fame as a man, displays in public a rigid seriousness of purpose unrelieved by outbursts of humor or amiability.

"He's been described in certain Democratic quarters as a splendid example of Reaganism without a human face.

"Bunning's abrupt and abrasive manner has irritated many people in all branches of state government in Frankfort, where he has served as Campbell County's state senator since 1979. . . ."

There didn't seem to be many votes in that article. But months of campaigning, complete with the slings and arrows of outrageous politics, had taught Jim to roll with the punches. Some of those fogbound airplane trips were harder to take in stride.

The worst was saved for the final stages of the race—a flight in an Aerostar that was scheduled to land at Sturgis, in extreme western Kentucky. It was an absolutely rotten day, with visibility at the little airport near zero. The pilot was Jim Clackett, who had flown Bunning before. "He's the guy who told me in Russell Springs that we've got a twenty-three hundred foot runway and our plane takes twenty-nine hundred feet, 'But don't worry, we'll get up OK.'"

And they did get up OK. But this was different. They were trying to get down, and nobody—and that included Clackett—could see a thing. Not surprisingly, as the intrepid travelers approached Sturgis the pilot was informed that the airport was officially closed. But having come this far, he decided to give it a try anyway. So down they went through the thick fog, lower and lower, seeing nothing but praying a lot.

"Visibility's two hundred feet at Sturgis," the pilot told Bunning and his companion. "It doesn't look good."

But he continued to descend, determined to attempt an instrument landing.

"I'll give it one try," he said.

Fortunately for all concerned, it was a successful try. "We couldn't see anything until we hit the ground," Bunning recalled. He wasn't exaggerating.

I still remember the surprised look of the man who met us at the airport when the plane landed. "It's amazing you could even see this place, no less the runway," he told the pilot.

Quentin Wesley had waited at the Sturgis Airport for Bunning's arrival. He was to drive the candidate to his scheduled destination, a nearby coal mine. Wesley had just about given up when, lo and behold, he heard the sound of an approaching plane.

"We were going to leave in ten minutes," he told Bunning. "The airport manager said, 'No way they can land.' Then I heard you go over. He said, 'That crazy guy!'"

All that so Bunning could visit Peabody Coal Company's Camp No. 11 Mine, southeast of Morganfield, a peculiar stop for a Republican candidate for governor. If the plane ride had been scary, the automobile trip wasn't exactly a pleasure junket. At one point, as his passengers held on for dear life, Quentin Wesley passed a big truck on a narrow road in a pouring rain and then remarked casually, "Wouldn't it be something if I killed you on the ground?"

"Especially," replied Bunning, "when we should've been killed up there."

The mine visit was a waste of time. Jim, wearing a hard hat, gave the obligatory pep talk. "Hi, I'm Jim Bunning," he told the miners. "I'd appreciate your vote on the eighth."

Sweating profusely, the miners—it's doubtful there was a Republican in the lot—stopped working long enough to listen to this man they almost certainly had no intention of supporting. Even if the sun had been shining and the Sturgis Airport had been open for business, this would have been a good place for candidate Bunning to avoid. Only one reporter bothered to show up and not a single television camera was in sight. Live and learn.

All in all, it was an eventful day, one in which a poll of 150 registered voters showed a whopping 23 percent undecided. It was also a day in which the Bunning people made plans to file a suit against six election boards that had no Republican precinct workers, a violation of election laws.

The visit to the coal mine out of the way, the Bunning party headed for Bowling Green. Arriving there, Jim shook hands with the four official greeters and remarked, "Most people I've seen today."

Things improved dramatically at Edmondson County High School. The students waited on bleacher seats on one side of the gym, and the adults sat on the other; a speaker's platform had been set up in the foul lane of the basketball court. When Bunning entered, the adults gave him a standing ovation. These were his people. At last.

Using no notes, Bunning gave an excellent speech, his left hand resting on the rostrum, his right hand chopping the air as he made his points in a manner reminiscent of John F. Kennedy.

"It's about time the people decided the old form of government, where they pay off their buddies, the old spoils system, has to leave," he declared.

"Four years from now there will be someone here campaigning for governor and education will not be the issue because I will have done something about it."

He waited for the applause to stop, then went on, using the ninth-inning, game-tied analogy again. "If the people are going to get their government back then I have to be elected," he told them. More applause. It was the high point of the day, and quite a long day it was. By the time Jim got around to eating lunch at Shoney's, it was 4:30 in the afternoon.

Back in Lexington, Joe Cowley reported that Channel 27 was taking a most unscientific phone poll. The way it worked, apparently, was that callers heard a recorded list of the two major candidates and one very minor one. The "B" choice was Bunning, the "C" choice Collins. If you wanted Bunning you said "Stop!" after B; if you preferred Collins it was "Stop!" after C. Sounded simple enough. But Jim was told of a call from his operatives downstate asking how the poll worked. Naturally, they planned to make several calls designed to boost their man's total.

"They called seventeen times," Edie Cook told him, "and said 'Stop!' after B, but it kept going through C. Finally, the eighteenth time, it stopped at B. I think," noted Mrs. Cook, "we voted seventeen times for Collins."

There was a poll being conducted on another station, as well. This one was less subject to error. If you wanted Collins, you were instructed to say "Yes." If you were for Bunning, you were to say "No." As might be expected, the Bunning backers weren't too thrilled with that arrangement, either.

Still, Jim seemed in a reasonably good mood as the final weekend before the election approached. Happily, dumb questions were at a minimum. As tired as he had to be, there's no telling how Bunning would have reacted if someone had pushed him to the breaking point. Like the time Jim delivered a long, detailed speech on education. The speech over, the points carefully covered, Bunning felt pretty good about things until a woman approached and said, "That's fine, but what are you going to do about education?"

Jim threw up his hands, muttered, "Nothing," and walked away. He went back to apologize minutes later.

The Friday tracking poll was the best yet. It read Collins 46 percent, Bunning 38.5 percent, undecided 15 percent. "It's still winnable," Jim decided, "but a lot of work has to be done. If the '64 Phillies could lose," he added, "anything can happen."

There was a visit to a senior citizens' home at noon. Jim talked to a 98-year-old man in a wheelchair, letting Thomas Lilly know that he had a father, 81, and a mother, 80. Then he visited with Emma Snyder, also in a wheelchair. A very alert 102, she told Bunning she was 84, proving that you don't have to be middle aged to fib about your birthdate. ABC News had a cameraman there, and Bunning asked him when the footage would be aired. "Six-thirty Monday evening," the man told him, "unless there's another invasion."

He was referring to the invasion of Grenada in October 1983.

"We get pre-empted by invasions," he warned Bunning.

Another plane trip was scheduled, so Joe Cowley drove Bunning to the Lexington Airport early in the afternoon. To gain entry to the area where private planes are kept it was necessary to announce yourself at the gate. Dutifully, Cowley pushed the button to speak.

"Should I say it's Governor Bunning?" he asked.

"Do what you want," Jim told him. "You will anyway."

"Governor Bunning here for his plane," Cowley chirped.

Nothing happened.

"Governor Bunning here for his plane," repeated Cowley.

The gate swung open.

"Governor Bunning sounds good," Cowley said.

"Now we have to make it happen," the candidate replied.

An editorial in the *Campbell County Recorder* brought some smiles to the Bunning camp. "Conviction, Purpose Distinguish Bunning as Best Bet for Troubled State," the headline read.

"Nowhere was the difference between these two candidates demonstrated more clearly than in the televised debate Oct. 12," the editorial stated. "When directly asked, Mr. Bunning said he would sign a right-to-work law. Mrs. Collins, on the other hand, sidestepped the question, delaying any decision until the state legislature has dealt with the proposal.

"It is this type of equivocation that Mrs. Collins has constantly demonstrated in her governmental experience. As lieutenant governor and president of the state senate she did not come forward as a spokesperson for the education and economic development programs she now characterizes as vital to the state. It is this silence in a position of power that makes Mrs. Collins' ability to govern suspect. We expect more from a governmental leader than good-will trips and ribbon cuttings.

"As a member of the senate, Mr. Bunning showed no reluctance in dealing with the realities of government. An outspoken senator, he was chosen to lead the minority party. He made known his stands and fought to make his voice heard. This is not the demagoguery Mrs. Collins has made it out to be. It is a strong legislator working for his constituents.

"It is that conviction, that purpose, which distinguishes Mr. Bunning in the gubernatorial campaign. . . . It is the time for a strong leader who has the courage of convictions. Jim Bunning is the only candidate to show that courage."

Bunning had, in fact, appeared to outpoint his opponent by a wide margin in their debate televised over the public network. But the impact of his showing was probably minimal; the viewing audience was not large. Still, it was nice to know that somebody had noticed — even if that somebody was a newspaper in his home district.

An interviewer from WAVE-TV cornered Bunning in a corridor at the Bethesda Senior Citizens Center and commented, "They [the Democrats] say the suit [charging fraud] is a desperation tactic."

"If doing what we can to ensure a fair election is an act of desperation, we need some acts of desperation," the candidate retorted.

Corruption was on his mind. His people — at least those who had been through the Kentucky political wars before in these statewide elections — had warned him what to expect; clearly they, and therefore he, expected the worst. One of his commercials late in the campaign was titled "Let's Make History"; of which Bunning cracked, "I'll tell 'em let's make history — have an honest election."

Among friends in the strongly Republican Fifth District, Jim hit hard at the corruption issue in a speech at the Anchor Motel in Monticello. His audience listened attentively, then gave him a standing ovation when he was done.

On to the courthouse he went, somehow keeping pace with the whirlwind schedule prepared for him on this last weekend. There was a voting booth in the courthouse corridor. "Pull it a few times," a man, obviously a Bunning backer, called out to Jim. "Get a head start."

"Just make sure nobody's done that already," the candidate replied in all seriousness. "We'll be happy to start off with zeroes for everybody."

In the courtroom, a Bunning for Governor sign was taped to the wall next to the American flag. These were Jim's people, all right.

There was no rest on the last Saturday before the election. If anything, the pace grew even more hectic. First, a visit to a senior citizens' apartment complex in Dayton, the site of a destructive flood nearly half a century before. Many of the residents had been born in the hospital that had stood on this spot until the flood of '37 damaged it beyond repair.

At noon Jim and Mary flew to Louisville to watch the homecoming football game against Southern Mississippi. Before the kickoff, of course, they made the rounds at the various tailgate parties. More hands to shake. More pleas for support.

"I'm a baseball fan," one enthusiastic man told the candidate. "I saw you pitch for the Phillies."

"We need your support Tuesday," Jim reminded him.

"OK," the man said. "Only trouble, I'm from Indiana."

Bunning's driver had overslept. Joe Cowley didn't show up until Jim and Mary were in the stadium parking lot with the tailgaters.

"I won't even tell you about the offer the Yankees made," Cowley told Bunning.

"What offer?" Jim asked his driver/client. "If you'd been in the car we could've talked all the way out."

Cowley, who would go on to pitch a no-hit game of his own for the White Sox a few years later, looked crestfallen over being late. "I've got a sick feeling like I missed a game in New York or something," he confided. "Like I thought it was a 7:30 game and I wake up at 2 in the afternoon and they're playing the national anthem on TV."

Not to worry. Bunning forgave him. Besides, there was no time to get angry; there was a livestock show to visit. Also, more chili to eat for supper. A guy selling beer and soft drinks stopped the candidate to inform him, "I'm voting for you. I don't care about your politics, but I like your baseball."

Finally, back to the Greater Cincinnati Airport. "This is an unbelievable emotional drain," Jim said when the plane landed. "I'm going to sleep two days when it's over."

There was a new tracking poll out, and it actually showed Bunning slightly ahead. An aberration? Possibly. But it sent hopes soaring. Maybe, just maybe, Martha Layne Collins was going to emulate the '64 Phillies after all and snatch defeat from the jaws of victory.

Just in case the Bunning backers were feeling too good about things, the *Kentucky Enquirer* (the commonwealth's edition of the *Cincinnati Enquirer*) greeted them with a front-page story on Sunday. Actually, it was a *Washington Post* article based on an interview conducted several weeks before. Headlined "Collins Likely Winner," the story had her ahead by 15 points.

Early Sunday afternoon the Bunnings were airborne again. No fog now, though. Not a cloud in the sky. If you ignored the pollution that hung over downtown Cincinnati in the distance, it was a perfect day.

Jim stared down at the Ohio River, admiring the peaceful scene. The Ohio looked like a huge, grayish blue snake basking in the Sunday sun. The pilot swung to the left, lowered the gear, and made a perfect landing on runway 36. Flying seemed so safe, so easy on days like this. That fogbound airport in Sturgis seemed a million miles away.

As usual, the news was mixed. On the positive side, the *Danville Advocate*, normally Democratic in its politics, had come out for Bunning. On the negative side, Gordon Wade, the finance director for the Republican Party in Kentucky, was irate over the refusal of the *Kentucky Post* to accept a full-page ad that would have reprinted part of an editorial the paper ran during the Democratic primary blasting Martha Layne Collins.

"They said they didn't want it taken out of context," Wade told Bunning. "It's thoroughly consistent with the entire editorial. I told them I'd blow up the building if they didn't take the ad."

He was only kidding. The only blowup was verbal; the building remained standing even though the ad didn't run.

That minor setback was followed by another. Bunning was scheduled to speak at a luncheon gathering at Fort Thomas's fifty-five-and-over club. These were his friends and neighbors. Upon entering, Jim walked around, greeting people by name. Nothing could possibly go wrong here. Or could it?

Shortly before the Bunnings arrived, a Collins representative had appeared, announcing that Martha Layne was treating everybody to lunch. You had to get up early in the morning to outfox those Kentucky Democrats.

"Collins predicts a two-to-one win," a lady from NBC told Bunning, mike in hand. "Do you think you have a chance to win?"

"Not only win," replied Bunning, "but I think I'm going to win going away."

He was entering the home stretch now. An appearance at Pioneer Park in nearby Covington, where a balloon race was in progress; an early evening trip to a church, where a bingo game was in full swing; and then the final weekend of campaigning would be history. Jim Bunning and his wife could go home and sleep the sleep of the weary.

"This is the last stop," Jim observed on the way to the church. The relief in his voice was evident.

Bunning's job at the church wasn't to deliver a rousing speech; it was to call out the bingo numbers. Even with an election so close, these bingo lovers had their priorities in order.

Up on the stage marched the gubernatorial candidate.

"Eye-28," he barked. "Gee-60. Oh-70. Bingo?"

More than a dozen hands shot up. The place was loaded with winners. Maybe they, at least, would ignore Martha Layne Collins's free lunch and vote for the man who called their numbers. One could only hope.

Jim's daughter Amy, sitting at one of the tables, reported the following conversation.

Lady: Is it true he has nine kids?
Second Lady: It's true.
First Lady: He must've done something besides play baseball.

Said Amy, "The whole table cracked up."

No question about it; the bingo players—especially the winners—were impressed with the Republican candidate.

"You're not only a good ballplayer and a good politician," a woman told Bunning, "you're a good bingo caller."

It remained for yet another woman to put matters in some sort of perspective.

"My husband always says if our bingo game gets raided, he'll bail me out," she declared. "Wouldn't it be something if the raid comes while the next governor is here calling the numbers?"

Let the record show there was no raid, and Bunning left to a rousing round of applause. Clearly, a winning bingo card outweighed a three-dollar lunch any day.

"The last one," sighed Bunning as he climbed in his car for the ride home. "It's in the hands of the electorate now, and it's scary. Boy, is it scary!"

On the way home, he drove past a building in downtown Newport owned by long-time Cincinnati Reds shortstop David Concepcion. Strung across the top floor was a big sign with Bunning's name on it.

"He said he owed me one," Jim explained. "He hit his first big league home run off me."

Before the Bunnings retired for the night there was one last call from party headquarters. The latest poll showed Jim about 4 points behind.

Election Day was clear, with temperatures in the mid-sixties. The candidate voted, then arrived at his Lexington headquarters around noon.

"Can you imagine the AP sending somebody from Cincinnati to interview me who knew nothing about the campaign and asks me to discuss the issues?" he asked. "I told him to get lost."

"We've got so many people praying you wouldn't believe it," Mary Bunning was saying. "So if the Lord wants us to win, we'll win."

Jim's campaign chairman, Jim Host, was trying his best to view things optimistically as the moment of truth approached. Running for governor in Kentucky as a Republican "is the most difficult situation that exists anywhere in the country," he stated. "To think we've come as close as we have. It's a miracle."

As the day wore on, reports kept coming in about payoffs in certain areas — especially the Fifth District, where the campaign expected to roll up a large plurality. After all was said and done, Jim's people estimated that $250,000 in cash was distributed in ten counties in the Fifth District, giving a new meaning to the phrase "Taking the Fifth."

"The fact of the matter is, they didn't tell them they had to vote for the Democrats," Bunning pointed out. "They told them they could just stay home, and that's exactly what happened. They surpressed the vote in the Fifth District by paying people not to go to the polls."

In some cases the payoffs were made out in the open, in full view of anybody who cared to look.

"They call them [the men handing out the money] 'haulers,'" Bunning explained. "They bring them to a polling place and they hand out twenty-dollar bills."

"They're buying so many votes," noted Mary. "They're paying twenty dollars and a bottle of booze in western Kentucky. We're just hoping they'll take the money and vote for us anyway."

Tension grew as darkness fell. Someone from *Nightline* called Bunning headquarters and asked if Jim would appear with Ted Koppel — if he won. Another ABC show, *Good Morning America*, phoned with a similar request. Bunning turned both of them down. They'd take him win or lose, or not at all. He'd had enough of that business during some of those Hall of Fame voting fiascoes.

There were the usual reports of machines breaking down, and as evening came and the polls closed the Democrats predicted that Martha Layne Collins would have things wrapped up by 8:30, 9:00 at the latest.

"This race is not over," Jim Host was telling his troops at 7:25 P.M. "I think we're in for a longer evening than some others have predicted."

Actually, some early results from selected precincts showed Bunning slightly ahead on the big board in the hotel ballroom, where a large Republican turnout came to root for a major upset. The room was packed. Red, white, and blue bunting and multicolored balloons decorated the walls. The setting was fine; the numbers weren't. Collins was pulling safely ahead. The Fifth District, in particular, was a disappointment. Bunning figured he had to win by forty thousand votes there. Instead, he won by only sixteen thousand. Although the statewide vote was the largest in history, the turnout in the Fifth District was disappointingly low; Bunning and his people were positive those twenty-dollar bills were the reason.

By 9 P.M. it was clear the Democrats had won. Jim, Mary, and the rest of the family faced the unpleasant prospect of making it official.

"Don't you cry," Jim told Bridget as they headed for the ballroom and all those supporters. "I'm the one who's supposed to cry."

Some of those early campaign speeches—before Bunning really had the hang of it—weren't easy to give, but this one was, by far, the hardest of all. He waited for the applause to subside, then plunged ahead.

"It's very, very nice for everybody to be here," he began. "Thank you for coming . . . " His voice cracked slightly. "Let me get my breath," he said.

He had lost, but he wasn't ready to throw in the towel. There would be other campaigns, he had already decided.

"This is the beginning tonight," he told that ballroom packed with Republicans.

He continued, "I want to relate to you a telegram I have sent to Mrs. Collins because the numbers have come in and the people have made a decision."

He read the concession wire, which contained the customary wording, then set his sights once more on the future.

"If you have a goal," he was saying, "and you work for it and you believe in it as strongly as I do, all the sacrifice we have made for the last eight months . . . "

It wasn't wasted, he told his audience as Mary and the kids stood at his side. "As sure as God made little apples, four years from now we'll be back. . . . Even those who cast their votes on the other side have got to know who Jim Bunning is and what he stands for, and that he's his own person. . . . Mary and I both enjoyed campaigning. I'll tell you right now I'm not going to quit until we win."

Jim had been outspent by his opponent by about three to one. When his money ran low in the closing weeks of the campaign he mortgaged his home for $150,000 and added that money to fuel the desperate drive of the last ten days. All that, and still he got barely 45 percent of the vote. As disappointing to him as that was, it represented the best showing for a Republican gubernatorial candidate in the last twenty years.

There had been mistakes. Plenty of them. But it hadn't been for lack of effort. And valuable lessons had been learned along the way. Never again, Bunning promised himself, would he start so late.

Getting over the defeat was difficult. "We tried so hard to make it work," Jim recalled. "It took Mary about nine months to get over it. It took me about as long."

All the while, he thought about what they had done right and what they had done wrong. He remembered a fundraiser in Louisville, where Jack Kemp was the featured speaker. "It was held at a farm, one of those fancy farms outside of the city," said Bunning.

The affair was staged in a barn, all spruced up for the occasion. They anticipated a good crowd; Kemp, after all, was a big name.

"I think we had more horses than we had people," Jim remembered.

At least more horses than *paying* people. Most of those in attendance were campaign workers and the like.

"We papered the house," Bunning said. "We had more ribs and meatballs and other things bought, and we didn't have any people (potential contributors, that is) to eat them. We lost money on the event. I remember that. *We lost money!* It wasn't because of Kemp. It was because of the organization that put the event on."

Those kinds of mistakes—fundraisers that didn't raise funds—couldn't be allowed to happen again.

Man of the House

Jim Bunning hated to lose, and what really griped him in the wake of the 1983 loss to Martha Layne Collins was realizing that he had never given himself a reasonable chance to win. In politics, as in baseball, you needed a team behind you. A good, solid, experienced team capable of swinging the odds in your favor.

"We didn't have a consultant in that race," Bunning said. "We didn't have a media person in that race. We didn't have a [full-time] pollster in that race."

In short, he didn't have a legitimate chance in that race. It was a hard way to learn an important lesson, a lesson he wasn't about to forget.

"I made a commitment to myself," he said. "If I got back into a political race I would never start late again, and never run a campaign where I was going to be outspent or underfinanced."

If the "game plan" called for six major mailings, he wouldn't settle for five. If it called for two thousand gross rating points on television or radio, he wouldn't settle for fifteen hundred. If the plan called for a phone bank, there would be a phone bank. No scrimping. No shortcuts. "I was never going to get into a campaign if I wasn't, in my mind, sure that I was going to be able to do all those things," Jim Bunning declared.

He wasn't a man to repeat past mistakes. If Mickey Mantle, batting lefthanded, had trouble hitting high inside fast balls, Bunning didn't feed him a diet of off-speed pitches out over the plate. If a man running for political office needed the best advisors, the most astute fundraisers, the most savvy media experts and ad agencies, that's what he was going to have—or else.

First, though, he had to decide what to run for. On the night of his defeat in the race for governor he had talked about running for the same office in four years. But then Gene Snyder, the Republican congressman from the Fourth District, came to him with the news that he was going to retire in 1986.

"You ought to take a look at the congressional race," he told Bunning.

Jim's immediate reaction was negative. "I said, 'I don't want to go to Washington,'" he recalled. "And he gave me all this baloney about how I was the only person who could hold the seat, and I said, 'Gene, a lot of people can hold the seat.'"

This was the summer of 1985; the congressional election was well over a year away. He didn't have to make a snap decision. There was time to weigh the pros and cons. And while he and Mary were weighing them, the phone calls began. There was a call from Vice President George Bush, a call from the White House, a promise from the National Republican Committee to give Bunning full funding if he decided to run. Jim learned later that Snyder had generated those calls to make sure the seat stayed in Republican hands. Even so, it was apparent that a lot of people—including some extremely influential people—wanted Jim to run. He and Mary talked it over and decided maybe Washington, D.C., didn't seem that bad.

Increasingly eager to plunge into another campaign, Bunning drew on his experiences in the gubernatorial race to make sure the mistakes of 1983 wouldn't be repeated. For starters, he asked the sharpest politicos he knew, both in Kentucky and in Washington, to name the best possible consultant he could hire. The vast majority cited Lee Atwater as the person best equipped to run his campaign.

When they met, Bunning told him, "I asked everybody I know in politics to give me the best person who could help me with the race, and that's you. I want you to be my overall consultant. No ifs, ands, or buts about it. I want you to do it."

Atwater told him he wasn't becoming involved in any House races, but Bunning wasn't about to take no for an answer. "I still want you to do this one," he told Atwater. "It's important. We'll work together well."

He must have been convincing, because Atwater agreed to take the job.

Getting Atwater meant also getting his media placement arm, National Media, which saw to it that the television and radio commercials were aimed at the right audiences, depending on the message. That was vital.

"The pollster and the media buyer have to work hand in hand," Bunning explained. "If you have a weak spot or you have a strength or you have a certain group of people that you're not getting to, they computerize all that. You put the plusses, minuses, male, female, age groups, religious groups, everything into that computer and it comes out and says you should buy two spots on the Sunday night movie, or you should buy *Wheel of Fortune*. So I got two things by getting Atwater."

One key member of the team was set, two more biggies to go. Jim wanted Roger Ailes. The problem was, Ailes normally wouldn't come unless he had the right to place the media messages, and Atwater and company were going to take care of that. But Ailes, Bunning knew, could be invaluable in directing commercials and advising on the media buys. He had met Ailes before; in fact, he had accompanied him to the Kentucky Derby a year earlier, and Roger's wife, Norma, and Mary Bunning had become good friends. Ailes agreed to join Atwater on the Bunning team. He would be responsible for creating the commercials, determining what they wanted to say and how they were going to say it. "In other words," explained Bunning, "the theme of the campaign."

Bob Teeter, the pollster who did some work for Jim in the gubernatorial race, was next. Now the major pieces were in place. Bunning had an overall consultant, one of the best in the business; he had a media guru; and he had a top-flight pollster and marketing researcher. By hiring them he delivered a message to the folks inside the Beltway. The moment they saw those names they knew Jim Bunning was going full speed ahead; that he was prepared to spend top dollar to get the top people.

"You can't hire Atwater, Ailes, and Teeter without having big bucks," Bunning pointed out. "That was the commitment I made to myself when we decided [in July of 1985], after looking at the governor's race and looking at everything, that we were going at the Congress. It's the best. We can serve more people for a longer period of time. I like legislation. I liked being a legislator when I was in the Kentucky senate."

No big mistakes this time. No late start while his opponent ran up a big early lead in dollars and in the polls. Bunning was charging ahead, his team in place, before his eventual opponent, Terry Mann, decided to run.

Because he had Atwater and Ailes, Bunning received a personal boost from President Reagan, who had worked with both of them in his campaign. Jim was the only Republican candidate running for a seat in the House of Representatives to get Ronald Reagan to deliver a television commercial in his behalf. True, Jim had a few anxious moments waiting for the spot to show up, but Reagan came through as the campaign moved into the home stretch.

"As a matter of fact, Lee told me the Reagan commercial almost fell through," Bunning remembered. "He [the president] had promised it to me. Lee said, 'Don't worry, I'll get it done. Just mark it down in your book.'"

With two weeks to go, Bunning told Atwater he was getting nervous about the Reagan commercial. "Don't worry about it," Atwater reassured him. "I've got it all set up."

As election day neared, with Jim getting more concerned, Atwater told him, "I've got some good news and some bad news. The good news is, you're getting the Reagan commercial. But you're not getting it until next Monday [the week before the election]."

In retrospect, the timing was fine, the commercial precisely what Bunning wanted. For a congressional candidate who had campaigned as a solid Reagan supporter, it couldn't have been much better, the president looking earnestly into the camera and extolling the virtues of the Republican from Kentucky's Fourth Congressional District and explaining how important his election was to Reagan and the party.

"You're the only person [running for Congress] in the country that's getting a personal message from the president," Atwater told Jim.

If the gubernatorial race had been an object lesson in how not to do things, this campaign ran like clockwork as the brightest Republican political minds called the shots. Terry Mann, who didn't decide to run for the open seat until February of 1986, started out thirty points behind and, in an effort to catch up, went through a succession of campaign managers. This time it was Bunning who knew what he was doing and where he was going every step of the way.

Which isn't to say that everything went smoothly. There was, once again, a scare in the air—an emergency landing in a private plane that was more frightening, by far, than the worst of the shaky landings in planes and helicopters that marked the race for governor in 1983.

Bunning was asked to speak at a Lincoln Day dinner in a Detroit suburb in February of '86, and he took off in a Cessna 310—the plane he had leased for his gubernatorial campaign—on a miserable, windy day complete with a tornado sighting. No sweat. The plane landed safely in Detroit, and Bunning headed for the dinner. He had agreed to go because the organizers told him they couldn't get anybody else. To Jim's surprise, Jack Kemp was there, too. "You didn't need me," Bunning told them, but he was happy to be a part of the dinner—until the return trip.

It was just Jim and the pilot in the Cessna 310 when they left from Detroit Metro. The takeoff was fine. They were about twenty minutes out of Detroit, nearing Toledo, fighting exceptionally strong head-winds, when the left engine stopped running.

"And that," as Jim learned, "is the critical engine, the one that controls the aircraft."

On a normal day the plane can fly on one engine, but this was no normal day—not with winds blowing at forty-five miles an hour.

"We were at about six thousand feet and we started to lose altitude," Bunning recalled. "We couldn't feather the left engine the way it should be feathered, and so it's a drag on the plane. The pilot said to me, 'The airport's seven miles away; we've got a shot at it.' I said, 'Good.' I didn't think anything of it. Not at all. I thought, 'He knows more about this than I do and he doesn't seem worried, at all.'"

Down they went, heading for the Toledo Airport. As they descended Jim became aware of familiar sights. Below them was the old ball park that served as home for the Toledo Mud Hens. The memories it brought back were not among his favorites.

"We get down to about three thousand feet and about three miles from the airport," recalled Bunning, "and he said, 'We're not going to make it to the airport. We've got to start looking around for a place to land.'"

Clearly, there was now something to worry about. Jim started looking around. No likely landing places were visible. What's more, they had run out of time to look.

"We're going to land now," the pilot suddenly announced.

"He saw the 'Circle Freeway'—the 465 freeway around Toledo," Bunning said.

The ball park was right off that. What a place to go down. For two years Jim Bunning, as manager of the Mud Hens, had felt hopelessly buried there. Now this.

According to Bunning, "What happened is, when his left foot controlling the rudder hit the floorboard, he had to do something immediately—in other words turn into that [wind]—or go into a spin. So he turned the aircraft left, right into the wind, and there's the darn 'Circle Freeway.'"

Their landing was something out of a James Bond movie, only this was real. The plane headed for the highway, lower and lower. So low that Jim shouted, "Better look out for that overpass."

"We're going to have to go under it," the pilot told him.

He was wrong. The plane flew above the overpass. "Whoosh, just like that," Jim remembered. "He landed with the traffic, which just cleared out of the way."

The Cessna rolled down the highway, and they pulled off in one of the little turnabouts.

"He made a smooth landing in a forty-five-knot windshear," marveled Bunning. "He's a US Air pilot now."

It wasn't until the plane was down, and safely stopped on the turnabout, that Bunning had time to be frightened.

"I couldn't move," he said. "It happened so fast I didn't have a chance to get scared until after we landed and I looked at where we were."

In no time at all, five Ohio state troopers were on the scene. They saw a plane with one engine shut down, leaking oil. One of the pistons had blown.

"That aircraft," Bunning learned later, "had just been serviced, totally redone and serviced."

Jim caught his breath and called his wife. "Due to some weather I won't be coming in tonight," he told her. "I'm coming in tomorrow morning."

He wasn't about to tell her what he had just been through. Not then, anyway.

He drove all night to get home, stopping to call Mary at six in the morning.

"If you hear that we landed on Interstate 465, I'm fine," he told her. "I'll be home very shortly."

It was one of those experiences that remains etched in a man's mind the rest of his life.

"I figured I was going to win that election after that," Bunning said. "The Good Lord had other plans for me if I didn't go down. He didn't want me right away."

Despite the close call near Toledo, Bunning has never ducked air travel. "I've flown over three million miles," he pointed out. "There isn't a lot you can do about it [once you're in the air], so I am totally and completely relaxed when I go on an airplane."

As time went on, he became a more relaxed public speaker, as well. Rick Robinson, Bunning's legislative director for six years, noted, "I think the biggest thing was being able to speak off the cuff. Initially, he was doing just about everything with prepared text. He got so he was able to get up and talk in front of a crowd without a text."

Jim's improvement in dealing with crowds—mingling with the people, chatting with them, asking for their votes—was readily apparent as his first congressional campaign progressed.

There was the brutally hot day in late July when he participated in the Oldham County Day parade in La Grange. Twenty-eight years before, almost to the day, he had pitched his no-hitter at Fenway Park. Now there he was, standing atop a handsome black wagon pulled by four equally handsome Clydesdales, a tiny American flag in the breast pocket of his light blue jacket. Surprisingly, he was beginning to look almost as comfortable pitching for votes as he used to look pitching for outs.

In many ways this was a tougher grind than pitching baseballs for a living. At least in his baseball days Bunning generally got three days off between appearances; in the political game there were virtually no days off, precious little rest for the increasingly weary. But if the candidate was being worn down by the political grind, he didn't show it that day. He stood there, waving and smiling, on his midmorning ride along the parade route, although upon closer inspection it was evident his shirt was soaked through with perspiration.

Behind him came the bands and the convertibles and the floats, and behind them came six fire engines making a tremendous racket with their screaming sirens and ringing bells. The parade was held up about twenty minutes to let a freight train pass through town, but only the skittish Clydesdales seemed to mind.

The parade finally over, Jim and Mary Bunning made their way through the town square. It was time to work the crowd.

"Hi," Bunning was saying, extending his hand. "I'm Jim Bunning.

I'm running for Congress." Again and again he did it, still sweating, still smiling.

As for Mary Bunning, that stellar campaigner was busy distributing Bunning stickers, suitable for wearing on shirts and dresses. Things were going swimmingly until she encountered a young man holding a leash, at the end of which was a large, brown goat.

Undaunted, Mary pressed forward. "Should we put a sticker on him?" she asked.

The young man shrugged noncommittally. "He'd probably eat it," he said. "He's eaten everything else today."

To take part in all this, the Bunnings had got up at 5:30 in the morning, extremely early for a couple who had attended a carnival in northern Kentucky the night before. No complaints, though. After all, there were 14,271 registered voters in Oldham County.

"Hi," the candidate was saying to a young woman holding a baby. "I'm Jim Bunning running for congress. I'd appreciate your help."

More and more, with each passing week, he was proving that he could do what so many who knew him for years thought he could never do. "I didn't do it very well at the start," he remarked. "I'll be the first to admit that. But it's like a lot of things that I did in my career. That's why it took me five years to get to the big leagues."

Watching him now, moving so easily from stranger to stranger, from handshake to handshake, it was hard to understand how difficult his first solo walk along the campaign trail had been the day Mary left him alone in 1979. The private man was making the most difficult transition of his life. He was becoming a public man. In baseball, he did what he had to do to maximize his chances of winning. In politics, he was determined to do the same.

"A sports background helps as far as staying with it after you find out what it takes," he observed. "There's a certain amount of sacrificing you have to do to be competitive. There's a certain amount of conditioning you have to do. There's an awful lot that goes into it."

His opponent, Terry Mann, had been elected to the general assembly fourteen years before at the age of twenty-four. The principal of the Chapman Vocational School in Covington, Mann didn't always ride in parades, the way Bunning did. "He used to run in the parades," Jim said, "and try to shake hands with the people on the side, while I would ride and wave to them. I never could figure out why he did it—maybe to show how young he was, how vital. He would always be tired at the end of the parade and I'd be comfortable.

Although Kentucky's Fourth District had been Republican for twenty years, the Democrats hoped to stage a strong fight with Mann, who lost to Gene Snyder by only twelve thousand votes and four percentage points in 1982. But their nominee committed a major blunder early in 1986, one the Republicans eagerly capitalized on.

With the Kentucky House of Representatives in session, Mann went to Louisville to meet with a Democratic congressman. Rather than be marked absent on the votes that were being taken, he came up with the bright idea of rigging his voting lever with a rubber band that automatically recorded twenty-three straight "yes" votes while he was many miles away. He didn't get away with it.

"Some of my good friends in the state house of representatives informed the press," Bunning recalled. "They went in and took a picture of it. That was the end of the race. I didn't ever have to say anything."

The press took care of that for him. Mann admitted his mistake, but the damage was done. Between the "Rubber-Band Affair" and his early organizational problems, the Democratic candidate found himself in a deep hole and never climbed out.

Running for federal office in Kentucky was nothing like running for governor. "I think it's a much cleaner race," Bunning noted. "Running statewide in Kentucky is always an adventure."

This was different. There were federal marshals to worry about. Get caught cheating and there would be big trouble. "They're fearful of what will happen to them," Jim said.

With Mann starting late, and shooting himself in the foot with the rubber-band caper, Bunning's high-powered advisors recommended an early, all-out media blitz. For ten days, television viewers were inundated with Bunning commercials—about 650 gross rating points worth. Atwater wanted to get his man's approval rating up to 55 percent. "If we get you there," he told the candidate, "the other side can't let you do that. They have to spend money [in an effort to counteract the Bunning surge]."

And the Democrats figured to be short of money.

"If we get you there [to 55 percent], I guarantee you nothing is going to happen in July, August, September," Atwater assured Bunning. "Nothing is going to change those numbers no matter what the other side does. They can go door to door, those numbers aren't going to change [in the summer]."

After that, if the opposition found the resources to hit hard on television and radio, the Bunning people would hit just as hard to hold them off.

"Just exactly what he said would happen, happened," Jim recalled. It paid to surround yourself with people who knew the business.

Raising money proved to be no great problem. Between July 1 and October 1, Bunning raised $223,000. During the same period Mann raised $34,000. By the time it was over, Jim had raised well over $500,000 from more than six thousand in-state contributors, a figure no Kentucky congressional candidate had approached before. Add PAC money and the Bunning campaign topped its goal of $850,000. He outspent Mann by as great a margin as Martha Layne Collins had outspent him.

One of the campaign's big early gatherings was what Jim called a "meet-and-greet affair"—not a fund-raiser, but a prelude to a fund-raiser, so to speak. It was to be staged in Washington, D.C.

Pete Rose and Tommy Helms had asked Bunning to play in a golf tournament in the summer of '85, about the time he decided to run for Congress. Jim played and was in the group directly behind Rose, the manager of the Cincinnati Reds at the time, and Helms, a Cincinnati coach. When the round was over, Bunning went up to baseball's all-time base-hit king, told him he was going to run for Congress, and mentioned that he was planning a midwinter get-together in Washington.

"I want to have a baseball motif instead of a political motif," Bunning told Rose. "I'd like you to help."

"I'll do it," Rose replied.

Pete's presence virtually guaranteed a successful effort. This was before his fall from grace for income tax violations and gambling; he was still one of the biggest names in the game.

Everything was go for an event that promised to lure many potential contributors to the Bunning cause. Then, ten days before it was to be held, Jim received a call from Reuven Katz, Rose's lawyer, who told him that Pete was not going to be there. "Something to do with a contract he had signed with a Japanese company," Bunning remembered.

Panic. The big occasion was going to be a big dud. The star attraction was going to be a no-show.

Bunning phoned Bob Summerall, a friend who ran a tire manufacturing and distribution business in the Cincinnati metropolitan area. Summerall was a good friend of Reds owner Marge Schott.

"I told Bob what happened," Jim said, "and he said, 'Maybe we can get Marge to go.'"

The plan had been to give away baseballs autographed by Pete Rose. Refreshments included peanuts, popcorn, Cracker Jack, hot dogs . . . everything associated with baseball. Marge Schott agreed to stand in for her absentee manager.

Marge showed up, as promised, and she was "great," according to Bunning. At least she was until she remarked, with Jim at her side, "I've only had an association with Peter Edward Rose for one year. He doesn't have much class because he didn't show up, so I'm here to substitute for him."

"I almost died," Bunning recalled, "because I knew what the story was going to be the next day, and it went coast to coast."

It wasn't the story the candidate wanted to read in the nation's press. Besides, Rose hadn't been a total washout; he *did* sign three dozen baseballs to be handed out.

"I didn't hear from Pete," Bunning said. "I haven't heard from Pete since. I didn't have anything to do with it. Marge said it. I thought it, but Marge said it."

It was a typical, off-the-cuff Marge Schott remark. She had this knack of opening her mouth and making headlines, all the while thinking that what she said would never go beyond her immediate audience.

That was the formal kickoff of Jim Bunning's first campaign for Congress.

Terry Mann's effort pulled itself together toward the end as the Democrat emphasized his fourteen years of experience in the legislature as opposed to Bunning's four. But Jim's conservative appeal was considerable in the district, and his support of President Reagan also helped against his more liberal opponent.

Mary helped too, of course. In addition to her face-to-face campaigning, which surely swayed countless voters, she hand-wrote a four-page letter, reproductions of which were mailed to registered women voters on pale blue personal stationery. Jim's advisors suggested the areas she should cover, and Mary took it from there, composing a letter that began:

"Dear Friend, I would like to take a minute to tell you a little about the man I married. He's my husband, Jim Bunning. We have been campaigning together across the 4th District to make sure Jim will be your next Congressman.

"I've known Jim just about all my life," she went on. "We met in grade school. He was in the fifth grade, I was in the fourth. In the beginning I think I was attracted to him because he was the only boy taller than I.

"But as I got to know him, even back then, I began to see the things in him that have helped keep us married for almost 35 years."

It was a lovely, loving letter. Nobody reading it could have doubted Mary Bunning's sincerity as she sang Jim's praises.

"Oh, I know," she wrote, "you expect a wife to say those things, especially when her husband is running for Congress. It really is true. Jim deeply cares about people. He's honest, and he stands by his word. . . . That's one thing I always admired about his dealings with our kids. He always did exactly what he told them he would do.

"Jim will make a really super Congressman. He's never been average at anything he's ever done. . . . I firmly believe that it won't be long before Jim's in a leadership role in Congress. That's just the kind of man he is.

"Jim's also a God fearing person. We did a lot of praying before Jim decided to run for Congress, and we start every day with a prayer together. There's no question that we're doing the right thing. I say 'we' because this campaign is really a family affair. I feel more a part of this Congressional campaign than just about anything we've done. And that's because we're really doing it together. Even in his speeches Jim says 'we're running'. And WE are!"

It wasn't like the gubernatorial race, Mary explained. They started so late in that one they "had to split up so we could cover more area."

"This time we're traveling together," she pointed out. "And it's a lot of fun. I travel with him just about every day. We even walked door-to-door together in the intense heat this summer. Our kids are getting into it, too. Amy and Dave, our 20-year-old twins, are heading up their dad's effort down at U.K. [University of Kentucky]. Another daughter, Cathy, is going door-to-door for us in Covington. . . .

"Jim knows the value of a dollar," Mary wrote, "because he's had to work hard for every penny he's earned. It's never been easy for him — even back when he was setting baseball records. He's always had to work a little harder, give a little extra effort. That determination will serve us well in Congress—just like it served constituents in the State Senate, and before that, on city council. . . .

"The election is only a few days away and Jim needs your help. Will you give him your support? Please, get to the polls, and better yet, take a friend with you and give Jim your vote on November 4th.

"Knowing him as I do, I know you'll be happy you sent him to Washington. Thanks for letting me take a few minutes to tell you about my husband, Jim. [Signed] Sincerely, Mary Bunning."

To win in Kentucky's Fourth Congressional District a candidate had to score heavily in the Louisville suburbs, at the western end of the district, and in northern Kentucky, just across the Ohio River from Cincinnati. Approximately 80 percent of the registered voters lived in those two areas; to reach them a candidate needed plenty of money to buy commercial time on television stations in Louisville and Cincinnati. It was an expensive business—especially since many who watched the Cincinnati channels lived in Ohio.

As expected, considering the expertise behind them, Bunning's commercials were exceptionally well done. They softened his image somewhat from the intense, often confrontational gubernatorial candidate of 1983 to the devoted family man who enjoys a cookout in his back yard in Fort Thomas.

"I feel more at home campaigning than I did then," Jim reflected. "I'm much more relaxed."

Off to a flying start, Bunning stayed comfortably ahead. Although registered Democrats outnumbered Republicans more than two to one, Bunning's wholehearted support of President Reagan played well in a district that gave Reagan 60 percent of its votes in 1984. Republican interest in retaining the seat was demonstrated by visits to Kentucky by such party luminaries as Vice President Bush, Congressman Jack Kemp of New York, Secretary of the Treasury James Baker, and, in late October, Frank Fahrenkopf, Chairman of the Republican National Committee, who appeared at a $25-per-person fundraiser at the Drawbridge Inn in Fort Mitchell to celebrate Jim's fifty-fifth birthday. Asked if the party had even bigger plans for Bunning in the future, Fahrenkopf replied, "That will be up to Jim and Mary."

When Vice President Bush agreed to come in for a Bunning fundraiser, a letter to potential contributors was promptly drafted. Jim sat down one day in his office to personally sign each letter, a rather tedious, time-consuming job. Apparently, fatigue had set in, because neither Bunning nor anyone else noticed that the letter's closing which should have read "Best Personal Regards," inadvertently came out "Bush Personal Regards."

As Jim's long-time district director, Debbie McKinney, recalled, Bunning had signed about two hundred letters before he noticed the mistake. He was so angry that he threw a handful of pencils in the air hard enough to implant a couple of them in the ceiling. Then he waited for the letter to be retyped and began signing all over again.

Such annoyances were no more than bumps in the road as the Bunning bandwagon rolled along. To top off the support from all those party bigwigs came President Reagan's personalized message, a major coup.

In an effort to combat that, Governor Martha Layne Collins appeared at a $100-per-person fundraiser for Terry Mann in mid-October. "The Fourth Congressional District needs to elect experience and not an experiment," she declared. For his part, Mann, with time growing short, made his most aggressive attack on Bunning, claiming his opponent had voted against every major piece of education legislation while in the state senate. Bunning countered by saying that a review of his voting record would show he had supported education legislation 85 percent of the time.

Things were finally getting a little nasty. Jim chided Mann for voting to raise legislative salaries and benefits in 1980 and 1982, saying, "I thought when you were elected to the general assembly, you were elected to serve the people and not be self-serving."

When the candidates met during a forum conducted before the Louisville Rotary Club, it was Mann—not Bunning—who brought up the by-now-infamous rubber-band incident. He tried to defuse the issue, once and for all, by asking, "Is there anybody here who over the last fourteen years has never made a mistake? Should you throw out fourteen years of substantive accomplishment because of a bad day?"

Bunning responded by saying he had never missed a vote during his career as a legislator. "I think you expect more out of your public officials," Jim remarked. He added, "Terry said if I use it [the rubber-band incident], it's gutter politics. But I call it gutter legislating."

Bunning's first congressional race was in the home stretch now, and virtually every poll showed him well ahead. One released by the state Democratic Party in late October had Mann leading 43 to 42 percent, but the sample used was so small as to render the finding meaningless.

"Last question," said a television interviewer after the Republican candidate spoke at a VFW hall in Alexandria on October 30. "Why should people vote for you?" Bunning, smiling, answered quickly. "Because I'll do a better job than the other fellow."

Several newspapers agreed. Among those endorsing Jim were the *Kentucky Post* and the *Cincinnati Enquirer* in its Kentucky edition.

Said the *Post*: "It comes down to a question of which one has best prepared himself for the race and instills confidence in his readiness to represent the 4th District in Congress.

"Our choice is Jim Bunning.

"Ask Mr. Bunning a question on a major national issue and you'll get a considered opinion on the causes and possible solutions. Often, his answers follow the thinking of the Reagan administration—but not always. . . .

"Mr. Bunning entered the race whole-heartedly, studying the issues, pounding the sidewalks, agreeing to a debate when he had little to gain in terms of political strategy.

"Some argue he would make a bad lawmaker because he's impatient with the legislative process. Where's the proof?

" . . . There also is some concern that Mr. Bunning would be an aloof, out-of-touch legislator. In this campaign, he has been neither, and he has promised town meetings, constituent polling and a liaison office in the district. . . . [He] has done more to demonstrate he has the energy and dedication to give the 4th District his best effort."

The *Enquirer* concurred: "As a businessman and state senator, Mr. Bunning has shown a keen insight into the concerns of his district and a capacity for constructive legislative leadership. He has earned the right to go to Washington."

The *Louisville Courier-Journal* saw it quite differently. Although lukewarm toward Terry Mann, acknowledging that he "has not waged as effective a campaign as his underdog position requires," the paper's editorial board liked him better than Bunning. The latter, they said, "is remembered from his one term in the Kentucky Senate primarily as an obstructionist who didn't even seem to like legislative service."

Ten years later, the *Courier-Journal* endorsed him for the first time. This created something of a dilemma for Jim, who had said if he ever got endorsed by the *Courier* he'd refuse the endorsement. As it turned out, the editorial came so late in the campaign that Bunning, rather than stir up an eleventh-hour controversy, decided to remain silent.

"If I was rich, I'd buy a newspaper," Mary Bunning said after reading one particularly negative story about Jim. "Well," she added after a moment's thought, "I guess I'd have to be very rich, because I'd have to pass them around free because nobody would subscribe to it."

Jim's wife, who found something good in just about everybody, had difficulty understanding how anyone could dislike her favorite political candidate, her husband, the father of her nine children. As the embroidered sign hanging in her kitchen put it, "God Must Have Loved Bunnings—He Made So Many of Them."

Four days after the election Jim told a receptive audience at a VFW function that he was proud of his twenty-two years as a professional athlete and the fact he competed to the best of his ability, and that he would work to be the very best congressman he could be in Washington.

"But I'm not always going to vote the way you want me to vote," he noted. "I'm going to examine every issue and vote my conscience. Please, please be understanding about that."

Still, he wasn't taking his election for granted. "Yogi Berra said it best," Bunning commented. "The game's not over 'til it's over. I want you all to remember that. . . . It's the sixth year of an incumbent president, and historically [his party] loses forty-five to forty-eight seats in the house. This president has done a very good job," Jim told his audience. "I don't want two years of vetoes for this president."

He asked each listener to "take one or two or three persons to the poll with you." And then, he said, "next Tuesday night I want to invite all of you to the Drawbridge Inn for the largest celebration we've had in northern Kentucky in a long time."

One day during the pre-election week Bunning drove across the river to have lunch at the Cincinnati Hyatt, where he bumped into sportscaster Bob Trumpy.

"Jim Bunning, how are you doing?' Trumpy called out.

"Fine, Trump."

"What can I do for you?" Trumpy asked.

"Don't mention my name [on the air]," Bunning replied. "you'd have to give the other guy equal time."

Things looked so good it was almost frightening. One night they were having dinner at Mike Fink's—an old riverboat transformed into an upscale restaurant—when Mary blurted out, "You don't think this will be 1964 all over again, do you?"

"You sound like Gus Triandos," Jim told her, recalling his catcher's prophetic comment made during the '64 stretch run: "You don't think we'll be like the Dodgers and blow it?"

As they left the restaurant, a woman spotted the congressional candidate and wished him luck. "I hope you win," she said. "Terry Mann's been saying some awful things about you."

"If I lose," Jim replied without a trace of a smile, "I'll move down to Florida."

That didn't seem likely. In comparison to the Republican candidate's well-financed campaign, Mann's seemed minor league, at best. His television commercials lacked the polish of Bunning's, as some of Jim's people were pointing out one afternoon.

"It isn't very funny when you don't have any money," Bunning told them. "I know. I went through that in '83. Buy one day [of television time], two days at a time. It's brutal."

One of Mann's television spots sought to depict Bunning's baseball background as a reason *not* to vote for him. It opened with a picture of an empty ball park, with a solemn voice intoning, "The baseball season is over." Then came a glimpse of one of Jim's Phillie baseball cards, followed by a comparison of Bunning's pitching record with Mann's legislative record. The Democrats were getting desperate.

A shipment of fifty-seven thousand door hangers (deep pink, with the words, "Urgent—Your Vote for Jim Bunning for U.S. Congress is Critical") showed up on the Sunday morning before election day. Hardly a door in Republican areas would be overlooked.

"Would you believe they hung one on my own door?" Jim said Sunday afternoon.

Considering the gung-ho attitude of the Bunning forces as election day approached, it was very believable. Thirty thousand door hangers were placed in northern Kentucky alone, and they weren't even part of the original "game plan."

"We've completed our 'game plan' and then some," Jim told Mary late that afternoon. "I never thought this time would arrive."

For some fifteen months they had been on the go, driving themselves to make the electoral strategy work, to make sure nothing was overlooked. Memories of the 1983 gubernatorial debacle danced in their heads. The Bunnings had been determined not to let that happen again. And now, finally, the end was in sight. Victory seemed within their grasp, if only the polls were right and people voted the way they said they were going to vote.

Much of that Sunday night was spent watching television to see two new commercials, one featuring Jim and Mary, the other starring President Reagan. Jim had a checklist to make sure the ads were aired as scheduled. Two appeared on ABC during a James Bond movie entitled *Never Say Never Again*, another on CBS during *Murder, She Wrote*, still another on *Sixty Minutes*. Viewers of the local late news shows saw them, too. The idea was to hit as wide an audience as possible. With that in mind, the Reagan commercial had made it onto *Hee-Haw* the day before.

"What really burns me [about the Mann commercial contrasting Bunning's baseball record with his opponent's legislative record] is they've got my record wrong, " Jim told Mary. "You'd think that they would research it better."

"What's wrong?" Mary asked.

"They left off my last year," Jim responded.

"That was a good year to leave off," Mary replied, recalling Bunning's 5-and-12 farewell season with the Phillies.

Jim gave her one of those looks. Mary smiled contentedly. "You've got to keep him humble," she said.

The braintrust decided it would be a good idea for Jim, Mary, and a few others to work the Cincinnati bus terminal Monday morning, targeting arriving commuters. At a few minutes before 7 A.M. Jim and his entourage were at their assigned post, ready to hand out literature and, in the case of the candidate, press the flesh. The first few buses weren't too crowded.

"You wanted us here at 6:30," Jim complained to John Salyers, who had set up this early morning outing. "We're going to outnumber the people at 7 A.M."

"We wanted you to beat the rush hour," Salyers told him.

"Well, we did," retorted Bunning.

By 7:25 things were picking up, although not fast enough for the candidate.

"Aw, they're coming by so fast you can't count them," Salyers explained.

Since Democrats are allowed to ride on buses, too, not every person who walked past that morning greeted Bunning with a cheery smile and a big hello. "You should stick to baseball," one man told him.

At 8, Jim and Mary departed to have breakfast. Enough was enough.

They ate at Bob Evans, where the waitress told them of being awakened at 9 o'clock Sunday morning by a caller from Bunning headquarters, reminding her to vote for him the following Tuesday. Despite losing her beauty sleep, she assured Jim he still had her full support.

Back at headquarters, Bunning looked over the list of financial contributors through the last day of October. In all, 5,711 persons and organizations had poured $868,188.51 into the Bunning war chest. Among the sports figures who had chipped in were Norman Braman, owner of the Philadelphia Eagles, who donated $200 to the cause, and Jerry Reinsdorf, owner of the Chicago White Sox and Chicago Bulls, who found himself $2,000 poorer after a conference call with Bunning, in which they were discussing Joe Cowley's contract.

"I understand you're running for congress," Reinsdorf said in the midst of the negotiations with Cowley's agent.

"That's right," Jim replied. "Why don't you send money?"

Reinsdorf did.

At 2 P.M. Monday Bunning spoke to the Republican state chairman, who said he had told both CNN and *USA Today* that "Jim Bunning is a 'lock.'"

"There's no such thing as a lock in politics," Bunning shot back. "You shouldn't have said that."

There was nothing to do now but wait for election day. Jim relaxed at home most of the afternoon, safely away from the incessant ringing of the office phones. If reporters call, Bunning had instructed Fred Wolf, his press secretary, "tell them I'm out campaigning." At long last, it was time to rest.

Mary wasn't resting; she was out walking. When she got home late in the afternoon, her husband kissed her and asked, "Do I have your vote?"

Mary assured him that he did. Must have been the Reagan commercial.

Tuesday, November 4, 1986 was a most special day in the lives of Jim and Mary Bunning. No matter what the polls said, this was a hard day on the nerves. The election was the only poll that counted.

Mary, too nervous to sleep, her calves sore from all that walking, was up at 4 A.M. At 8:30 the Bunnings cast their votes at a church up the street from where they lived. Jim was voter number one hundred at that Fort Thomas location.

"I wonder if it's OK for Jim to drive today, or if he's too nervous," Mary was saying as the morning advanced.

Their grandson Ryan, age four, was working on his list to Santa Claus. "I can't wait 'til Christmas comes," he told Mary.

"I can't wait until seven o'clock comes," Mary replied.

The waiting was a cruel form of torture. Mary decided she wasn't going to sit around doing nothing.

"When I get nervous I go shopping," she said.

"And then I get nervous," Jim told her.

Shortly after 1 P.M. they had lunch at the Carrollton Inn in Carroll County where Jim's parents lived. "Have you voted yet?" Mary asked a fellow diner she happened to meet on the way to the ladies' room. "I wish you would. My husband's running for Congress."

A little later, Jim's press secretary got up to go to the men's room. "Get a vote," Mary said as he left the table.

The hours crawled by. There was an early evening party scheduled at the Brownsboro Ramada. The Bunnings arrived at 5:50; another ten minutes and the polls would be closed, the counting would begin. A big sign said, "Welcome Jim Bunning."

It was raining hard when Jim and Mary got there. They set up temporary headquarters in room 278, the candidate sitting on the bed next to the phone, waiting to get the early reports from his people, his wife stretched out on the other bed, trying to listen to the television reports and Jim at the same time.

At 6:15 Mary got up and started pacing. "I can't stand this," she declared.

Jim kept repeating numbers, jotting some of them on a pad. To someone who didn't know precisely where they were coming from, the numbers were meaningless.

"It isn't good, is it?" Mary asked.

"Mary, sit down," was Jim's reply.

"I can't stand it. I feel like you're pitching," Mary told him.

More numbers. From the expression on Jim's face, they were mostly good numbers. Mary sat there, her hands clasped in front of her. Each time Jim took a call, she looked at him, saw his expression, and murmured, "Thank God!" They were ahead. At 6:45, WHAS in Louisville was reporting that Bunning had a 61-39 lead in Jefferson County with 24 percent of the votes in. The tension had lifted in room 278. Jim looked increasingly relaxed, saying, "That ain't too bad," as he wrote down the latest numbers.

"Have we won?" his wife inquired at 7:20.

"Mary, we've won big," Jim answered.

At that very moment, Terry Mann was being interviewed on television. He was saying how good things looked for his side.

"We're looking at the numbers," Bunning remarked. "He's looking at the heavens."

Five minutes later, Fred Wolf was commenting to a television interviewer that signs pointed to a big Bunning victory. At 7:30 Jim was on the phone, telling one of his people, "How can I go downstairs and say that? I don't have a count. What can I tell them?"

He didn't want to jump the gun, least of all when his opponent was still talking optimistically. But victory was his; that much seemed certain.

"I'm not going down until I know the count," Bunning was saying. "It's just a case of how big."

At 7:45 there was a knock on the door. "Is Mr. Bunning here?" the man asked. "Here's a bottle of champagne courtesy of the hotel."

"We've won?" Mary asked once again, just to make sure.

"Yes," Jim answered.

Mary's eyes grew misty. "Congratulations, Congressman," she said, kissing him.

Shortly thereafter, Gene Snyder arrived at room 278 with a message to call George Bush just as Bunning was getting ready to go downstairs.

"I thought you might want to do that first," Snyder suggested.

Bunning nodded and went back into the room to make the call.

At precisely 7:52 the newly elected congressman from the Fourth District of Kentucky walked into the Indian Hills Room downstairs, where the party was going full blast. He was wearing a charcoal gray, pinstriped suit and a victorious smile. His daughter Bridget Lamb stood on one side of him, holding his two-month-old grandson Daniel. Mary stood on the other as he told the happy audience, "This sure beats 1983!"

His right arm around Mary's shoulder, he went on, speaking with undisguised emotion. "I've never had an elation like this," he said. "I'll tell you, even pitching a perfect game can't compare with having so many people work for you towards [reaching a goal]."

The night had just begun. At 8:45 the Bunnings were boarding a Lear jet for Louisville. An hour later, they were at the Drawbridge Inn in Fort Mitchell, where another, bigger victory party was under way in the Canterbury Room. Channel 9, the CBS station in Cincinnati, projected a Bunning victory at 8:53.

"Well, father," Jim said to his dad, "now you can relax."

The earliest returns had been anything but relaxing, showing Mann ahead. Even though the lead quickly evaporated, there had been some anxious moments for Jim's family, friends, and supporters. At the very time the numbers Bunning was receiving indicated a solid victory, one radio station reported that "Jim Bunning has not yet conceded." The station was right, of course; he hadn't. But Jim, hearing that, was momentarily taken aback. "The numbers couldn't be wrong," he said. "They couldn't be."

They weren't. Still, as he mentioned later, "My mom and dad almost had heart attacks."

In the end, Bunning won handily enough, topping Mann by nearly 14,000 votes out of the 121,000 cast, winding up with 55 percent to his opponent's 44. Jim decisively won suburban Jefferson County, took Boone and Kenton Counties, and finished in a near dead heat with Mann in Campbell County. The Democrat carried seven of the eight rural counties.

"I just really think we did more of everything better," Bunning told a *Kentucky Post* reporter during the victory celebration at the Drawbridge Inn. "I'm talking organization, fundraising, planning, county organizations, the whole grass roots."

What's more, the Republican Bunning won his first congressional race in a district that was strongly Democratic in registration, this on an election day that saw the incumbent Democratic U.S. senator, Wendell Ford, win a sweeping statewide victory, getting more than 70 percent of the vote.

An obviously elated Jim Bunning stood on the rostrum, a huge American Flag covering the wall behind him, a smaller American flag, a Kentucky flag, and an assortment of red, white, and blue balloons decorating the area directly in front of him. Surrounded by his children and grandchildren, an arm around his wife, Bunning began to speak. "People ask me, "What does it feel like? What can I compare it to?' I think it feels a heck of a lot better than pitching a perfect game against the New York Mets."

The look on Jim's face, and on Mary's face, showed how happy they were. All the planning, all the fundraising, all the walking and hand shaking and traveling and speech making had paid off, just as the hard work had paid off in baseball. As a ballplayer, it had taken time for the results to show. As a politician, it had also taken time. There were setbacks along the way, but they only served to make success, when it finally came, that much sweeter.

"I'm very proud of the campaign we ran," the congressman-elect told the crowd. "A lot of campaigns around the country have been very negative. I don't think you saw one campaign comment, one negative statement out of Jim Bunning or any of his team during the whole campaign. I want to congratulate Terry Mann tonight. I think he ran a very strong campaign. I know how it feels to be on the other side, because I've been there.

"It's been a long race," he noted. "Fifteen months ago we started this thing. It's been extremely exciting. I feel so darn . . . " He stopped for a couple of seconds, groping for the words to express how he felt. "I've never had an elation like this in my life," he finally went on. "I'll tell you, even pitching perfect games in baseball does not compare with the exhilaration you get in winning a campaign and having so many people work so darn hard to accomplish one goal."

He thanked the six thousand plus who gave money to his campaign—"I'm talking about a buck to a thousand bucks," he observed. "That's what made the difference, the individual people that were interested in making sure that the Fourth Congressional District stayed in conservative hands."

Later the local CBS affiliate called to get the congressman-elect on their morning news show. It was all arranged. The station promised to send a limousine to pick him up at 7:30 A.M. Jim was dressed and ready to go when the phone rang about twenty minutes before the limo was scheduled to show up.

"You can relax," he announced after taking the call. "CBS canceled. They said the Senate races were too important. Can you believe it? Twenty minutes before and they called Fred Wolf and said they were canceling. I told Fred to tell them to go to hell."

Bunning was accustomed to getting stood up by those television morning shows. They did it to him when he failed to make the Baseball Hall of Fame in 1986. This time he won, and they did it to him again. It did little to boost his opinion of the media, which wasn't too high to begin with. "If the *CBS Morning News* wants me on in January, I'll tell them to stick it and tell them why," he declared, relishing the prospect.

Actually, as Fred Wolf reported later, the local CBS affiliate had made several calls in the course of the night and early morning. The first few were to make sure everything was all set for Bunning's appearance. Then came another call, at about 3 A.M., that Wolf described as "a little tentative." Finally, someone phoned Wolf at his home at 6:30 A.M. to tell him Bunning was no longer scheduled "because the Senate changed hands."

"I hope you understand," the caller said to Wolf.

"We don't understand," the press secretary replied. "You call me at six-thirty. Jim's home, getting ready. I hope you don't think we'll ever let this happen again."

"Sorry you feel this way."

"We do," Wolf snapped, and hung up.

But not even CBS could spoil this exhilarating time in Jim Bunning's life. The man who wanted to be a major league baseball manager had become a United States congressman instead. The earlier goal seemed awfully trivial now.

Keeping a seat in Congress is easier than getting one. There are tremendous advantages in incumbency. The 1986 election was, as he and his advisors expected, the toughest of Jim Bunning's six campaigns to represent the Fourth Congressional District of Kentucky.

It's an expensive place to wage a campaign. To run successfully these days, a candidate needs to make wise use of television, and that costs money. As Bunning explained, the way the district is configured it is necessary to buy time on television stations in Louisville. Even though the city proper isn't part of the Fourth District, several of the surrounding counties are. The even more expensive Cincinnati market, across the Ohio River from northern Kentucky, is also a must. "The Cincinnati market is outrageous," Bunning remarked. "It cost $7,000 for thirty seconds on *Home Improvement*, and $6,000 for *Sixty Minutes*. Throw in the Lexington market and Huntington-Charleston [West Virginia] and it costs about $11,000 to buy thirty seconds in those areas on *Sixty Minutes*." As a result, Bunning spent nearly $400,000 in his sixth—and final—congressional campaign, which he won by a better than two-to-one margin.

"So you have to raise a lot of money in this district," Bunning explained. "It's to the disadvantage of a challenger."

Especially when the challenger is running against an incumbent who takes nothing for granted. Congressman Bunning didn't coast in 1988, when he rolled up a 74-26 percentage margin over his challenger, Richard Beliles. Two years later, Jim whipped the Democrat Galen Martin, 69 to 31 percent.

The Fourth District got a new look in 1992, a look that figured to make things more difficult for its Republican congressman. Under the revamped configuration, Louisville's heavily Republican Jefferson County suburbs were gone. In their place was the territory east of the Cincinnati suburbs, in which all but one county voted for Bill Clinton over George Bush in 1992. President Bush barely carried the Fourth District against Clinton; so (in retrospect, at least) there was reason for concern that year when Bunning took on the challenge of Dr. Floyd Poore.

Except for his initial congressional race against Terry Mann, this was Bunning's most difficult—and his most unpleasant—contest. Dr. Poore, the secretary of transportation under Governor Martha Layne Collins, had finished a decent third in the 1991 Democratic primary for governor, carrying the counties that were switched to the Fourth Congressional District a year later. So how did Bunning manage to win by fifty-three thousand votes (62 percent to 38 percent)? "They forgot that northern Kentucky, those three counties up here, are becoming more and more Republican-registered because of the unbelievable economic boom," he explained. Indeed, Boone County, which was four-to-one Democratic when Jim first ran, is almost even now, and Campbell and Kenton Counties, about three-to-one for the Democrats in '86, were less than half of that six years later when Bunning faced Dr. Poore.

"We thought he was going to be a very difficult opponent for the simple reason that he finished a very strong third (27 percent) in the gubernatorial primary," Bunning pointed out. "He had carried the newly constructed Fourth District against the other two candidates. So we thought, 'Gee, this is going to be a tough race.'"

It was certainly a nasty race. Bunning accused Dr. Poore of failing to provide sufficient financial support for the children from his first marriage. Dr. Poore raised Bunning's anger dangerously close to the boiling point when, during a televised debate, he suggested that Jim was an adulterer.

"It was horrible," Mary Bunning said. "He surmised, since Jim was a ballplayer and they all did this, that Jim did this. I knew it wasn't true. I thought, 'How can you lie like that?' Jim was very angry."

Rick Robinson, who spent six years in Washington as Bunning's legislative director, recalled: "After the debate both sides have a press conference. Their press conference, by flip of the coin, went first. While he was holding his press conference he did, in fact, apologize to Mary, but not to Jim. He said it was a rumor and unsubstantiated. Mary was sitting upstairs, waiting to go to our press conference. Jim was walking back and forth, trying to get his anger under control."

It was at that tense point that David Bunning walked up to his mother and said, "Hey, Mom, are you ready for that Manhattan and a cigarette right now?" According to Robinson, David's crack broke the ice, bringing smiles to the faces of some very upset people.

Dr. Poore was a flamboyant character, a physician who changed his name legally so that "Dr." would have to appear on the ballot. "In the early years of his medical practice," explained Rick Robinson, he was very well known for his bright sports coats, his Rolls-Royces, bragging about how much money he made. But now that he was running for office, suddenly he was a populist, just one of the folks."

The Bunning braintrust, looking for a way to cut Dr. Poore down to size, came up with a television commercial that did the trick. It was designed to remind voters that the doctor wasn't so poor after all and that he certainly wasn't one of the folks.

"We were looking for a way to spoof that," Robinson commented, "and we came up with an ad that was a knockoff of a Grey Poupon [mustard] commercial."

"We were trying to construct an ad which would give the people humorously a picture of what Dr. Poore said he was like and what he was really like," Bunning remembered.

And they were trying to do it without being overly negative. Jim didn't want to use negative ads unless they were absolutely necessary — he held them in reserve, just in case; Mary absolutely hated them.

"A hard negative ad does have an impact," Bunning said, "but something that can make fun of your opponent and get people to laugh at him is devastating."

The commercial showed a Rolls-Royce being driven down a country road, approaching a farmer on a tractor. The car pulled up, the window came down, and the driver, wearing a loud sports jacket, looked out at the farmer and said, "Pardon me, do you have any mustard?" The farmer (a real one) gave him a funny look and said, "What?"

"Then you see the window rolling up and the car pulling off," Robinson said, "and on the back of this Rolls-Royce is a Poore bumper sticker, and the farmer looks at it and says, 'Poore? Poore, my [bleep]!'" Except the "Poore" when he says it, obviously isn't meant to have an "e" on the end.

Poor Dr. Poore became known in some circles as "the Mustard Man." This was fine with Bunning, who thought he was something of a hot dog, anyway.

When the idea for the commercial had been suggested, Jim thought it might be too subtle, but he agreed to give it a try. As things turned out, it became the defining advertisement of the race, winning an award as the best political commercial of the year. The more he campaigned in the days after it ran, the more Bunning came to realize how effective it was.

One day he walked into a tiny restaurant in Brooksville (in Bracken County), a town of about four hundred people. Jim introduced himself to the young lady behind the counter and shook hands. "You know," she told him, "your opponent was in here and I offered him some mustard and he got madder'n heck." As Jim recalls it, he said, "Well, I know one thing, that commercial's getting into all areas of my district." Not to mention getting under Dr. Poore's skin.

Bunning took no chances in that campaign, raising over $984,000. His landslide victory over "the Mustard Man" was followed, two years later, by an even bigger win—74 to 26 percent—over Sally Harris Skaggs. In 1996 he got 68 percent of the votes in defeating Denny Bowman, the mayor of Covington. In his five contests as an incumbent, the 62 to 38 percent victory over Dr. Poore in 1992 represented Jim Bunning's closest race. He had turned the Fourth into a safe district.

As his seniority increased, so did his role on Capitol Hill. After serving two terms on the Banking Committee, Jim was elected to the prestigious Ways and Means Committee in December 1990. After his victory over Dr. Poore two years later, he was elected to the Budget Committee. But it was after the 1994 election, when the Republicans gained control of the House, that Bunning really got a chance to be productive.

"It's really been rewarding to be able to work in the majority and be able to write legislation," he declared. "For instance, the senior citizens' earnings bill [increasing the amount seniors may earn without reducing their Social Security payments]. We worked on that eight years and never got it through the Democratic Congress. Now we got it through and the president signed it into law."

Bunning has been a leader in the fights for welfare reform, balancing the federal budget, giving the president the line-item veto, and, as chairman of the Social Security subcommittee, trying to put that system on a sound footing. He has also infuriated some of his old acquaintances in baseball management by trying to get the sport's antitrust exemption overturned.

As you might expect, Jim has never steered away from controversy. Saying what he thinks, however strong those opinions may be, is part of the Bunning charm, although his opponents don't consider that trait particularly charming. You always know where Jim Bunning stands, and where you stand with him.

Jim made no secret of his dislike of House Democratic leaders or of President Clinton. Outraged by his colleagues' overdrafts on the House bank—a scandal that rocked Capitol Hill—Bunning, as a member of the Ethics Committee, led the successful charge against committee chairman Mathew McHugh's proposal to name only the twenty-four worst offenders. Jim was the lone dissenter in a 12-1 vote not to require members to report overdrafts as loans or gifts on their financial disclosure statements.

In September 1993, speaking at a Republican rally in northern Kentucky, Bunning voiced his opinion of President Clinton, calling him "the most corrupt, the most amoral, the most despicable person I've ever seen in the presidency." That comment, wrote the veteran political columnist Jack Anderson in November, "jarred some of Washington's most seasoned hard-ball players. . . . One Senate Democratic leader, echoing a sentiment expressed by many on Capitol Hill, said, 'I think even bitter partisans recognize that there is a line beyond which you just don't go, and he crossed it.'"

If you're going to say what you think, you'd better have a thick skin. Bunning has developed a very thick one. All those years playing baseball helped. "I've heard him say several times, 'When you've been booed by fifty thousand people at Yankee Stadium, you can handle [a negative phone call from a constituent or a negative newspaper article] pretty well,'" Rick Robinson pointed out.

For a man who didn't think about getting seriously involved in politics until he was in his fifties, Jim Bunning has become every bit as dedicated to his new career as he was to his old one. "The competition, the competitive spirit got me more involved and more involved," he said. And he's as deeply committed to politics as he was to baseball in his twenties and thirties. The two businesses have some strong similarities. Competitiveness, for one thing. Also the undeniable fact that the public has come to view both professional ballplayers and politicians in an increasingly dim light. Bunning is well aware of that. He hates to see all ballplayers painted with the same brush, accused of being greed-driven ingrates. And he hates to see all politicians viewed as men and women whose word means nothing, who do what's expedient rather than what's right, who make promises they have no intention of keeping in their lust for power.

"The fact of the matter is 85 percent of the people [in Congress], maybe 90 percent are just hard-working stiffs trying to do a good job at what they do," he said. "It's just like any other profession. If you have an outstanding professional athlete and he goes the cocaine route, the whole team and the whole league are painted with that. The same thing happens when a lawmaker breaks the law.

"The profession has a broad-brush bad name because of certain people making promises they can't keep and deliberately breaking promises they make. So I'm very careful about what I say when I campaign. I think the people of my district are fully aware they're going to get exactly what they expect out of me."

Rick Robinson recalled the time a lobbyist for an organization Bunning generally supported referred to Jim as a "swing vote" in a fundraising piece. The congressman had said all along that he was in favor of that particular legislation, and now the phone calls began, angry constituents saying, "Hey, Bunning told us he was for this; why did he lie to us?"

Jim was furious. He called the executive director of the organization and asked him to come over.

"We're sitting in the office," Robinson recalled, "and Jim pulled out the piece and said, 'I want you to explain this.' The guy tried to make a joke of it. I thought Bunning was going to come over the desk at him.

This is a very powerful lobby group we're talking about. I don't think this guy had ever seen anybody stand up to him like that before."

You can always tell when Bunning is getting angry. The red starts coming up on his neck, the eyes glint.

"He leveled this guy," Robinson said. "You could just see him sinking back in the chair, shocked. 'I want to know what you're going to do to make this better,' Jim said to him. 'What are you going to do to tell people in my district you're the liar?'"

"He ended up sending another letter, and he made it right. I remember him walking out of the office and saying to the guy with him, 'Well, I still have a piece of my ass left,' and the other guy looked at him and said, 'Not much.'"

Like the great majority of people who have worked for Bunning in his congressional years, Rick Robinson became totally committed to the man. "I had a blast," the legislative director said of his six years with Jim in Washington. "He's very committed, very principled. I've always said there are only two or three people I could work for in Congress. He's one of them. There's no gray with Jim. It's either black or white. In these days of money politics, it's great to have people who are principled about whom to take a contribution from."

One of Bunning's "golden rules," Robinson said, was to never accept money from somebody who also gave to the other side. That's a common occurrence in today's politics. You give to the Democrat, you give to the Republican; whichever one wins, you're a "supporter."

Not with Bunning. He has his staff check the lists of contributors. As soon as a "double contributor" turns up, he or she receives a letter explaining why the money earmarked for Bunning's campaign is being returned in full. A typical letter plucked from Jim's office files, dated July 17, 1992:

"Dear Ed and Debbie, I'm sorry to learn that you have contributed $500 to my opponent in the upcoming election. According to Dr. Poore's Federal Election Report, the donation was made on May 15, 1992.

"I have a policy of not accepting contributions from people who contribute to the other side. I wish you would have told Mary when she called about the fundraiser at Jerry and Marge Deters' home.

"Enclosed you will find a 'Citizens for Bunning' check as a refund. [Signed] Respectfully, Jim Bunning, Member of Congress."

Jim started returning such donations in his gubernatorial campaign against Martha Layne Collins and has continued the practice ever since. As Robinson explained, with Bunning there is no gray, only black and white. He doesn't appreciate "backers" who hedge their bets.

Jim made an effort to downplay his celebrity as a former baseball star on arriving in Washington. He was determined to be known as a congressman, not a ballplayer who became a congressman.

"We were all kind of touchy about the baseball thing," Robinson recalled. "Then the first day we were there one of the older ranking congressmen showed up with a young kid at a swearing-in party we had in Jim's office. He said, 'Jim, this young man is the son of my treasurer and he wants to have his picture taken with a real congressman, one that has a hundred victories in both leagues.' Right away Jim, I think, realized this baseball thing was going to be a little more benefit to him than he thought."

There was no way Jim Bunning could put his baseball career completely behind him. It was his second week in Washington, or maybe his third, when carpet was being laid in his new congressional office. Jim was in his inner, private office, the door closed. Two men—one young, one not-so-young—were laying carpet in the outer office. The older man was from Baltimore, a fact that became apparent when he remarked to his co-worker, "You know whose office this is? 'Buckles' Bunning."

"I'm sitting there listening to this," Rick Robinson said. "I know that was one of the incidents in his life. Mary calls it the worst week of her life. I'm thinking, 'Guys, you don't want to talk about this too loudly.' And this guy's going, 'Buckles Bunning is one of the greatest pitchers to ever play the game of baseball. You know what he did in Baltimore? He would take baseballs and notch them on his belt buckle.' Every other word is 'Buckles Bunning.'"

Robinson kept listening, and hoping that they'd lay the carpet and leave before good old "Buckles" opened the door. No such luck. The bell rang. A vote was coming up. The door flew open and there was "Buckles" staring that carpet-laying Oriole fan straight in the eye.

"I'll be damned," the man said, "Buckles Bunning," and he stuck out his hand.

It got so quiet in that office you could have heard a resin bag drop. As Robinson remembered it, everybody stopped and looked around, waiting to see if the new member of congress was going to shake the guy's hand or punch him in the nose.

"Jim laughed," said Robinson, "and then he looked at him and said, 'Oh, you're from Baltimore, huh?' and shook his hand."

He even signed a baseball for him. A fresh, clean, unmarked baseball.

The original Baltimore incident had died a quick death in baseball circles, where charges of pitchers doctoring balls were nothing new. But oddly enough—or maybe not so oddly, when you consider what goes on in political campaigns—the "Buckles" business surfaced as a minor issue in Jim's race with Dr. Poore in 1992. Believe it or not, Jack Anderson began one of his columns this way a year later:

"Is 'Belt Buckle Bunning' up to his old tricks?"

"Rep. Jim Bunning, R-Ky., who was given that nickname by his opponent during last year's election, has long been accused of sharpening his belt buckle to doctor baseballs during his major league pitching career. Bunning denies the allegation, but a 1990 book by Dan Gutman, 'It Ain't Cheatin' If You Don't Get Caught,' nominates Bunning for the 'Scuffball Hall of Fame.'"

The column went on to criticize Bunning for his remarks about Bill Clinton.

Despite their great differences, the Republican congressman from Kentucky's Fourth District and the Democratic president from Arkansas did find themselves championing the same cause on occasion. Jim had been pushing an adoption bill, one that Clinton was eager to claim as his own in '96. So it was that one memorable Saturday morning Jim Bunning answered the phone in his congressional office.

"This is the White House," the voice at the other end said. "The president would like to . . . "

"Oh sure," the congressman interrupted. "Who is this?" And with that he slammed down the receiver, in no mood for practical jokes.

The phone rang again. Jim picked it up and heard: "This really is the White House."

It really was.

Another long-time Bunning adversary—baseball, not political—has a conspicuous place of honor on the wall in his Kentucky office, where Ted Williams' picture is prominently displayed.

"The only autograph I've ever asked for," Jim said. "I told him that when I asked for it."

On the bottom of the picture, which shows Ted standing next to Bunning at a Florida fundraiser, the last .400 hitter wrote, "To Jim Bunning, a great pitcher who struck me out three times in one game [signed] Ted Williams."

Love of the Game

When Bill White made up his mind to step down
as president of the National League, a position
he had held for five years, he began thinking
about a successor. He was the first African American to hold
such a high-visibility job in professional sports in this country. Bill's first choice was Bob Watson, a former player. "I
wanted a black guy to succeed me," he explained.

Watson had other plans. He wanted to be a general manager, an ambition he realized with the Houston Astros and,
later, with the New York Yankees. So Bill White looked
elsewhere. He wanted a strong president, one who would
stand up to the owners when necessary. And he preferred a
man with a background in the game. Ultimately, the National League did choose an African American, electing
Leon Coleman in March 1994. A Princeton graduate, with
a master's degree from Harvard, Coleman had a varied and
impressive professional background that included stints as a
teacher, a politician, an investment banker, and, beginning
in 1992, Major League Baseball's executive director of marketing development. Known as an excellent administrator,
Coleman ranked high on Bill White's list of candidates.

So did Jim Bunning.

A former player himself, and a highly successful one,
White understood the advantages of having a league president who knew the game from the perspective of one who
had played it at the top level. Bill phoned Bunning, his

former teammate on the Phillies, and broached the subject. "They would never consider me," Bunning told him.

White wasn't so sure. "I got support," he observed, reflecting on what Jim said in that phone call. "I was not an angel. Why would they go for me? Bunning had more administrative experience than I had. If they would support me, why not Bunning?"

The reasons could fill a book.

The owners—certainly those who remembered Bunning's involvement with the Players Association—saw him as a loose cannon, a man who made a habit of saying what he thought instead of what they thought he should be saying. They had already selected a fellow owner, Bud Selig of Milwaukee, to replace the ousted Fay Vincent as interim commissioner. The idea that the owners would tolerate a league president who had been so outspokenly critical of them for years and who had spearheaded a fight to strip Major League Baseball of its antitrust exemption was far-fetched, to put it mildly.

Bunning did, however, have at least one vocal supporter in management's ranks—George Steinbrenner, principal owner of the New York Yankees, never one to blindly follow the party line. Other owners might quake at the mention of Bunning's name; not George. He saw in Jim precisely the type of leadership qualities and feeling for the game that baseball so sorely needed.

George, in fact, considered Bunning an ideal choice for baseball's highest office—commissioner.

"Here you have a guy who was one of the greatest competitors that I ever saw in the game, and one of the best pitchers I ever saw," Steinbrenner declared. "On top of that he has an intelligence you could put up against anyone. I can't think of too many athletes who have those qualities. If we could get a guy like Bunning we wouldn't have to wonder about whether he's for the players or for the owners. Get Jim Bunning, you get a standup individual. He would be a great commissioner."

Steinbrenner had similar feelings about Bill White, who teamed with Phil Rizzuto on telecasts of Yankee games before taking over as National League president. Bunning and White, George knew, were very much alike—both no-nonsense, tell-it-like-it-is types who stood up for what they believed was right, even if they ruffled a few feathers along the way. But White did most of his fighting behind the scenes.

Except for one occasion when he felt obliged to publicly comment on then Commissioner Vincent's lack of support in a dispute involving an umpire, Bill kept his name, and any disagreements he might have, out of the headlines. No so Bunning, who said and did things on numerous occasions that upset baseball's hierarchy. Jim, after all, had been battling the owners for years as a leader in the Players Association. His rhetoric was strongly pro-union, anti-management. Modern-day baseball owners, determined to run the game their way, with often reckless disregard for the long-term consequences, weren't likely to accept a man who had been instrumental in hiring Marvin Miller and, as congressman, was a constant thorn in their sides.

But Bill White, like Jim Bunning, had a mind of his own and a realization that what the majority of owners considered best for them was not necessarily best for baseball. So it wasn't all that surprising that White, despite his expressed desire to pick an African American to succeed him in the National League president's chair, would think of Jim as a good choice for the job. When White met with the search committee—the Dodgers' Peter O'Malley, the Mets' Fred Wilpon, and the Braves' Bill Bartholomay—at the Waldorf-Astoria in New York, he brought up Jim's name. "I felt outside of Watson, Bunning would be the one to stand on his own two feet," White recalled. "He didn't need the job."

Neither did White when he took it. To Bill, that was important. A man who couldn't afford to get fired would be putty in the hands of the owners. As he put it, if you needed the job "you were going to be dancing." Bunning, he felt confident, had the strength to run the league the way the outgoing president believed it should be run—in the best interests of the game.

"I didn't see why they couldn't choose the best person available," White said.

But Bunning had alienated too many baseball people to be considered seriously. Not that he really wanted the job, anyway. His political career was flourishing, and his lack of respect for the owners, and what they were doing to the game, bordered on contempt.

Some thin-skinned baseball "leaders" were incensed when Bunning pointed out in his Hall of Fame induction speech: "For over four years now, baseball has been rudderless. For God's sake and for the game's sake, find a rudder. Pick a course and stick with it, and get your internal problems resolved before the Congress of the United States gives up on you and intervenes. The only thing that could be worse is if the fans give up on you."

Baseball ownership bridled at such remarks, seemingly unwilling to accept responsibility for what has happened to the game in recent years at the big league level. Perhaps rather pointedly, nobody from the commissioner's office bothered to show up at Jim's Hall of Fame induction. Instead of seeing Bunning for what he was—a man who loved baseball and was dismayed over what the game's leadership was doing to it—they viewed him as the enemy, a man intent on hurting the game at which he had excelled.

Certainly, that was the way former Phillies president Bill Giles viewed him.

Bunning had not endeared himself to Giles with some of the comments he made about baseball in general and the Phillies in particular. Giles, who stepped down as the club's president in June of 1997 in the midst of a disastrous Phillies season, must have held his breath every time Congressman Bunning opened his mouth to comment on the state of baseball.

"I like Jim Bunning as a person," Giles commented in his office overlooking the playing field at Jack Russell Memorial Stadium in Clearwater, Florida, during 1997 spring training. "I enjoyed him as a player and he was a great competitor and a great family man. But why he has been on this tirade, so negative about baseball, is bothersome. I love the game and I see no reason for people who have made a nice living off the game to be so critical, and I think Jim's been way off base on much of his criticism. I'm very disappointed in his public stance and negativism toward ownership and whatever."

And yet Giles' Phillies had held a special night for Bunning at Veterans Stadium the year before to salute his election to the Hall of Fame. "I don't dislike him as a human being," Giles explained. "I just dislike some of things he does."

Jim Bunning Night at the Vet in the summer of '96 was a pleasant occasion. The honoree gave a speech that not even Giles could find fault with, and the Phillies presented him with, among other things, a videotape of the entire proceedings. It was all done with consummate class.

"He really enjoyed that evening," said Giles.

Indeed, both Jim and Mary Bunning enjoyed it immensely, right down to the climactic ride around the stadium in an open car, waving to the fans. It was a touching affair, one handled beautifully by the

Phillies and the Bunnings. But when it was over, the hard feelings on Bill Giles's part remained.

Asked why he hadn't taken the opportunity to discuss their areas of disagreement, Giles replied, "He's impossible to talk to. He's so stubborn and so set in his ways on what's wrong with baseball and how people have screwed up and all that. I talked to him two or three years ago when we were going through all the antitrust stuff; he was one of the people assigned to me in the Congress to call and he was very ugly toward me and very ugly toward baseball."

"Very ugly toward *you*?" Giles was asked.

"Not personally," he replied. "Ugly toward ownership. . . . When you love something like I do and people blast it all the time, it hurts, and I don't like it, that's all."

Asked how his fellow owners reacted when he told them the result of his lobbying call to Bunning regarding baseball's antitrust exemption, Giles replied, "They said, 'We're not surprised. We kind of knew he felt that way.' I just said, 'Forget Bunning being willing to help on that antitrust exemption.'

"I mean, it's not just Jim Bunning. It would disappoint me no matter who it is to be as harsh as he's been. Baseball takes such punishment as it is, it bothers me that somebody as great as Jim was is so outspoken. I respected him as a player. That's what's so sad. I'd always held him up as something special, and then to have one of my heroes as a kid criticize so much, it hurts. . . . He's always been a strong union guy. I guess a lot of people in baseball have always had a little animosity toward him for his involvement in hiring Marvin [Miller]. But I have never had animosity toward him until the last two or three years when he's been so outspoken and critical."

What Giles and others can't seem to understand is that Bunning loves the game every bit as much as they do. No doubt more than many of the newcomers to baseball's ownership ranks. It's what he feels they're doing to the game he loves that causes him to be so critical. In any event, Jim Bunning might be the last guy baseball would choose to fill a high-profile position.

Giles's feelings about Bunning run so deep that he walked out during Bunning's speech at the Philadelphia Sports Writers Banquet in February 1997 when Jim poked fun at baseball's lack of direction.

Those who disapprove so strongly of Bunning's negative comments don't seem to hear the many positive things he has to say about the game itself.

To the fans listening to his Hall of Fame speech in Cooperstown, he stated, "You made baseball our national sport. Please don't give up on it now. . . . Baseball is still the greatest game in the world."

Typical of Bunning, the Cooperstown speech that angered some owners contained remarks that didn't sit well with former Players Association head Marvin Miller, either.

"To the owners and players alike, I would say, get a commissioner," Bunning declared. "Come up with a way to mutually share the cost of the commissioner's office, and mutually hire, if necessary through a third party, a real commissioner with restored powers. . . ."

"I told Marvin what I was going to propose about the commissioner's office," Bunning remembered. "He said, 'Oh God, that's awful. That's a terrible thing to say.' I said, 'Well, Marvin, you and I disagreed before. We're going to disagree again.' He thinks the commissioner's office should be weak and should be adversarial; therefore the Players Association office is elevated. Which in my opinion creates all the controversy, and right now baseball doesn't need that."

Back in his playing days, Bunning had disagreed with Miller on the steps the Players Association should take, specifically on a proposed boycott of spring training.

"Roberto Clemente got up [at a players association meeting] and made a great speech," Bunning recalled. "He asked, 'If we take the first step, what follows after that?' It needed to be said and he said it very well. Then I got up and said, 'If two people can't sit down and negotiate, there's got to be something wrong with the two people.'"

Bunning's suggestion in his Hall of Fame speech that the baseball commissioner should represent both sides, not just management, was nothing new. Another early leader in the Players Association, Robin Roberts, has long advocated the same idea—the one Miller called "awful" and the owners, no doubt, called even worse. In a perfect world, it would be an ideal solution. But the baseball world is far from perfect, as the cancellation of the 1994 World Series demonstrated so conclusively.

Nothing Bunning has done or said angered baseball ownership as much as his outspoken stand against the antitrust exemption.

When Bud Selig, the owner who has doubled as acting commissioner since Fay Vincent was run out of office, sent an informational packet and accompanying letter to members of Congress in 1994, Jim Bunning promptly responded by sending a letter to each of his colleagues that dismissed Selig's arguments as poppycock. In his letter of January 12, 1994, Congressman Bunning wrote:

" . . . Mr. Selig's letter was so rife with errors and misleading statements that I felt compelled to point them out to you.

"Error #1—Major League Baseball does not operate as an economic cartel. Wrong! MLB operates as a cartel in classic monopoly fashion. The owners, not market economics, dictate how the supply of its product will be allocated. The antitrust exemption shields MLB from having to react to market forces and makes competition to MLB impossible. . . . The final arbiter of disputes in the world of Major League Baseball is the commissioner's office, an office now filled by Mr. Selig, one of the owners. The era of an independent commissioner overseeing the game is long gone. Now, suppliers of the product of baseball answer only to themselves, completely control the allocation of their product, and suffer no competitors. Sounds like a monopoly to me!"

Bunning went on to debunk, in considerable detail, the acting commissioner's other arguments in defense of the antitrust exemption. Disputing Selig's claim that the players should agree to a salary cap because it is good for baseball, Bunning pointed out:

"Wrong yet again!

" . . . Big league baseball has a problem because small-market teams take in less gate and television revenue than big-market teams and have a harder time competing when it comes to paying salaries and expenses. . . . The owners' solution to this dispute is to limit expenses by artificially limiting how much they have to spend on salaries. In short, the owners are trying to forge a resolution to their internal argument on the backs of the players instead of working out the big-market/small-market squabble among themselves."

Of Selig's claim that the antitrust exemption has not hurt the players, Bunning noted:

"As wrong as wrong can be! Because of the exemption, the players worked as virtual slaves until the last several decades. The only place that the players could go to sell their services was the existing major leagues; the exemption effectively protected MLB from facing competition and the formation of new teams and leagues with which the players could negotiate. The players had to play for the major league monopoly or for no one at all.

"It was not until the union asserted itself through the collective bargaining process in the past several decades that players' salaries rose and they began to win some of the rights that other American workers have. Salaries have gone up but the players still work for a monopoly that has a great deal of power over their livelihoods. . . . I know that it is hard to sympathize with workers whose median salary is around $500,000 per year, but because a player earns a high salary does not mean that he should have fewer rights than other Americans. The antitrust exemption enslaved the players in the past and lurks as a constant threat to their future. To say that it has not hurt them and does not jeopardize their future is just not true. In America, professional athletes might make more money than most other people, but it does not mean that they deserve less protection under the law."

Of the claim that repealing the antitrust exemption would hurt baseball, and the fans and communities that have big league franchises, Bunning observed:

"After eight work stoppages in the last 24 years, it is hard to imagine anyone or any force doing worse damage to baseball and the fans than the havoc that the owners have wreaked. . . . How could the fans be treated any worse than they have in the past?"

(Note that Jim wrote this nine months before the World Series of 1994, the one that wasn't played.)

"Obviously, Mr. Selig, one of the members of the owners' cartel and a beneficiary of the exemption, wants to keep the exemption," Congressman Bunning wrote. "John D. Rockefeller and Standard Oil did not want Congress to pass the Sherman Antitrust Act either.

"But, it is indefensible that MLB, which under the protection of the antitrust exemption has compiled an awful track record of mismanagement and suffers from abysmal labor relations, can claim with a straight face that it has to have the exemption to survive. It is the exemption that has led major league baseball to the brink of extinction.

"After helping organize the players union and negotiating contracts with the owners, I know firsthand that the antitrust exemption has instilled in the owners an arrogant and contemptuous attitude. Although we are about to enter the 21st century, the owners still want to have the power to act like the 19th century robber barons. . . .

"In America, our economy has always worked under the principle that competition and markets are good things and that unregulated monopolies are inefficient and unresponsive to consumers. But Major League Baseball, one of the last unregulated monopolies left, claims that it needs antitrust protection so that it can continue its sad record of mismanagement and unresponsiveness to the fans. If Mr. Selig's contentions were not so misguided and indefensible, they would be laughable. . . .

"Mr. Selig is dead WRONG! It's time to repeal baseball's antitrust exemption. [Signed] Jim Bunning, Member of Congress."

And yet, for all of that, the congressman's Hall of Fame speech was interpreted by some sportswriters as the opening salvo in his bid to be considered a candidate for the commissioner's job. That's pretty funny when you stop to think about it.

"I laughed because they didn't know what they were talking about," Jim said. It was not only that the owners wouldn't consider him for the job. Bunning wouldn't take it under present conditions, even if, through some extraordinary set of circumstances, they somehow offered it to him.

As Jim sees it, "The person they hire now will be a figurehead and do whatever the darn owners say he will or else he'll get fired.

"I think Bill White would make a hell of a commissioner. All I can tell you is, he has about as much chance as I have. When he called me and said, 'I'm going to recommend you to take my place,' I said, 'Go ahead, Bill, it won't do any good. I'm flattered that you think I can do it. The fact of the matter is, no chance.' He said, 'It's worth about 450 grand a year.' I said, 'That's not important to me.'"

Bunning recalled telling White, "No one [owner] in his right mind would vote for me. They think of me as somebody who is hostile to them, not realizing I'm not hostile to any of them—except that I want the game to be preserved."

Bud Selig is not the only titular head of the game who has had problems with Bunning. And vice versa. The baseball commissioner Jim came to distrust and dislike the most was Peter Ueberroth, a man whose desire to boost his personal image was so transparent he could stand in front of you for nine innings and you wouldn't miss a pitch. Ueberroth's legacy to the game he led from October 1984 to March 1989 was his role in orchestrating collusion by the owners in their dealings—or lack of same—with free agents.

Ueberroth and Bunning first met in January of 1986 in New York City. Jim was still an agent at the time, and one of his clients, Lonnie Smith, had asked the St. Louis Cardinals the year before for help in combating a drug problem. Under the terms of the drug agreement in effect then, Smith could go through rehabilitation and rejoin the club within thirty days with no loss of pay.

Lonnie was one of the players who testified in the highly publicized Pittsburgh drug trial involving several major leaguers, doing so only after the federal government granted him immunity. Ueberroth, waiting until the last day of February, announced that Smith and the others had to turn over 10 percent of their salaries to drug-abuse programs if they wanted to play baseball in 1986. In Smith's case, Ueberroth's decision meant 10 percent of $850,000, or $85,000. Bunning was furious. "I'm at a loss for words to understand the commissioner of baseball reacting after the federal government procured Lonnie's testimony with the understanding there would be no punishment," he said. "Fining him $85,000 now, I think, is unreasonable and outrageous. I think it's totally unjust."

Ueberroth's decision came down the day before big league players were required to report for spring training. Bunning and Ueberroth had met for the first time the previous month in the commissioner's office at a hearing called to determine the next step to be taken in the Lonnie Smith case. Jim and Warren Scovil, an attorney he had hired, were there to protect Lonnie's rights. They assumed, since immunity had been granted, no further punishment would be meted out. What Ueberroth did—a grandstand move to protect the image of baseball, Bunning felt—convinced Jim that the man in the commissioner's office could not be trusted.

"His dealings with Lonnie Smith just turned me sour," Bunning remembered. "That's one of the reasons I didn't like Peter Ueberroth—the shoddy, dishonest treatment of Lonnie Smith after the attorney general of the United States gives him immunity to testify at the Pittsburgh trial. It was totally unfair. Ueberroth was just covering his backside. He had no regard for Lonnie Smith. He didn't know who Lonnie Smith was. He didn't care about Lonnie Smith personally. He was only concerned with the image of baseball. . . . This guy [Ueberroth], I don't think he knows one thing about baseball. I don't think he understands the significance it has in the overall lifestyle of the American people. I don't think he understands anything about the people who play the game. . . . I think he's taken a very selfish approach to baseball: 'How can it be used to better my interests?'"

Bunning said that, and more, about Peter Ueberroth in the aftermath of the commissioner's decision. Then, in September 1987, the congressman and the commissioner of baseball met again, this time in Bunning's office in Washington. Ueberroth had heard and read some of the things Jim was saying about him, and he wanted to change Bunning's mind. Instead, he managed to alienate him even further.

"The funny thing about it," recalled Bunning, "is that when Peter and his attorney came to my office, it was like the first time he had met me. He said, 'I don't know why you're saying bad things about me; this is the first time we ever met.' The meeting went downhill from that point on."

As Rick Robinson recalled it, Ueberroth said, "So Jim, I hear you're telling everybody I'm an S.O.B.," to which Bunning retorted, "No, that's not true, Peter. I've been telling everybody you're a no-good, lousy S.O.B."

Bunning promptly informed the commissioner that they had, in fact, met previously. "I told him that we had spent about two hours across the table from each other in the Lonnie Smith hearing," Jim said. "I told him, 'I got a letter from your office inviting me to come and visit with you, and I was there at the designated time.'"

That must have been an embarrassing moment for Ueberroth. To Bunning, it was a revealing one. Surely, you would expect a commissioner of baseball to remember that he had met one of the game's big names under circumstances that could hardly be described as routine. That is, if the commissioner in question knew anything about the game he was commissionering. Bunning was no fan of the former commissioner Bowie Kuhn, but after dealing with Ueberroth he began to realize that Kuhn wasn't so bad after all.

"Bowie Kuhn had some background in baseball," Jim remarked. "He had operated [as an attorney] in the National League office. I got along with Bowie. I had dealt with him so many years as part of the management team on the National League staff. But this guy [Ueberroth], he doesn't care about the game."

In the course of their rather heated meeting in Washington, the commissioner reminded Bunning that he was from the same political party.

"I can't help that," Jim replied. "It's an accident."

No, it did not go well.

Asked about Ueberroth years later, Bunning commented, "He was fluff. I didn't think he ever acted in the best interests of the game. He acted in the best interests of Peter Ueberroth. . . . He sure cost the owners a great deal of money by [some of his actions]. All the collusion [agreeing not to sign free-agent players for big money], he was the ringleader. Management wasn't smart enough to know they were colluding. I'm serious. I don't think Bill Giles to this day thinks he colluded. I don't think Bill Giles would have broken the law if he knew he was breaking it. He's that honest a guy. In private meetings he was led to believe this was the thing to do. Ueberroth was the reason."

It remains Bunning's firm belief that "the commissioner of baseball should become something other than a management tool. The last commissioner who looked at the game and said, 'You know, the guys that are playing are as important as the guys that own the clubs, and somehow we've got to get them together and make it work,' was Happy Chandler," he said. "Why do you think Happy lasted such a short time?"

When Major League Baseball tried to curry favor with congressmen in its fight to save its antitrust exemption, Jim Bunning saw red. There was the day in early June of 1993 when a letter arrived at Bunning's Washington office. It was similar to those sent to 434 other members of the House of Representatives and 100 United States senators by acting commissioner Bud Selig, the Milwaukee Brewers' owner who is chairman of baseball's executive council.

"On behalf of Major League Baseball," it began, "it is my pleasure to invite you to the 1993 All-Star game on Tuesday, July 13, at Oriole Park at Camden Yards. . . ."

Bunning's first reaction was to laugh at what he considered an obvious attempt by Major League Baseball to win friends and influence politicians who were considering legislation that would eliminate the sport's precious exemption from antitrust laws.

"If that isn't legalized bribery, I don't know what is," he stated.

Even having the members of the House and Senate pay the list price of $60 for each of the hard-to-get tickets didn't change his mind. If the tickets were offered as outright gifts, Bunning pointed out, they would have to be reported. To Jim, the overriding fact was that in a 48,000-seat stadium that is routinely sold out for regular season games, more than 1,000 tickets were being set aside for an All-Star game in what he construed as a blatant attempt to influence votes.

"We have done our best to reserve good seat locations," Selig promised in his letter.

"The fact is, it's something that's frowned upon," Bunning noted of Selig's invitation to buy tickets. "It's not politically correct."

Maybe the commissioner should have scratched Bunning's name from the list of congressmen receiving his All-Star letter. Jim had testified on March 31 of that year at a hearing on baseball's antitrust situation before the House Subcommittee on Economic and Commercial Law. As usual, he pulled no punches.

"Mr. Chairman," he began, "it is a bit difficult to describe, in just two minutes, the injustice which has stretched over seven decades due to the decision of the Supreme Court in 1922, which granted antitrust exemption to Major League Baseball.

"The question today should be very straightforward and simple. Is that exemption justified? Is there any basis in logic, reason, or law that the players, fans, or the members of the general public with an interest in baseball should not enjoy the same basic protections provided by our nation's antitrust laws to everyone else?

"The answer is equally clear. And the answer is no."

Bunning went on to say, "Major league baseball is not—as it was determined [by the Supreme Court] in 1922—a local exhibition. It is a big business. . . . As it stands, twenty-eight owners totally control the destiny of the sport and the lives of those it affects like so many Roman Gods sitting comfortably on their thrones."

Acknowledging that major league players have managed "because of a good union to overcome many of the problems caused by the antitrust exemption," Bunning mentioned some of the injustices that "still permeate the system."

"Minor league players are subject, for the most part, to the traditional, pre-free agency reserve system," he testified. "Essentially, the players in the minor leagues have no recourse, no free choice. The clubs, through the draft, tell the players which club they can negotiate with. And they have to take it or leave it.

"And finally, potential ballplayers . . . are also affected adversely by the antitrust exemption [because it] allows the owners to artificially limit the number of franchises and opportunities available. Seventy years," he concluded, "is a long time for a bad law to be on the books."

Bud Selig's offer, two months later, to set aside good seats for the All-Star game did not change Jim Bunning's opinion.

"I'll tell you, I've mellowed out as far as baseball is concerned. I really have," Bunning said recently. "I feel so sorry for the game because it is, without an argument, still struggling. Management and ownership are not capable of making the decisions that have to be made. I am frightened to death that we are going to lose this great game.

"Mismanagement, mis-marketing, whatever you want to call it. If you look at franchises like Cincinnati—veteran franchises—and look at those all across the country, it's only because we have new stadiums and new franchises that we have the people coming to the park. If we didn't have a new ball park in Cleveland, or if we didn't have one in Baltimore, in Arlington [Texas], in Colorado. . . .

"The baseball direction is not very good because of the executive council [the ownership group that runs the game], and I know that's where Giles and I differ. It's sad, the lack of understanding about what people want in baseball. . . . I just sit back and observe it. People get mad when you tell the truth.

"I love baseball. I love the game better than Bill Giles ever hoped to. The problem is, what they're doing to it is screwing it up for generations. I thought the game couldn't be screwed up, but the players have cooperated with owners to screw it up."

No, the men who run baseball were not likely to give serious consideration to Jim Bunning as the next president of the National League. But if most of the owners aren't crazy about him, those players who remember what Bunning did for their union remain his staunch fans.

Al Kaline, the Detroit Tigers' Hall of Fame outfielder, recently talked about the time and effort Bunning, his onetime teammate, put in on behalf of the Players Association in those early days. "Guys like myself, I just wanted to play," remembered Kaline. "I didn't worry about fifteen, twenty, thirty years in the future. We all appreciate what Jim did. In fact, I think Jim Bunning would make a great commissioner."

Rest assured, we will never find out.

The Biggest Challenge

Jim Bunning, politician. A couple of decades ago, the very idea would have seemed absurd to those who knew him in his baseball days. But the man who had no thought of turning to politics as a career became a city councilman, and then a state senator. The man who "didn't want to go to Washington" became a six-term United States congressman, chairman of the Social Security Subcommittee of the Committee on Ways and Means and a member of the House Budget Committee.

"Could you have imagined any of this happening twenty years ago?" he was asked.

"No, I can't," he replied. "Even in my wildest dreams."

He had turned himself into a political big leaguer the same way he turned himself into a baseball big leaguer—through good old-fashioned determination, dedication, and hard work. He learned how to pitch to men like Ted Williams and Willie Mays and Mickey Mantle, and he learned how to raise money and give speeches and campaign for votes and deal with the everyday problems and decisions of political life. Now here he was at age sixty-five, his House seat secure in Kentucky's Fourth Congressional District. There was every reason to believe he could hold it as long as he desired. But twelve years in one place is a long time. Besides, there was another goal to reach, another hill to climb, and he had the energy and the will to climb it.

"I think twelve years in one institution is enough," Bunning decided.

Of course, there was always retirement. People his age, even those with his vigor and vitality, *did* retire.

"I don't want to sound pretentious," he said, "but let me put it this way. Obviously I have scraped and scrounged and saved enough money where I can retire, without any sweat, and play golf five days a week if I so choose. I may choose to do that sometime, but I'm not ready to do that yet. I think I can still do something and contribute."

The question was how. Another try for the governor's office? Or a bid for a seat in the United States Senate?

Another gubernatorial race seemed inviting when the subject came up in 1995. The first time, in 1983, Bunning was a rookie in big-time politics, not at all prepared to fight the good fight. Short on experience and short of cash, he had little chance to win. Now he had the experience, the political name recognition, and the ability to raise enough money to be competitive.

"I was thinking about running [for governor]," Bunning said. "It was a 'free shot.' You didn't have to give up your congressional seat to run."

Mary talked him out of it. Memories of the '83 race still lingered. It had not been a pleasant experience.

"Mary was the one who said, 'I don't want to go through the governor's race; it's too dirty, too ugly,'" Jim explained. "So I said no."

He gave no serious thought to running for the U.S. Senate until completing his successful re-election campaign in 1996. First things first. In politics, as in baseball, Bunning believed in leaving nothing to chance, taking nothing for granted.

"I was concentrating on my re-election and Bob Dole's successful election in Kentucky," Bunning said. (Dole wound up losing the commonwealth by seven-tenths of a percentage point to Bill Clinton in the presidential race, a fact that disturbed Bunning greatly.)

Once the 1996 elections had ended, the pressure started. Senator Mitch McConnell called and suggested that Jim take a long, hard look at the race for the Senate seat held, for four terms, by the Democrat Wendell Ford.

"He said, 'I think if we put pressure on Ford, he'll retire,'" Bunning recalled.

When Senator McConnell talked, people listened. "I knew going into it that a statewide race in Kentucky for a Republican is very, very difficult," Bunning said. "Only one person has been successful since 1967."

That person was Mitch McConnell, who had done it three times. His support and encouragement was a major factor in Bunning's decision to run.

"He was in the background," Jim said, "but he was very influential in getting, I would say, twenty-five other U.S. senators to call me and urge me to run."

Not everyone thought he would. "Some said, 'Bunning will never run for the Senate because he's number five on Ways and Means, and he's number five on the Budget Committee,'" Jim pointed out. "'He has twelve years' seniority. He'll never run for the Senate.'"

They were wrong. "I'm running to get out of the House," Bunning declared. "I've done my time in the House. In think I can accomplish a lot more in the Senate. If I'm going to affect every piece of legislation I think is important, I can't do it in the House. [In the House] I can do taxes, I can do trade, I can do Medicare. I can do important things, about 50 percent of the legislation. But the other 50 percent I can't touch.

"In the Senate you can affect every piece that comes up. I get to vote on treaties, I get to vote on judges. I get to vote on very important things to me personally."

The more he thought about it, the more sense it made. "I've been in the majority [in the House] now four years," he noted. "I've served in the minority eight years. I'd like to serve in the Senate. I think it would be a perfect way to get out of politics eventually."

Simply put, Jim Bunning decided he could "serve Kentucky and the country better in the Senate than in the House."

Also, as he was careful to tell Mary, a Senate campaign in Kentucky would be much cleaner than a gubernatorial race. "People in Kentucky have a high respect for federal marshals, federal law enforcement," Bunning explained. "They look at federal marshals differently than state election officials. In other words, people know if you go to jail in a federal prison, you don't get paroled; you stay for your full sentence. So they're very careful about doing anything illegally in federal elections."

At the time the decision was made to try for Wendell Ford's seat, Bunning and his people didn't know if Ford, then seventy-three, would run for a fifth term. The behind-the-scenes maneuvering was fascinating. As Bunning described it:

"Twice a Ford person came and said, 'Tell Bunning we're in.' He came to a friend of mine, John Cooper, and he told him, 'Tell Bunning, Ford is running definitely.' Ten days later they came to the same guy and said, 'Is there anything to do to get Bunning out of the race?' He [Cooper] said, 'Are you kidding? The more you try to get him out of the race, the deeper he digs in. He's going to run. Mark it down.' That was on Friday. Ford announced he was retiring the next Monday. He said it had nothing to do with me being in the race, and God Bless him. I think he served nobly and for an awful long time."

That was precisely what Bunning went out of his way to tell the media when he formally announced his candidacy. To his political enemies, the kind words sounded strange coming from the congressman's mouth. Senator Ford's initial reaction was to ask if someone had written the complimentary words that Bunning spoke. No, he was told, the congressman did it on his own.

"Why make Senator Ford mad at me?" Bunning wanted to know. "He's gracefully served four terms in the senate, one term as governor, one term as lieutenant governor and in the state senate. Almost forty years of public service."

Bunning announced his candidacy in a statewide tour, dashing by jet from airport to airport, from press conference to press conference, from Fort Mitchell to Lexington to Hazard to Bowling Green to Hopkinsville to Paducah to Owensboro to Louisville. Reporters and editorial writers seemed somewhat surprised by what they termed his "moderate" stance.

"We want to balance the budget," he remarked at the airport in Louisville, hitting in on one of his favorite themes, "but we are going to fight equally as hard to make sure that Kentucky doesn't get shortchanged."

At his stop in Hopkinsville, Bunning spoke of his desire to become the third Republican in recent memory to win a statewide election in Kentucky. "[Former governor] Louis Nunn did it," Jim said. "Mitch McConnell has done it three times. I'm looking forward to being the third."

Bunning's supporters wore baseball caps emblazoned with the words "The Bunning Team," leftovers from the 1983 gubernatorial race. Al Cross, political writer for the *Louisville Courier-Journal* observed, "At Bowling Green, Bunning was greeted by 75 people who hooted and hollered as if at a baseball game and displayed such signs as 'Put a star on the Senate mound.'" One Bunning supporter, aged eighty-two, was quoted as saying, "We knew he was coming back. And that's the reason we hung on to these caps."

One thing about politics: throw your hat in the ring and somebody is going to step on it. So it was that shortly after announcing his candidacy, Jim found himself in the headlines again—as a target for one of the most popular figures in the state, University of Kentucky (now Boston Celtics) basketball coach Rick Pitino.

For someone running for political office in the commonwealth, feuding with Rick Pitino is not recommended. Kentuckians love their basketball, and—with the exception of University of Louisville undergraduates, alumni, and boosters, and coach Denny Crum's immediate family—they love their Wildcats. Pitino took a struggling Kentucky basketball program and, in a remarkably short time, led it back to the very top. His Wildcats won the national championship in 1996 and, despite key personnel losses, reached the title game in '97. When Pitino spoke, Kentuckians listened. When Pitino sneezed, Kentuckians said gesundheit.

But one Kentucky political figure stopped being a Pitino fan on May 20, 1996. That's the date Kentucky's national champions (and Tennessee's championship women's team) were invited to the White House to be honored by President Clinton. Nothing unusual about that; championship sports teams—be they World Series winners or Super Bowl winners or NCAA basketball champions—are routinely given a presidential salute in Washington.

Naturally, Kentucky politicians were asked to participate in the happy ceremonies. Some Kentucky politicians, that is. James Paul David Bunning was, let us say, overlooked. Or, as the overlookee himself put it, "There were selective invitations."

Whatever the reason, Congressman Bunning was sitting in front of a television set when the president was shaking hands with Pitino and the Kentucky players. What he saw and heard made his blood boil.

"I watched Rick Pitino walk up to the microphone and endorse Bill Clinton for a second term," Jim declared. "Maybe he felt pressure to do it, but whatever it was, he's wishing the president luck in his run for a second term. That, to me, is an endorsement."

To Bunning, eager to see Bob Dole carry Kentucky, it was also a low blow.

The White House affair was not the only reception held for the Kentucky basketball team in Washington that day. A second one was planned later in the afternoon. One problem: nobody seemed able to find a room big enough to handle it.

"Somebody from the university called my office and said, 'Do you think Congressman Bunning can get a room—a *big* room—for us to honor the Wildcats?'" Bunning remembered. "They called me out of desperation. I said, 'Of course. We'll try to get the Ways and Means Committee room.'"

The mission was soon accomplished. Jim, rather amused that he'd been asked to help after being overlooked when invitations went out for the White House reception, was glad to do his part. After all, he was a native Kentuckian whose last five kids graduated from the university.

Anyhow, the post-White House reception in the Ways and Means Committee room was a success. Or so Bunning heard. Although he provided the room, he was not invited to attend that function, either.

Nothing to get that upset about. Mistakes happen. It wasn't until the night before the 1996 election that Jim really got angry. With the Clinton-Dole race a virtual tossup in Kentucky, the president made an appearance at the university and Pitino introduced him. The coach said his introduction of Clinton at the election eve rally did not constitute an endorsement, but Bunning remembered Pitino's endorsement of the president five and a half months before at the White House.

The minute Jim heard that Pitino planned to introduce Clinton he fired off a Mailgram to the Kentucky basketball coach. As usual, he did not mince words. The wire read:

"I just wanted you to know how disappointed and disgusted I was to see you personally rap [sic] Bill Clinton's candidacy in the cloak of respectability of UK basketball the day before an election. You might well have cost Bob Dole the election in Kentucky. You definitely have lost me as a UK fan. [Signed] Congressman Jim Bunning."

The word "rap," of course, was a typo. It was meant to be "wrap," but the Western Union operator who took the message over the phone left off the "w." Pitino, who knows his English as well as his basketball, did not let the slip go unnoticed. On November 11, four days after Bunning's Mailgram, Pitino sent the following letter:

"Dear Congressman:

"I just wanted *you* to know how disappointed and disgusted I was to receive your telegram. I have every right to welcome anyone I choose to our state, city, and campus. I *did not* 'rap Bill Clinton's candidacy in the cloak of respectability of U.K. basketball.' Had you attended the event or if you would read the papers you would see that I did not endorse his candidacy.

"For your additional information, the President of the United States welcomed our team and my family and friends this year to the White House at what was a non-partisan event. It was attended by Senators and Congressmen from Kentucky and Tennessee. I don't seem to recall that you were present, so obviously whether you *were* a U.K. fan is in question to begin with. [Signed] Sincerely, Rick Pitino."

Obviously, the coach assumed that Bunning had, in fact, been invited to the White House reception and chose to stay away. It was a reasonable assumption for him to make, but it was incorrect.

So both men were angry, and the fact that Clinton narrowly carried Kentucky did little to soothe Jim's feelings. Still, the Bunning-Pitino war of words was hardly of earth-shattering significance. It was a strictly private disagreement. Neither Bunning's wire nor Pitino's answering salvo was released to the press. Months went by without the public knowing anything about the dispute that, in a way, seemed almost comical.

As Bunning has learned, however, there's a big difference between being a starting pitcher and a politician. As a starter, you only have to worry about getting hit every fourth or fifth day. As a politician, you never know when you're going to get knocked around.

The apparently dead issue involving Pitino and Bunning became the stuff of headlines and editorials in early April 1997, shortly after Pitino's basketball team lost its bid for a second straight national title against Arizona. And, perhaps more significant, shortly after Bunning announced his candidacy for the U.S. Senate.

Pitino, appearing on a radio show in Lexington, responded to a question about a possible future in politics by attacking Bunning for what had occurred the previous November. As the Associated Press reported: "Rick Pitino has soured on politics and Hall of Fame pitcher Jim Bunning is part of the reason why."

Pitino, saying he was "highly insulted" at the wording of Bunning's Mailgram, added: "it's just that I don't think [politics] is a noble profession."

The "dead issue" became a lively topic in Kentucky. "It was ugly," Jim recalled. "He released his letter along with mine."

What bothered Bunning most was the curious timing.

"He saved it [Bunning's Mailgram and the reply] for five months," Jim pointed out. "If he was so upset about it, why wouldn't he immediately say, 'That dirty, rotten Bunning . . .' But no, he saved it for five months."

And waited until Bunning's candidacy was announced.

"Now, does that look like it was orchestrated?" Jim asked.

Orchestrated or not, the story had a long shelf life in Kentucky. Editorial writers had a field day. Even though Pitino soon left for the Boston Celtics, he remained a hero to legions of Kentucky basketball fans.

All in all, it was a lot to do over very little, but that's nothing new in politics. To tackle a political career, Jim Bunning has discovered, is to turn a private life that had been guarded zealously for years into public property. One time it's an opponent in a congressional race making wild accusations, calling you an adulterer, basing his foolish and blatantly false charges solely on the fact you were a professional ballplayer. Another time it's a dispute with a hugely popular basketball coach that gets blown hopelessly out of proportion. You never know the next time you're going to get blasted, fairly or unfairly. There have to be more pleasant ways to go through life—especially for someone in a position to leave the rat race far behind.

So why do it? Why subject yourself and your loved ones to the ever-growing negative side of political life? Why participate in a profession so many Americans view with disdain, even loathing? Why, in your mid-sixties, commit yourself to a contest you know will be extremely difficult, a race you may very well lose?

"It's not ego," Bunning commented. "The ego's over. The thing that motivates me now is that I'm in a position where I can actually do something about what's going on in the country. I can really make some kind of impact on real people's lives, so maybe some day somebody can say, 'Hey, he showed up and under his watch, while he was in Congress, he was able to get some things done,' like securing Social Security for the next seventy-five years or so, or at least get it going in that direction."

Yet he is only too aware of the widespread public perception of politicians, and it bothers him. "I get mad," he admitted. "I get mad for the simple reason most of it is self-inflicted. You've got to play by the rules. If you're going to be a lawmaker you can't skirt the laws. You can't illegally raise money. You can't illegally give information to a committee of Congress."

Of course it upsets him that all politicians, good or bad, honest or dishonest, are sometimes painted with the same brush, in much the same way that professional athletes are often vilified as a group. But to Bunning, as painful as some of his political experiences have been, the good outweighs the bad. He is ready—make that eager—to throw himself into another campaign, one in which he's going to have to raise perhaps four to five million dollars if he expects to win.

And if he loses?

"No matter which way the election turns out, I'll be perfectly happy," the candidate told someone who knows better. Jim Bunning, whether as a baseball player or a politician, has never been "perfectly happy" losing. Or the slightest bit happy, for that matter. The competitive fire that drove him to Hall of Fame brilliance in his pitching days still burns inside him.

"I want to serve in the U.S. Senate," he said. "I think I can do a good job in the U.S. Senate. But if the people of Kentucky say no—well, Mary's been wanting me to stay home for a while.

"No, I'm not going to be happy if I lose, but like when Paul Owens and those [Phillies] people decided it was time to fire me, to get rid of me, it took me about nine months to get over that. Yet I don't hold a grudge against Paul Owens and Dallas Green."

If anything, he owes them a vote of thanks.

Appendix

The No-Hitters

The First No-Hitter
(July 20, 1958, at Fenway Park; first game of a doubleheader)

The starting lineups:

Detroit Tigers		Boston Red Sox	
Harvey Kuenn	cf	Gene Stephens	cf
Billy Martin	ss	Pete Runnels	2b
Al Kaline	rf	Ted Williams	lf
Gail Harris	1b	Frank Malzone	3b
Gus Zernial	lf	Jackie Jensen	rf
Frank Bolling	2b	Dick Gernert	1b
Ozzie Virgil	3b	Lou Berberet	c
Red Wilson	c	Billy Consolo	ss
Jim Bunning	p	Frank Sullivan	p

TIGERS 1st: Kuenn grounded to second. Martin singled. Kaline grounded into a double play, Consolo to Runnels to Gernert. 0 runs, 1 hit, 0 errors, 0 left.

RED SOX 1st: Stephens flied to Kaline in deep right. Runnels grounded to third. Williams flied to right. 0 runs, 0 hits, 0 errors, 0 left.

TIGERS 2d: (Ted Lepcio replaced Runnels at second base.) Harris flied to right. Zernial grounded out, pitcher to first. Bolling grounded to third. 0 runs, 0 hits, 0 errors, 0 left.

RED SOX 2d: Malzone struck out. Jensen was hit by a pitch. Gernert grounded to third, Jensen moving to second on the play. Berberet struck out. 0 runs, 0 hits, 0 errors, 1 left.

TIGERS 3d: Virgil flied to right. Wilson struck out. Bunning grounded to short. 0 runs, 0 hits, 0 errors, 0 left.

RED SOX 3d: Consolo struck out. Sullivan popped foul to first. Stephens walked. Lepcio struck out. 0 runs, 0 hits, 0 errors, 1 left.

TIGERS 4th: Kuenn fouled to first. Martin called out on strikes. Kaline struck out. 0 runs, 0 hits, 0 errors, 0 left.

RED SOX 4th: Williams flied to Kuenn in right center. Malzone flied to right. Jensen lined to center. 0 runs, 0 hits, 0 errors, 0 left.

TIGERS 5th: Harris tripled to right. Zernial doubled to left, scoring Harris. Bolling fouled to first. Virgil struck out. Wilson singled, Zernial scoring. Bunning singled to right, Wilson stopping at second. Kuenn singled to center, scoring Wilson, and when Stephens fumbled the ball in center Bunning took third. Martin lined to right. 3 runs, 5 hits, 1 error, 2 left.

RED SOX 5th: Gernert grounded to third. Berberet struck out. Consolo was called out on strikes. 0 runs, 0 hits, 0 errors, 0 left.

TIGERS 6th: Kaline grounded to short. Harris fouled to first. Zernial fouled to third. 0 runs, 0 hits, 0 errors, 0 left.

RED SOX 6th: Marty Keough batted for Sullivan and struck out. Stephens walked. Lepcio was called out on strikes. Williams forced Stephens, Harris to Martin. 0 runs, 0 hits, 0 errors, 1 left.

TIGERS 7th: (Bud Byerly pitching for Boston.) Bolling struck out. Virgil singled to center. Wilson forced Virgil, Lepcio to Consolo. Bunning grounded to second. 0 runs, 1 hit, 0 errors, 1 left.

RED SOX 7th: Malzone fouled to the catcher. Jensen grounded to short. Gernert flied to center. 0 runs, 0 hits, 0 errors, 0 left.

TIGERS 8th: Kuenn doubled to left. Martin grounded to short and Kuenn was thrown out at third on fielder's choice. Kaline was called out on strikes. Harris lined to second. 0 runs, 1 hit, 0 errors, 1 left.

RED SOX 8th: Berberet was called out on strikes. Consolo popped to second. Billy Klaus batted for Byerly and struck out. 0 runs, 0 hits, 0 errors, 0 left.

TIGERS 9th: (Ted Bowsfield pitching for Boston.) Zernial singled to right. Johnny Groth ran for Zernial. Bolling lined to left. Virgil forced Groth, Lepcio to Consolo. Wilson forced Virgil, Lepcio unassisted. 0 runs, 1 hit, 0 errors, 1 left.

RED SOX 9th: (Groth playing left field for Detroit.) Stephens was called out on strikes. Lepcio struck out. Williams flied to Kaline in right. 0 runs, 0 hits, 0 errors, 0 left.

FINAL TOTALS	R	H	E	Left
Tigers	3	9	0	5
Red Sox	0	0	1	3

BOX SCORE

Detroit	AB	R	H	RBI		Boston	AB	R	H	RBI
Kuenn, cf	4	0	2	1		Stephens, cf	2	0	0	0
Martin, ss	4	0	1	0		Runnels, 2b	1	0	0	0
Kaline, rf	4	0	0	0		Lepcio, 2b	3	0	0	0
Harris, 1b	4	1	1	0		Williams, lf	4	0	0	0
Zernial, lf	4	1	2	1		Malzone, 3b	3	0	0	0
cGroth, lf	0	0	0	0		Jensen, rf	2	0	0	0
Bolling, 2b	4	0	0	0		Gernert, 1b	3	0	0	0
Virgil, 3b	4	0	1	0		Berberet, c	3	0	0	0
Wilson, c	4	1	1	1		Consolo, ss	3	0	0	0
Bunning, p	3	0	1	0		Sullivan, p	1	0	0	0
						aKeough	1	0	0	0
						Byerly, p	0	0	0	0
						bKlaus	1	0	0	0
						Bowsfield, p	0	0	0	0
Totals	35	3	9	3		Totals	27	0	0	0

aStruck out for Sullivan in 6th
bStruck out for Byerly in 8th
cRan for Zernial in 9th

Detroit	000	030	000	-	3	
Boston	000	000	000	-	0	

	IP	H	R	ER	BB	SO
Bunning (WP, 8-6)	9	0	0	0	2	12
Sullivan (LP, 8-3)	6	6	3	3	0	4
Byerly	2	2	0	0	0	2
Bowsfield	1	1	0	0	0	0

ERRORS- Stephens. 2b- Zernial, Kuenn. 3b- Harris. DP- Consolo, Runnels, and Gernert. LEFT- Detroit 5, Boston 3. HBP- By Bunning (Jensen). UMPIRES- Umont, Summers, Honochick, and Soar. Time- 2:22.

The Perfect Game

(June 21, 1964, at Shea Stadium; first game of a doubleheader)

The starting lineups:

Philadelphia Phillies		New York Mets	
Johnny Briggs	cf	Jim Hickman	cf
John Herrnstein	1b	Ron Hunt	2b
Johnny Callison	rf	Ed Kranepool	1b
Richie Allen	3b	Joe Christopher	rf
Wes Covington	lf	Jesse Gonder	c
Tony Taylor	2b	Bob Taylor	lf
Cookie Rojas	ss	Charley Smith	ss
Gus Triandos	c	Amado Samuel	3b
Jim Bunning	p	Tracy Stallard	p

PHILS 1st: Briggs walked. Herrnstein sacrificed, Kranepool to Hunt. Callison struck out. Allen singled to left, scoring Briggs. Covington grounded to second. 1 run, 1 hit, 0 errors, 1 left.

METS 1st: Hickman called out on strikes. Hunt grounded to second. Kranepool popped to short. 0 runs, 0 hits, 0 errors, 0 left.

PHILS 2d: Taylor walked. Rojas sacrificed, Stallard to Hunt. Triandos doubled to left, scoring Taylor. Bunning lined to short. Triandos to third on wild pitch. Briggs popped to first. 1 run, 1 hit, 0 errors, 1 left.

METS 2d: Christopher flied to center. Gonder fouled to the catcher. Taylor flied to right on 2-0 pitch. 0 runs, 0 hits, 0 errors, 0 left.

PHILS 3d: Herrnstein struck out. Callison lined to right. Allen walked. Covington lined to right. 0 runs, 0 hits, 0 errors, 1 left.

METS 3d: Smith struck out. Samuel lined to short. Stallard flied to left. 0 runs, 0 hits, 0 errors, 0 left.

PHILS 4th: Taylor bunted and was thrown out by Stallard on a close play. Rojas singled to center. Rojas thrown out at second attempting to steal, Gonder to Hunt. Triandos grounded to third. 0 runs, 1 hit, 0 errors, 0 left.

METS 4th: Hickman struck out. Hunt struck out on 3-2 pitch. Kranepool popped to Triandos in fair territory. 0 runs, 0 hits, 0 errors, 0 left.

PHILS 5th: Bunning grounded to short. Briggs grounded out, Gonder to Kranepool. Herrnstein grounded to second. 0 runs, 0 hits, 0 errors, 0 left.

METS 5th: Christopher popped to short. Gonder robbed of a hit by Tony Taylor, who knocked down his hard-hit ball with a dive to his left and threw him out. Bob Taylor grounded to third. 0 runs, 0 hits, 0 errors, 0 left.

PHILS 6th: Callison homered over the 371-foot sign in right center, his ninth of the year. Allen struck out. Covington walked. Bobby Wine ran for Covington. Taylor singled to center, Wine stopping at second. Rojas flied to right. Triandos singled to left, scoring Wine and sending Taylor to second to give Phils 4-0 lead. Bunning doubled off Hickman's glove in deep left center, scoring Taylor and Triandos to make it 6-0. Bill Wakefield replaced Stallard for the Mets. Briggs flied to left. 4 runs, 4 hits, 0 errors, 1 left.

METS 6th: (Bobby Wine goes to short for Phils and Rojas moves to left.) Smith flied to center. Samuel popped to Wine in short left center. Rod Kanehl batted for Wakefield and grounded to short. 0 runs, 0 hits, 0 errors, 0 left.

PHILS 7th: (Tom Sturdivant pitching for Mets.) Herrnstein popped to Gonder. Callison lined a single to center. Allen flied to center. Wine flied to center. 0 runs, 1 hit, 0 errors, 1 left.

METS 7th: Hickman struck out on a 0-2 pitch. Hunt grounded sharply to Allen at third on 0-1 pitch. Kranepool struck out on 1-2 pitch. 0 runs, 0 hits, 0 errors, 0 left.

PHILS 8th: Taylor popped to Sturdivant on a bunt attempt. Rojas struck out. Triandos struck out. 0 runs, 0 hits, 0 errors, 0 left.

METS 8th: Christopher struck out on 1-2 pitch. Gonder grounded to Tony Taylor on first pitch. Bob Taylor fouled off a 2-2 pitch, took outside pitch for 3-2 count, then called out on strikes. Triandos dropped third strike and threw him out at first. 0 runs, 0 hits, 0 errors, 0 left.

PHILS 9th: Bunning, after getting standing ovation, flied to right. Briggs struck out. Herrnstein grounded to first. 0 runs, 0 hits, 0 errors, 0 left.

METS 9th: Smith fouled to Wine on 2-2 pitch. George Altman batted for Samuel and struck out on 0-2 pitch. John Stephenson batted for Sturdivant. He swung and missed a curve ball for strike one, then took a curve for strike two. Stephenson took another curve ball just outside for ball one, and another outside curve for ball two, then struck out on 2-2 pitch, another curve ball. 0 runs, 0 hits, 0 errors, 0 left.

FINAL TOTALS	R	H	E	Left
Phils	6	8	0	5
Mets	0	0	0	0

BOX SCORE

Philadelphia	AB	R	H	RBI	New York	AB	R	H	RBI
Briggs, cf	4	1	0	0	Hickman, cf	3	0	0	0
Herrnstein, 1b	4	0	0	0	Hunt, 2b	3	0	0	0
Callison, rf	4	1	2	1	Kranepool, 1b	3	0	0	0
Allen, 3b	3	0	1	1	Christopher, rf	3	0	0	0
Covington, lf	2	0	0	0	Gonder, c	3	0	0	0
[a]Wine, ss	1	1	0	0	R. Taylor, lf	3	0	0	0
T. Taylor, 2b	3	2	1	0	Smith, ss	3	0	0	0
Rojas, ss-lf	3	0	1	0	Samuel, 3b	2	0	0	0
Triandos, c	4	1	2	2	[c]Altman	1	0	0	0
Bunning, p	4	0	1	2	Stallard, p	1	0	0	0
					Wakefield, p	0	0	0	0
					[b]Kanehl	1	0	0	0
					Sturdivant, p	0	0	0	0
					[d]Stephenson	1	0	0	0
Totals	32	6	8	6	Totals	27	0	0	0

[a]Ran for Covington in 6th
[b]Grounded out for Wakefield in 6th
[c]Struck out for Samuel in 9th
[d]Struck out for Sturdivant in 9th

| Philadelphia | 110 | 004 | 000 | - | 6 |
| New York | 000 | 000 | 000 | - | 0 |

	IP	H	R	ER	BB	SO
Bunning (WP, 7-2)	9	0	0	0	0	10
Stallard (LP, 4-9)	5.2	7	6	6	4	3
Wakefield	.1	0	0	0	0	0
Sturdivant	3	1	0	0	0	3

2b- Triandos, Bunning. HR- Callison. SAC- Herrnstein, Rojas. LEFT- Philadelphia 5, New York 0. UMPIRES- Sudol, Pryor, Secory, and Burkhart. Time- 2:19.

Index

Aaron, Henry, 3, 74, 77, 94-95, 97-98
ABC News, 221
Abrams, Cal, 37
Adcock, Joe, 108
Agee, Tommie, 131
Ailes, Norma, 232
Ailes, Roger, 232-33
Alexander, Gary, 200-201
Alexander, Grover Cleveland, 87
Alexander, Hugh, 184-86, 190
Allen, Maury, 66-67
Allen, Richie, 60-61, 72, 76, 81, 83, 87
Allison, Bob, 103-5
All-Star Game, 38, 50, 59, 75, 93-99, 106, 118, 273-74
Alston, Walter, 56, 97
Altman, George, 62-63
Amaro, Ruben, 56, 58, 61, 71, 77, 83-84, 175, 194
Anderson, Jack, 257, 261
Anderson, Sparky, 123
Aparicio, Luis, 51
Arroyo, Luis, 50, 58
Ashburn, Richie, 57, 102-3, 180
Associated Press, 37, 226-27, 282
Astrodome, 193
Atlanta Braves, 141
Atwater, Lee, 231-33, 238-39
Avila, Bobby, 33

Bailey, Ed, 94
Baker, Del, 43-45
Baker, James, 242
Baldschun, Jack, 75, 77-78, 81, 85-86
Baltimore Orioles, 37, 49, 123-24

Banks, Ernie, 94
Bannister, Alan, 154-55, 165
Bartholomay, Bill, 264
Baseball Hall of Fame, 1, 9-18, 20, 45, 66, 69, 85-86, 97, 102, 107, 114-15, 117, 122, 154, 192, 208, 227-28, 253, 264-65, 267, 270, 282, 284
Baseball Writers Association of America, 9
Bastable, Jack, 176
Bavarian Beers, 19, 24
Bavasi, Buzzie, 13, 89
Bedell, Howie, 178, 181-84, 186-89, 191-92
Beliles, Richard, 254
Bennett, Dennis, 74-75, 79-80
Berra, Yogi, 13, 15, 48, 50, 98, 122, 245
Birtwell, Roger, 43
Blackwell, Ewell, 48
Boltano, Danny, 176
Bolling, Frank, 22, 53, 77, 94-95
Bolling, Sue, 53
Bond, Walter, 59
Boone, Bob, 133, 181
Boozer, John, 76
Borski, Robert, 8
Bosetti, Rick, 176-77, 193, 199-201
Boston Celtics, 280, 283
Boston Red Sox, 38-44, 48-50, 55
Bottomley, Jim, 37
Bowa, Larry, 118-19, 132, 181
Bowman, Denny, 256
Boyer, Ken, 95, 98
Braman, Norman, 248
Brandon, Darrell (Bucky), 148, 172
Bristol, Dave, 179-80

291

Broeg, Bob, 13
Bronson, Jimmy, 138, 142
Brooklyn Dodgers, 64, 72, 115–16
Brown, Dick, 121–22
Brown, Joe L., 13, 102, 125, 129
Brunet, George, 156–57
Bryant, Clay, 142
Bunning, Amy, 16, 207, 226, 241
Bunning, Barbara, 16, 27–29, 32–33, 60–65
Bunning, Bill, 16, 28
Bunning, Cathy, 16, 28–29, 91, 241
Bunning, David, 16, 29, 207, 241, 255
Bunning, Jim (James Paul David): as All-
    Star pitcher, 4, 93–99; on baseball's anti-
    trust exemption, 266–70, 273–74; break-
    ing into politics, 202–4; as campaigner,
    7, 206–8, 211–26, 236–48, 254–56; co-
    existing with Max Patkin, 141–44, 150–
    51, 173–74; decision to run for U.S. Sen-
    ate, 276–79, 283–84; with Dodgers,
    128–29; duels with Ted Williams, 38–
    39, 42–44, 261; election to Hall of
    Fame, 9–18; feud with Peter Ueberroth,
    270–73; fighting for players' rights, 100–
    105, 110–14; fired as manager, 6, 179–
    82; first no-hitter, 39–48; Hall of Fame
    induction speech, 107, 264–65, 267; Jim
    Bunning Night at Veterans Stadium,
    265–66; managing Eugene Emeralds,
    147–57; managing Oklahoma City
    89ers, 175–78; managing Reading Phil-
    lies, 135–46; managing Toledo Mud
    Hens, 5, 158–74; managing winter base-
    ball, 196–201; as minor league player,
    20–24, 27; perfect game, 60–66; with
    Phillies, 54–91; with Pirates, 127–28;
    playing winter baseball, 28, 31–35; run-
    ning for governor, 209–29; as state sena-
    tor, 205–9; with Tigers, 27, 36–53, 121–
    22; as U.S. Congressman, 230–61
Bunning, Jimmy (son), 16, 28, 32–33
Bunning, Joan, 16, 32–33
Bunning, Laura, 27
Bunning, Mr. and Mrs. Louis, 17–19, 24
Bunning, Mark, 16, 28
Bunning, Mary, 3, 7, 11–13, 16–17, 19–20,
    22, 25–30, 31–33, 42, 52–53, 60, 64–65,
    83, 91–92, 135–36, 171, 184, 187–88, 192,
    196, 200, 202–3, 205–10, 212–15, 218,
    223–24, 226–29, 231, 235–37, 240–42,
    245–50, 252, 255, 259, 265, 277–78, 284

Burdette, Lew, 94, 123–24
Burgess, Smoky, 69, 95
Busch Memorial Stadium, 96
Busch Stadium, 93
Bush, George, 231, 242–43, 250, 254

California Angels, 55, 75, 175, 185
Callison, Johnny, 62–63, 72–73, 76, 78, 87,
    96
Campanis, Al, 117, 128–29
Campbell County Recorder, 212, 222
Campbell, Jim, 52–53, 129, 159
Campbell, Paul, 22
Candlestick Park, 69, 94
Cannon, Judge Bob, 103–10
Cannon, Helen, 108
Canseco, Jose, 121
Carbray, John, 150
Cardenas, Chico, 81
Caribbean Series, 34–35
Carlton, Steve, 132, 179
Carpenter, Bob, 102, 110, 137
Carpenter, Ruly, 110, 179, 181, 184
Cartwright, Al, 185
Carty, Rico, 77
Casey, Ben, 124
Cash, Norm, 49, 95
Cater, Danny, 60, 64–65
Cater, Gail, 60, 64–65
Cates, Steve, 172–73
CBS, 11, 110, 251–53
CBS Morning News, 11, 253
Cepeda, Orlando, 94–95, 98
Chandler, Happy, 273
Chicago Bulls, 248
Chicago Cubs, 58, 87, 97, 130, 188
Chicago Tribune, 64
Chicago White Sox, 37, 39, 44, 205, 224,
    248
Christenson, Larry, 154, 197
Christopher, Joe, 62, 67
Cincinnati Enquirer, 224, 244
Cincinnati Reds, 22, 73–74, 77, 80–81, 90,
    123, 129–30, 180–81, 205, 226, 239
Clackett, Jim, 218–29
Clark, Ron, 162, 165–66
Clemens, Roger, 121
Clemente, Roberto, 57, 69, 89, 94–95, 267
Clendenon, Donn, 87
Cleveland Indians, 49
Cleveland Municipal Stadium, 95

Clinton, Bill, 3, 207, 254, 257, 261, 277, 280-82
CNN, 248
Cochrane, Mickey, 10
Coggin, Chuck, 128
Cole, Nat (King), 35
Coleman, Ken, 13
Coleman, Leon, 262
Collins, Eddie, 10
Collins, Martha Layne, 210-15, 217-18, 220-22, 224-25, 227-28, 230, 239, 243, 254, 259
Concepcion, David, 134, 226
Connie Mack Stadium, 58, 68, 71, 76, 78, 86, 88, 90-91, 98, 131-32, 165
Cook, Edie, 210, 215, 221
Cook, Jack, 203-4, 210-11, 215
Cooper, John, 278-79
Courtney, Clint, 5
Covington, Wes, 59, 61
Cowley, Joe, 213, 220-22, 224, 248
Crandall, Del, 94
Cronin, Joe, 10
Crosley Field, 80-81, 83
Cross, Al, 279
Crum, Denny, 280
Culp, Ray, 67
Culver, George, 165-66, 179

Dalrymple, Clay, 67, 85
Danville Advocate, 224
Dapper Dan Dinner, 108
Davis, Tommy, 95
Davis, Willie, 70, 73
Day, Boots, 133
DeBusschere, Dave, 44
DeLuca, Duke, 138
Demeter, Don, 53
Detroit Free Press, 66, 100, 124
Detroit Tigers, 8, 19-20, 22-24, 29, 31, 36-53, 55, 60, 64, 66, 100, 102, 115, 121, 129
Detroit Times, 41
Dewey, Thomas E., 104
DiMaggio, Joe, 9, 49
Dodger Stadium, 76, 185
Doerr, Bobby, 39
Dole, Bob, 277, 280-81
Downs, Dave, 140-41
Doyle, Denny, 132
Dressen, Charley, 51-52, 55-56, 58, 64

Driessen, Dan, 139
Drysdale, Don, 86, 93, 96, 101, 115, 117-21, 123
Durocher, Leo, 70
Dwyer, Jim, 193
Dykes, Jimmy, 49, 51, 80

Ebbets Field, 72
Ed Sullivan Show, 64-65
Elia, Lee, 116, 153-57, 163, 165, 168-73, 176, 191, 194
Elliot, Larry, 58
Erps, Bob, 21
Erschell, Fred, 203
Escogido Leones, 196, 199-201
Estadio Quisqueya, 199, 201
Eugene Emeralds, 5-7, 147-57

Fahrenkopf, Frank, 242
Fairly, Ron, 70
Falls, Joe, 100-101, 124
Fehr, Don, 106, 111, 113-14
Feller, Bob, 7, 41, 103
Fenway Park, 12, 38-40, 43-46, 61, 64, 95, 236
Ferrell, Rick, 129
Figueroa, Ed, 196-97
Fingers, Rollie, 85
Flood, Curt, 66
Florida Marlins, 130
Ford, Dan, 152
Ford, Gerald (Jerry), 104, 203
Ford, Wendell, 251, 277-79
Ford, Whitey, 123-24
Fox, Nellie, 13-14, 51, 59, 97
Foytack, Paul, 22, 33-34, 42
Franklin, Tony, 178
Franks, Herman, 124
Fred Hutchinson Cancer Fund, 153, 155-56
Freehan, Bill, 97
Fremuth, Mike, 7
Friend, Bob, 103-5, 108
Fryman, Woodie, 127, 131-32
Fuentes, Tito, 134

Gaherin, John, 109
Gaines, Joe, 69
Galbraith, John, 102-3, 108-9
Garrett, Wayne, 131
Gentile, Jim, 49
Gernert, Dick, 40

Giamatti, Bart, 113
Gibson, Bob, 7, 66, 79, 83, 115, 117–21, 152
Giles, Bill, 265–66, 273, 275
Gomez, Preston, 89
Gonder, Jesse, 60–62, 87
Gonzalez, Tony, 58, 89
Good Morning America, 227
Gossage, Goose, 85
Gran Stadium, 35
Green, Dallas, 78, 137, 148, 150, 159–60, 163, 176, 178–79, 181–92, 194, 284
Green, Sylvia, 184, 188
Griffey, Ken, 139
Griffith, Calvin, 102–3, 112
Grote, Jerry, 79
Gullett, Don, 194
Gutman, Dan, 261

Hale, Bob, 50
Haller, Tom, 86
Hamilton, Jack, 53
Harkness, Tim, 58
Harrelson, Bud, 131
Harris, Bucky, 23–24, 37, 51
Hart, Jim Ray, 86, 97
Havard, Mac, 201
Hawaii Islanders, 147, 156
Helms, Tommy, 239
Henrich, Tommy, 42–43
Herman, Billy, 44
Hernandez, Jackie, 134
Herrnstein, John, 75
Hickman, Jim, 60–61
Hill, Quency, 176
Hitchcock, Billy, 123–24
Hoak, Don, 94
Host, Jim, 210, 226–27
Houk, Ralph, 58, 142
House of Representatives, 15, 230–61
Houston Astros, 91, 193, 203, 262
Houston Colt '45s, 59, 69
Howard, Elston, 50
Howard, Frank, 69
Howell, Jay, 125
Hunt, Ron, 58, 60–61, 67, 119
Hunter, Catfish, 11
Hutchinson, Fred, 23, 58, 73, 82
Hyde, Henry, 15

Internal Revenue Service, 14

Iorg, Dane, 167, 175–77
Irvin, Monte, 13

Jack Russell Stadium, 265
Jackson, Al, 67
Jackson, Grant, 132
Jensen, Jackie, 37–39, 41, 46, 98
John, Tommy, 123
Johnson, Alex, 81
Johnson, Don, 204, 209
Johnson, Walter, 4, 7, 24, 152
Johnstone, Jay, 167–70, 172–73, 175
Jones, Cleon, 131

Kaat, Jim, 125
Kaline, Al, 18, 37–38, 40, 43, 46, 275
Kansas City Royals, 113, 167
Katz, Reuven, 239
Kaye, Danny, 88–89
Keane, Johnny, 58, 75, 96
Kell, George, 18
Kemp, Jack, 229, 234, 242
Kennedy, John F., 95, 220
Kentucky, University of, 218, 280
Kentucky Enquirer, 224
Kentucky Post, 225, 244, 251
Kilgallen, Dorothy, 89
Killebrew, Harmon, 36–37, 96
Kiner, Ralph, 10, 62
Kingman, Dave, 118
Kirk, Jim, 117
Kiser, Larry, 165
Klaus, Billy, 42
Kniffen, Chuck, 164
Knoop, Bobby, 97
Koegel, Pete, 155
Koppel, Ted, 227
Koppett, Leonard, 13
Kosc, Greg, 198
Koufax, Sandy, 41, 47, 68, 87–89, 93, 96–97, 101
Kranepool, Ed, 58, 62
Kubek, Tony, 121
Kuenn, Harvey, 41, 102–5
Kuhn, Bowie, 272

Lampard, Keith, 155
Landes, Stan, 131
Lanier, Hal, 67
Larsen, Don, 64
Lary, Frank, 20, 22, 48, 56, 122

Laxton, Bill, 127
Lefebvre, Jim, 127–28
Legends Field, 185–86
Lemon, Bob, 12
Lepcio, Ted, 40, 42
Lerch, Randy, 176, 193
Lersch, Barry, 132
Lewis, Allen, 13–16, 46, 79
Lexington (Ky.) Herald Leader, 2
Lezcano, Sixto, 196
Lilly, Thomas, 221
Lis, Joe, 151
Liscio, Joe, 82
Lock, Don, 98
Los Angeles Dodgers, 68–70, 86–91, 123, 125, 128–30, 246
Louisville, University of, 19, 218, 280
Louisville Courier-Journal, 218, 244–45, 279
Lucadello, Tony, 185
Lucchesi, Frank, 130–33, 191
Luzinski, Greg, 137, 181
Lynch, Jerry, 69

Mahaffey, Art, 20, 57–58, 73–75, 77, 79
Major League Players Association, 18, 33, 52, 83, 100–114, 187, 193, 263–64, 267, 275
Maloney, Jim, 81, 194
Malzone, Frank, 39, 43–44, 46, 95
Mann, Terry, 233, 237–40, 243–44, 246–47, 250–52, 254
Mantle, Mickey, 36, 48–50, 94, 96, 98–99, 121–22, 230, 276
Marichal, Juan, 9
Maris, Roger, 49, 122
Marshall, Dave, 131
Martin, Billy, 40, 57
Martin, Galen, 254
Martin, Jerry, 5, 169–70
Mathews, Eddie, 10, 67, 74, 76–77, 87
Mauch, Gene, 38, 54–60, 67–70, 72–75, 77–80, 82–86, 90, 96, 133, 142, 188
May, Lee, 90
Mays, Willie, 94–98, 276
Mazeroski, Bill, 87, 94
McCarver, Tim, 80
McConnell, Mitch, 277–79
McCovey, Willie, 11, 98
McCoy Stadium, 161–62
McHale, John, 29
McHugh, Mathew, 257

McKinney, Debbie, 243
McLain, Denny, 52
McMillan, Roy, 94
McNally, Dave, 110
Medwick, Joe, 10
Merrill, Durwood, 198–99
Messersmith, Andy, 110
Metzger, Roger, 134
Mexican Winter League, 23
Mexico City Reds, 31, 33
Miami (Florida) Stadium, 117
Michael, Gene, 120
Mile High Stadium, 178
Millan, Feliz, 196, 198–99
Miller, Marvin, 18, 103–4, 106, 108–12, 114, 264, 266–67
Miller, Stu, 94
Milwaukee Braves, 58, 67, 74–79, 87
Milwaukee Brewers, 55, 113, 273
Mitchell, John, 104
Mitchell, Ron, 128
Molush, Ed, 5, 164–65
Money, Don, 127
Montanez, Willie, 196
Montreal Expos, 119
Moon, Wally, 94
Moore, Charley, 21
Moore, Mrs. Charley, 21
Morales, Jerry, 196
Moreland, Keith, 193
Morrison, Jim, 176–77, 193, 199–201, 203
Mosler, Ed, 95, 142
Mossi, Don, 44, 53
Mossi, Louise, 53
Mota, Manny, 200
Mullin, George, 46
Munzel, Edgar, 13
Musial, Stan, 13, 94, 96

NBC, 11, 225
New York Daily News, 107
New York Mets, 12, 45, 48, 57, 59–64, 66–67, 80–81, 83, 86–87, 90, 131, 166, 185, 205, 209, 252
New York Yankees, 48–50, 54, 64, 66, 75, 93, 96, 116, 121, 135, 224, 262–63
Niekro, Phil, 90
Nightline, 227
Nixon, Richard Milhous, 103–4, 203
Nolan, Gary, 194
Nordhagen, Wayne, 172–73, 177

Norman, Bill, 23, 39, 43
Nunn, Louis, 279

Ohio-Indiana League, 20
Oklahoma City All-Sports Stadium, 177
Oklahoma City 89ers, 175-78, 183, 193
Oliver, Gene, 67
O'Malley, Peter, 264
O'Malley, Walter, 105-7
O'Neil, Buck, 13
Oriole Park at Camden Yards, 49, 273
Otero, Reggie, 74
Owens, Paul, 58, 71, 76, 140, 159-60, 167,
    179-86, 190-91, 206, 284
Ozark, Danny, 180-81

Patkin, Max, 141-44, 150-51, 167, 173-74
Patrick, Van, 41
Paul, Mike, 5
Pepitone, Joe, 96
Perry, Gaylord, 123
Peters, Hank, 13
Philadelphia Eagles, 248
Philadelphia Inquirer, 2, 13-14, 46, 79
Philley, Dave, 37
Phillie Phanatic, 141
Phillies, 2, 4-7, 14, 20, 29, 52, 54-92, 100,
    102, 107, 118, 120, 126, 128, 130-35,
    137, 141, 145, 147-48, 154-55, 158-59,
    165-66, 168, 176-93, 196, 202, 205-6,
    209-11, 223-24, 247, 263, 265-66, 284
Piersall, Jimmy, 50
Piniella, Lou, 135
Pinson, Vada, 73-74, 81, 90
Pitino, Rick, 280-83
Pittsburgh Pirates, 57, 86-89, 102, 125,
    127-29, 135
Poff, John, 193
Poore, Dr. Floyd, 254-56, 259, 261
Pope, Dave, 37
Portland Oregonian, 156
Power, Vic, 70-71

Quad City Tigers, 21
Quincy (Ill.) Gems, 21
Quinn, John, 58, 67-68, 101-2, 110-11,
    126-27, 129-30, 134

Ranew, Merritt, 67
Reading Municipal Stadium, 137
Reading Phillies, 4, 136-46

Reagan, Ronald, 233, 240, 242-44, 247-48
Reese, Pee Wee, 13-15, 115-16
Reid, Scott, 5-6, 130-31, 136, 149, 160-61
Reinsdorf, Jerry, 248
Republican National Committee, 231, 242
Richardson, Bobby, 95, 121
Richmond Braves, 5
Rigney, Bill, 58
Ripken, Cal, Jr., 15
Rivera, Jim, 34
Rizzuto, Phil, 263
Roberts, Robin, 57, 103, 105, 107-9, 111,
    113, 132, 187-89, 267
Robinson, Brooks, 96
Robinson, Frank, 73, 81, 94
Robinson, Jackie, 117
Robinson, Rick, 236, 255-56, 258-60, 272
Rodgers, Bob (Buck), 200
Roebuck, Ed, 58, 69, 85-86, 188
Rogodzinski, Mike, 4, 148-49, 162
Rojas, Cookie, 56, 59, 61
Rojas, Larry, 138, 140, 144-46
Rose, Carolyn, 83
Rose, Peter, 90, 239-40
Roseboro, John, 71, 90
Ruiz, Chico, 73-74
Runnels, Pete, 40, 46
Rupp Arena, 213
Ruthven, Dick, 158-59, 193, 197, 202,
    204-5, 217
Ryan, Nolan, 41, 47

Sadecki, Ray, 80
Safewright, Harry, 156, 172
Salyers, John, 247
Sandberg, Ryne, 140
Sanford, Jack, 119
San Francisco Giants, 67, 69, 86, 88-89,
    118, 124
Santana, Blas, 139
Scarce, Mac, 140, 152
Scheffing, Bob, 50-52
Scheffing, Mary, 51
Schmidt, Mike, 181
Schoendienst, Red, 125
Schott, Marge, 240
Scott, Frank, 64
Scovil, Warren, 271
Scully, Vince, 89
Seattle Mariners, 135
Selig, Bud, 113, 263, 268-70, 273-74

Selma, Dick, 131–32
Seminick, Andy, 145
Senger, Charley, 159–60
Severson, Rich, 155
Shantz, Bobby, 77
Shea Stadium, 12, 41–42, 45, 59, 61, 63–
  64, 66–67, 86, 93, 96, 209
Shepard, Larry, 127–28
Sherman Antitrust Act, 269
Short, Chris, 55, 58, 67, 69, 72–76, 79, 81,
  88, 101, 132
Sievers, Roy, 51
Simmons, Curt, 80
Simpson, Wayne, 196, 200–201
Singleton, Ken, 133–34
Sisler, Dick, 73
Sixty Minutes, 247, 253–54
Skaggs, Sally Harris, 256
Sloane, Harvey, 212, 214
Smith, Al, 3
Smith, Charley, 63, 67
Smith, Hal, 37
Smith, Lonnie, 177–78, 193, 203, 216,
  271–72
Snider, Duke, 86
Snyder, Emma, 221
Snyder, Gene, 231, 238, 250
Southern Association, 22
Spahn, Warren, 86
Spence, Bob, 151
Spoelstra, Watson, 101
Sportsman's Park, 93
Stack, Ed, 13–14
Stanky, Eddie, 142
Stargell, Willie, 57, 69, 87, 98, 133–34
Staub, Rusty, 6
Stearns, John, 166–67, 185, 197
Steevens, Morris, 70, 73
Steinbrenner, George, 223
Steinman, Jack, 203
Stengel, Casey, 62, 93–94
Stephens, Gene, 40, 42
Stephens, Vern, 39
Stephenson, John, 12, 58, 62–64
Stevens, John, 50
St. Louis Cardinals, 67, 75, 77–81, 83–84,
  90, 96, 152, 167, 271
St. Terese Parochial Grade School, 25
St. Xavier High School, 19
Sudol, Ed, 62
Sullivan, Ed, 64–65

Sullivan, Frank, 41, 45–46
Summerall, Bob, 240
Sutter, Bruce, 85
Sutton, Don, 123

Taylor, Hawk, 58, 62
Taylor, Tony, 56–57, 60, 62, 73, 77, 81
Teeter, Bob, 232
Temple, Johnny, 50, 94
Terre Haute Phillies, 21
Texas Rangers, 5
Thomas, Frank, 67–68, 70, 83
Thornton, Andy, 151
Three-I League, 21
Tiger Stadium, 36, 39, 50, 52, 99, 121, 158
Tigertown, 22
Tighe, Jack, 22
Today show, 11
Toledo Mud Hens, 5–6, 158–74, 234–35
Torborg, Jeff, 89
Toronto Blue Jays, 205
Torre, Joe, 74–78, 116, 119–20, 135
Triandos, Gus, 37, 52, 59, 61–64, 78, 189,
  246
Trucks, Virgil, 46
Trumpy, Bob, 245
Tsitouris, John, 73, 81, 83
Turley, Bob, 121–22

Ueberroth, Peter, 270–73
Umont, Frank, 42
United Press International, 50
USA Today, 248

Valentine, Harry, 193
Vander Meer, Johnny, 48
Vaughns, Chico, 156
Veale, Bob, 127
Venturi, Ken, 65
Vernon, Mickey, 57
Veterans Committee (Hall of Fame), 13–
  15, 97
Veterans Stadium, 19, 132–33, 199, 265
Vincent, Fay, 13, 263–64, 268
Virdon, Bill, 69
Virgil, Ozzie, 40
Vukovich, John, 117–18, 133

Wade, Gordon, 225
Wager, Kit, 2
Walk, Ned, 19

Wallace, Dave, 148, 151-53, 163-67, 169-73, 176-77
Wallace, Mike, 148
Washington Post, 224
Washington Senators, 48-49
Watson, Bob, 262, 264
Weldon, Curt, 15
Wertz, Vic, 51
Wesley, Quentin, 219
West, Joe, 178
Wharton School of Finance and Commerce, 103
White, Bill, 13-14, 95-95, 262-64, 270
White, Mike, 59
Wilhelm, Hoyt, 123
Williams, Billy, 11, 87, 97
Williams, Ted, 12-13, 38-39, 42-46, 48-49, 97-98, 206, 261, 276
Wills, Maury, 68, 89, 95
Wilpon, Fred, 264
Wilson, Billy, 131
Wilson, Red, 42-43
Wine, Bobby, 56, 61, 63, 196
Wise, Rick, 64
Witt, Mike, 55

Wolf, Fred, 248, 250, 252-53
Woods, Tiger, 133
Woodward, Woody, 67
World Series, 48, 50, 54-55, 59, 64, 71, 76, 83-84, 87, 89, 93, 106, 111, 113, 167, 180, 267, 280
Wright, Jim, 120, 193
Wynn, Early, 94
Wynn, Jimmy, 59

Xavier of Ohio, 19, 22

Yankee Stadium, 48, 110, 200, 258
Yawkey, Tom, 112
Yee, Dr. Samuel, 156
York, Rudy, 39
Yost, Eddie, 102
Young, Cy, 4
Youngblood, Joel, 139

Zernial, Gus, 41
Zimmer, Don, 116-17
Zipeto, Ted (Red), 144, 149-50, 153, 156, 165, 171